Ver -

Thank you for your
FRIENDSHIP !

Manfred

HELIX *of* FATE & LOVE
An Immigrant's Story

MANFRED TATZMANN

ISBN 978-1-66782-948-7 eBook 978-1-66782-949-4

CONTENTS

PART III
Two Special Decades: Career, Loss, And Reunion   **215**

THIS BOOK IS DEDICATED TO MY CHILDREN, Tracy, Steve, Anna, and Marie; to their children, Marion, Joey, Nick, Greyson, Ellie, and Clara, once they are old enough to understand it; to my stepchildren, Amanda and Bob; and grandchildren yet come!

And to Maria, without whom this book would have never been. Thank you for your love!

PREFACE

The essayist Emily Grosvenor says, "Memoir can only really happen when time passes, and the self reflects back differently on what occurred . . . the reflective self-piecing together meaning from life's sometimes random events."

Was it random events or fate that brought Maria and me together? Was it random events that allowed both of us to grow into adults who could appreciate our individualism? We believe it was fate.

This book is a reflection on the events that shaped my life and Maria's. It would be boring and narcissistic to think one could share every moment that influenced our lives. So here are key moments in our lives and what role fate appeared to have played in bringing us together. Fate, in our minds, being the irony of two people who grew up at almost opposite poles meeting, falling in love, losing and then finding each other makes this story remarkable. Was it destiny that split us apart and fate that brought us back together after almost four decades? Indeed, we think so.

Some readers may find the level of historical context excessive at times. Hopefully, someday our grandchildren will read this book and find the description of the McDonald's of my high school days and say, "Wow, that's what it used to be like?" For other readers it may bring back fond memories.

The details are not for us who remember, but for those who still need to learn them.

INTRODUCTION

"I will tell you about myself and other members of this family we both belong to, but don't ask me to be precise, because inevitable errors will crop in. There are places, dates, and names I don't remember; on the other hand, I never forget a good story. . . . My life is created as I narrate, and my memories grow stronger with writing; what I do not put in words on paper will be erased by time."

From *Paula*, by Isabel Allende

Maria and I are fascinated with popular TV genealogy shows like *Finding Your Roots* and *Who Do You Think You Are?* When asked about specific relatives, guests on the show often state, "I don't know much," especially if that family member was an immigrant to the United States. Maria and I, as immigrants, proudly treasure our backgrounds and diverse cultures. We want our children and grandchildren to have a glimpse into who we were and what made us who we are so that, in the future, they may have insight into who they are.

I am so grateful to have been able to write this story. I hope that it will provide some understanding about both Maria and me for Tracy, Steve, Anna, Maria, Amanda, Bob, and our grandchildren.

PART I

Manfred's Story

CHAPTER 1

COMING TO AMERICA

The summer evening sun that had enveloped the partiers had set some time ago. Nevertheless, by the dim light of the streetlamp, the party went on. I rested my head on my arms as I peeked out between the horizontal two-by-four slats of the balcony, hoping that my parents and the other revelers on the street would not catch me spying on them. It was 1957; my parents and I were moving to America, and this was our going-away party.

I should have been in bed, resting for the adventure we were about to embark upon the next day. Sleep was the last thing on my mind; I was excited in spirit and body. The air was warm and thick, and insects buzzed around me. "Sleep, rest, ha!" I thought. "I have the rest of my life to sleep. Tonight is a night to remember." It was my last night in the only home I'd ever known.

Dad in front of house where I grew up, with balcony that was my play area.

The balcony was on the second floor of the house where I'd lived my entire life, all eleven years of it. I knew this balcony well. It was my elevated fortress, my hideout. With blankets placed strategically, it became my playhouse. Occasionally, it even served as one end of a cable-car system lifting toy soldiers and bandits up from the garden. The balcony had been my refuge as long as I could remember. Tonight, though, was the last time my hands would touch the slats and my eyes look down from this stronghold.

Although I could not identify each person in the light of the moon, stars, and streetlights, I heard my dad's voice over the noise. I knew there were many partygoers, but I could not make out how many in the dark. The longer I watched, the louder and more familiar the previously indistinguishable voices grew. Never having been up this late, I wondered if all parties sounded like this or if, as the evening became quieter, I could just hear more.

Earlier in the day, I had overheard my parents mention that their lifelong friends, including my dad's brother's family and neighbors, would be there. The tables had been laid with many traditional foods: sausages, ham, cheeses, salads, fresh bread, and rolls, along with free-flowing beer, wine, and schnapps, the traditional fiery Austrian brandy. As the youngest, I had gone to bed first—or at least that is where my parents assumed me to be. My cousin, a year older than me, had been shooed off next to sleep in my grandmother's bed downstairs. But I had no illusions that my mother believed I would get some rest, as she directed, and pay no attention to all the noise from the party below. How could Mutti expect me to simply go to sleep, as if it were any other night? I was extremely excited about my new adventure and life to come, but at the same time I was extremely sad to leave.

My grandfather Franz Tatzmann built the house shortly after he married my grandmother, Rosa. Sadly, he had passed away five years before our going-away party, but my grandmother still occupied the ground floor.

Our home was a two-room apartment situated right under the A-shaped roof. By today's standards it would not even be called a studio apartment. It had no running water or bathroom. To the right, as you came up the stairs, was kitchen, dining room, and living room all squeezed into one small space. The left side of the roofline served as a pantry and storage area. Under the right side of the roofline, behind the wall dividing the small space from the kitchen area, we kept a bucket that served as our toilet; the house had a proper toilet on the first floor only.

To the right of the kitchen was the door to the bedroom, which was the larger space. My parents' bed was against the opposite wall. A large, European-style credenza held our clothing and other belongings. In the back wall was a large window looking out to our backyard and the mountains beyond. When I was little, my crib stood next to my mom's side of the bed, just to the right as you walked into the room; that way, after putting me to bed, she could just open the door and peek in to check on me.

In the kitchen, a wood-fired stove provided heat in the wintertime and a cooking surface throughout the year. When I was about seven, my parents finally had enough money to buy an electric stove. Mutti, as I called my mother, was overjoyed; it was almost like a miracle for her. My dad spent one afternoon getting it hooked up, and at about five thirty it was ready to be tested. It had a shiny, light-caramel-colored glaze on the exterior; a small oven, just big enough to hold one slim roasting pan; and two burners with heavy metal plates on top. After my dad finished the installation, we all just stood there, looking at it, for the longest time. Finally, Papa suggested that Mutti should try it out. Appearing almost afraid to touch it, Mutti carefully bent over, reached for the knob, turned it to "ON." In an instant she could feel the heat rise, and we noticed the smell of metal as the burners seasoned.

The first thing she made was a pan of milk. Somehow, the warm milk tasted better that day than it ever had before! Next, Mutti called my grandmother up from downstairs to show off her new joy and how easily it worked. My grandmother—Oma, as I called her—was old-fashioned and not open to change. She was not impressed with the new device. Looking at it, she harrumphed that her wood stove was much better. Mutti was disappointed, but she knew my grandmother was not one to show emotion. Nevertheless, Mutti was delighted and invited her friends to a party the following weekend so she could show off her new appliance.

The living area also held a medium-size table with four chairs and, against one wall, a fold-out couch. The biggest piece of furniture in the room was the hutch. In true European fashion, it was highly lacquered. Tall, from floor to ceiling, with drawers on the bottom half. Above drawers on the bottom half, a door in the middle section dropped down to reveal a backlit minibar. Above the bar was the radio, a large and elegant-looking instrument that was our only form of entertainment. We listened to music and radio plays, and I particularly enjoyed the children's stories. Good radios in those days were the status symbols equivalent to today's expensive, large-screen TVs.

The house had no central heat, so winters proved challenging. For years, the kitchen's coal stove was the only heat source for the upper floor. Even after the electric stove arrived, we kept it for that purpose. Soft, billowy down comforters and thick blankets kept us warm during most nights. On very cold nights, Mutti would fill a metal container shaped like a flattened watermelon with about a gallon of hot water and "iron" the flannel bedsheets with it, so that the entire bed was warmed just before we jumped into bed. I also had a large rubber water bottle the size of a deflated football to keep my feet warm as I went to sleep.

In the wintertime our upstairs toilet bucket saved us the long walk down to the first floor to the house's single, unheated toilet. Still, on very cold nights, the bucket presented a problem when its contents froze. I always took the ice on top as a challenge: could my pee melt through the top? I made a game out of hitting one spot to see if I could make a hole. Our apartment also had no shower. On Saturday nights, Mutti heated a large pot of water and poured it into a washbowl so I could sponge myself down thoroughly. Twice a month she fired up the large woodstove in the basement to do the family laundry. It looked much like the expensive built-in brick BBQ grills of today, but instead of a grill, it supported a large bowl of water in which she would do the laundry by hand, using a washboard. In the evening, when the laundry was done, Mutti would fill the bowl with fresh water and use a bucket to dump the heated water into an old, free-standing bathtub. The cast-iron tub probably absorbed at least half of the heat, so I always rushed to get into the tub while the water was still hot. Each minute while the warm water lasted was a joy; luxuriating in the bath was not something you could do every day! While I was in the tub, Mutti heated another batch of water so that she and Dad could take baths. We treasured these occasions. Once, we visited friends who lived in a newer apartment that included a full bathroom. I begged to luxuriate in their bathtub while the adults played cards.

My parents spent a lot of time with their large and close circle of friends. On weekend evenings, Oma would babysit me downstairs when they were gone. As far as I knew, she never bothered to check in on me once I was asleep—although probably she did. When I woke out of a bad dream, scared and crying, Oma heard me sometimes, but at other times not. Eventually, I made a game out of going back to sleep once my terrifying dream had passed. I believed I could push the wall next to the crib and make it move, and I reached my hands through the bars and pushed as hard as I could. Why that helped, I don't know, but I always drifted back off to sleep. Perhaps feeling powerful enough to move the wall drove away the fears that woke me in the first place. On the few nights my parents tucked me into my grandmother's bed before they left, her old-woman smell and loud snoring did not make those nights much better.

My Childhood

I was born immediately after the turmoil of World War II, marking a new beginning for my parents, who had met in Germany during the war. Fate brought them together in the most improbable way. My mother, Gertrud Lenk, who was born and lived in Germany, had attended a culinary school before the war. When the war started, she got a job at a displaced children's camp near Germany's north coast, a safer area for children from the industrial areas where Mutti had grown up. She enjoyed preparing meals for the hundreds of children in the camp. Mutti hoped that she could use this experience to obtain a good job with a restaurant or a hotel after the war.

My parents had met two years earlier in Gelsenkirchen-Horst, her hometown. Herbert Tatzmann, my dad, was stationed with the anti-aircraft batteries protecting the Ruhr area's coal mines and factories. Mutti's parents did not initially approve of her dating him. Her parents hoped she would marry someone from within their church. Papa, unfortunately, met neither criterion: he was from Austria and raised Catholic. Still, the two had fallen in love and stayed in touch during the war by writing to each other. During one leave from duty, he had asked Mutti's parents for her hand in marriage after the war. Her parents reluctantly agreed, seeing how much my parents-to-be were in love. However, the war continued, and they remained separated for almost two years. As the war was ending, Papa fled north to a displaced persons camp to escape the remnants of the German Army. He knew she worked at some camp in the north, but not which; still, they were in love and he wanted to see her again.

My aunt Helga Arndt captured the story of how my parents were reunited in her book, *Growing Up under the Third Reich: Helga Arndt and Her Sisters*. During a rare get-together over coffee one afternoon in the garden of my aunt's home, the sisters—each now old, with grown children, and in Mutti's case, widowed—described their childhood experiences on a tape recording later used for the book. Here is how my mother described the events leading up to the wedding:

When the war ended, I was still employed at the boys' home in the northeastern part of Germany. Not too far from home was an army post where soldiers returning from the Eastern Front were resettled. Somehow, Herbert heard that I was working at the home. He was excited to find out if it was true. As soon as he had the opportunity, he asked his superior officer for permission to visit me. I could not believe my eyes when I saw Herbert in the lobby. How could this be? I thought he was in France.

My questions could wait—first, I ran into his arms. Our tears mingled on our cheeks as we embraced each other. When the other soldiers found out there was an engaged couple in their midst, they persuaded us to get married. Everybody thought it would be wonderful to have a happy celebration after all the misery we had been through. This was not how I envisioned my wedding. I had dreams of marrying in a white gown but did not see any possibility of doing that. How could I? Such items were not available where I was—or were they? It so happened that an actress was staying at a hotel to entertain the troops. She generously offered me one of her white evening gowns to wear. Now my heart was filled with joy and anticipation. As for Herbert, he could still wear one of his better uniforms; it would be a suitable substitute for a tuxedo.

My aunt Elsbeth, who was also in the boys camp at the time, takes up an important piece of the story. *Could they have waited? Of course! However, there was more involved in the decision than being reunited in love. Being married to Traute* [my mother's nickname], *Herbert could use her address as his home address. As an Austrian soldier, he would have been sent to France as a prisoner of war. So Traute and Herbert were married in front of a justice of the peace on June 24, 1945. Marriage gave him the rights of a German citizen, allowing him to stay until the Allies created order out of the postwar chaos.*

Thirteen months later, five minutes before midnight on July 31, 1946, on what had been a beautiful summer day, I made my official entrance into this world. By all reports, the birth was uneventful, without any complications. The happy event took place with a *Hebamme,* or midwife, not far from our home in Graz, Austria. Hospitals were just recovering from the war, so it was commonplace to use a midwife for delivery. Later, I realized that one of the bus stops on my way to school was in front of the house where I was born.

Midwife (r), assistant, mother and I.

The years immediately after the war were not easy for the family. The country had suffered greatly, and Graz, an industrial city, had been bombed extensively, leaving limited infrastructure in place. On the day I was born, an article in the local newspaper, *Die Kleine Zeitung,* encouraged people to "obtain woodcutting permits, or find a friendly farmer to allow them to cut enough wood for the winter." Citizens were urged to "start the job of cutting early so the wood would dry." Households were allocated fifty kilograms, or a little over one hundred pounds, of coal for heating each winter month; considering coal's weight, that was barely enough.

Food was extremely hard to come by, so each family had a coupon book to purchase certain rations of food per week. The newspaper announced, "During this week 40 grams of onions [1.5 ounces] could be had" and "about a half-pound of apples." My mother was eligible for extra rations, having just delivered a baby; still, that was not enough for the entire family. Fortunately, there was a small underground black market for food, and the women bartered for various commodities. For example, Mutti traded some of her cheese rations for lard, then used as a cooking oil. In her later years, she related to me with great delight that, on the way home from the barter, she hid the lard in her bra so that the soldiers from the occupying forces would not see her carrying it. She had to hurry home to avoid the lard from melting.

Mutti was creative when it came to putting food on the table. When I was about five, she taught me how to dig out dandelions with a knife. We'd throw away the stems and flowers and make a salad out of the greens. Red Cross and UN food rations, from such organizations as CARE (Cooperative for American Remittances to Europe), were also available. Unfortunately, few people could read the English labels, and many of the supplies remained unopened or unused. Even before we left our home eleven years later, I recall seeing what I now know to be Gerber baby food jars on a shelf in the basement. None of us ever knew what they were.

We also faced rolling electricity outages. People were notified each day what part of the city would have outages for two or three nights in a row.

Getting about the city was difficult because British and Russian forces occupied it. No American forces were stationed in that part of Austria. Less than a quarter mile from our home was a large UK military base, and a few miles farther away was the Russian base. The Russian troops were few but had a bad reputation for harassing people without cause. British troops were more numerous and friendlier. Their barracks were on the other side of a gravel pit close to our home.

Occasionally, the Brits would practice tank maneuvers in the woods or fields nearby. My friends and I loved to see and hear the tanks rumbling down the streets, although I'm sure our parents, who had gone through the war, did not share our excitement. The uncertainty created by the occupiers, especially the Russian troops, was one reason why my parents wanted to move to America.

When I was about six months old, my young life was almost cut short. Dad had found a job as an auto body repairman. One Sunday, Papa borrowed a shiny black car from his boss to visit his sister Frieda, who lived about two hours away. These were the days before seat belts, so my mother held me in her lap. As he began driving, my father noticed that the passenger door was not fully closed. My mother opened it a bit to pull it shut and latch it. But in those days, car doors swung out in the opposite direction of today's cars. Thus, when Mutti opened the door, the wind caught it and whipped the door backward, pulling her to her right. As she tried to close the door, I bounced off her lap, ricocheted against the door, and tumbled out of the car. Fortunately, I fell to the pavement next to the car, rather than under its wheels, and did not suffer any cuts or abrasions. Mutti had wrapped me in a blanket, and I wore a cap in addition to my clothing. The fall knocked me out, however, and the doctor who examined me told my parents to take me home and keep close watch, making sure to wake me every few hours. Thankfully, my infant skull was still pliable, and the injury was not as severe as it could have been. Nevertheless, as my mother described it, I was in and out of sleep for about two days.

Basic services such as health care were almost nonexistent, and illnesses were common. During my first four years, I had whooping cough, measles, diphtheria, and the most serious, scarlet fever. The only hospital in the city was the Landeskrankenhaus, a large complex of many buildings run by the state but staffed by Catholic nuns. It housed twenty children per ward, each in metal beds with sides resembling cages. We ate from metal plates and drank out of tin cups. The feel of the tin cup against my lips is still a very vivid memory. The sight of all the other children, and the sound of metal clanging, left a lasting fear of hospitals in me.

I was afraid to be away from my parents, and the stern nuns, with their black habits and high, winged white hats, struck a lifelong terror into me. They forced each child, however ill, to get out of bed twice a day, kneel down next to the bed, and pray to get better. For years to come, I would hide behind my mother if we encountered a nun. Even as an adult, while working at my first job, I almost turned down a desirable presentation because it would have meant speaking before a large group of nuns at a convent in Berea, Ohio. Eventually, I relented. I was the only lay male there among three hundred nuns from all over the world and three Franciscan friars. Some of the nuns wore their habits, but others were in street clothes, which helped me with my fears. The last evening there, after watching *All in the Family* in black and white on the only TV set in the convent, we celebrated with gallons of wine, liquor, pretzels, chips, and cheese. Today, I'm still skeptical but no longer fear them.

Once my hospital days were behind me, I had a wonderful early life, growing up in a loving family, surrounded by friends and neighbors who cared and looked out for each other. The grassy street in front of our house and the back yard was my world. Werner was a second-generation friend because his father and Papa had been childhood friends themselves. Our families vacationed together and otherwise spent a lot of time together. We considered ourselves to be brothers because we were each the only child in the family.

Our favorite place was the gravel pit behind my neighbor's house, across the street. Every day, trucks came to haul away sand and gravel for the postwar construction. These dunes of dirt and rocks, an area the size of several football fields, became our imaginary cities and roads. At the top of the pit was a berm of the topsoil removed in digging the deep pit. We spent hours and days on end playing there—for us, it was one gigantic sandbox. The soil was dark brown and smelled like fresh earth after a rain, and it was moist enough that we could pack it hard, yet it was not muddy or sticky like clay.

We carved roads and hollowed out holes that became pretend factories and homes. We used sardine cans instead of toy trucks and cars, which none of our families could afford. Holes punched on either end of a can with a nail and threaded with string made our truck-and-trailer combinations. Weather permitting, while my parents still slept, I escaped to our cities created of dirt. It was a safe and fun time for me.

We also challenged each other to see who could jump the farthest down the side of the pit. Screaming like we were leaping into a pool, we launched ourselves high into the air, pretending we were test pilots shooting into the sky and coming down on the side of the pit, the sliding dirt breaking our fall. Then we'd climb back up to repeat it all over again. Lederhosen, those ubiquitous Austrian or Swiss leather pants, were great; they cushioned the impact somewhat, and the dirt could simply be brushed off, aging them in the process. No kid wanted perfectly clean lederhosen unless they were those worn on formal occasions. Fearlessly leaping into the unknown may have set a pattern for my later life, when I dove into challenges without considering the possible consequences.

Gravel pit was our pool and play area.

In the summer, once the groundwater level had risen enough, the bottom of the quarry became the neighborhood swimming pond. After work and on weekends, neighborhood families relaxed there and cooled off from the heat. The water was warm, clear, and refreshing, a respite from homes that did not have air conditioning or even a single fan. Occasionally, a security guard would call the police, but before the police car could make it to the bottom of the pit, everyone had scrambled up the sides and hurried back to their homes.

These times are the most memorable of my childhood. Even today, seeing a gravel pit, I want to jump out of the car and play. The freedom we had to enjoy ourselves without the fears that shape kids' lives today was wonderful. I'm afraid that the carefree childhood we experienced is a thing of the past.

In the winter, the same hills and paths in the pit became magnificent sledding locations—and dangerous, in my case. My sled was old-fashioned, made of wood more than an inch thick and bent in front into an oval shape that made the sled look like a figure nine laying on its back. It was more than five feet long had had a woven bamboo grass seat that could easily accommodate three people. My friends called it the "tank." Occasionally, I would deliberately crash into things—old sheds or leftover wooden crates—so that my friends could watch the destruction. I envisioned myself a tank driver crashing myself into a target. I was never afraid to take a risk.

One afternoon, as the winter's light was closing in on the day, I decided to make one more run, urging my friends to watch as I crashed into a mound of snow at the end of a short, steep road. Dressed in three layers of my mother's handknit sweaters, with zippers at the top of the neck that always pinched the skin under my chin, plus mittens, leather ski boots with laces, and a cap, also knit by my mother, I was ready to charge that hill. Like a bobsledder at the Olympics, I grabbed the handles at the back of the sled. My boots dug into the snow as I charged down the hill. As the sled picked up speed, I threw myself onto the sled headfirst, to cut down on the wind resistance, or so I imagined. As loud cheers erupted from my friends, I raced down the steep roadway.

My sled picked up more speed than expected. I tried to drag my feet off the back end to slow or stop myself. Normally, I could use my feet like rudders and provide some steering, but my speed was too great to alter the course. I crashed into the snow mound, which turned out to be a large pile of rocks covered by a thin layer of snow. The sled came to an instant stop. I kept moving forward, straight off the front of the sled and headfirst into the pile of rocks. My friends ran to see how I was and found me sprawled there, unresponsive and bleeding from my forehead. Afraid, they placed me on the sled and pulled it to my house. My mother heard the boys cry out to her from a distance, and she ran out to meet them. Scared by what she saw, though happy I wasn't dead, she took me into the house, cleaned up the cuts and gashes, and put me to bed—none of which I remember. I slept until the next day and woke with a tremendous headache. The following day, Werner came to my house to check on me and told me what happened. Neither Mutti nor I knew that one day that in the future, I would be working with people who had suffered traumatic brain injuries. Fate?

During the winter months at the beginning of the week, I would take my skis to school and not take them home until the weekend. As was the custom in Austria, boys' and girls' classes were separated, with boys going in the morning and the girls the afternoon. The boys got out of school about twelve thirty, so many of us enjoyed a few hours of skiing before it was time to go home before dark. Places to ski were all around. Farmers and landowners let families use their hills—although, once you went down a hill, you had to walk back up again. There were no formal ski areas with lifts near our school, so we had to do it ourselves. By the time we went home, we were exhausted.

Sledding, skiing, and the third *S* sport, swimming, were my favorite outdoor activities. I learned to swim by watching how others did it at a local public pool. My parents would take a picnic basket, spread a blanket on the grassy section near the pool area, go for a swim, and then enjoy one of my mother's delicious meals.

Swimming was not all I learned at the poolside. One sunny, warm summer day, when I was about four, we were at the pool. The sky was blue, without a cloud, and a slight breeze kept the air temperature warm and comfortable. My parents had found a shady spot under a tree to spread a blanket about ten yards from the pool's edge. The pool was fed with water from a mountain stream that ran slowly in at one end and out the other end. As I remember, the pool was about four times the size of an Olympic pool, with a small, raised cement play area on one side. The far end accommodated a diving well. All around the pool was a metal railing consisting of two bars, each about a foot apart and no higher than about three feet, to prevent people from accidentally falling or running into the pool. I had already spent some time in the kids' play area when I anxiously ran up to my mother, informing her that I had to pee.

"Well, just go over by the pool," my mother responded, intending that I use the bathrooms next to the pool. Next thing, she heard laughter near the pool. When she looked up from her blanket, she saw me standing by the edge of the pool, relieving myself into it. She ran to where I was standing and tried to pull me away, by the time she got there, it was too late! The stream flowing through the pool continuously flushed it, so my small addition of liquid caused no tidal wave, tsunami, or health problem. The embarrassment my parents suffered was the only harm done that day.

Unlike in the United States, we had no school buses. Instead, kids used the public transit system to get to school. I was luckier than other kids because my father was a bus driver, which entitled me to a free pass to travel anywhere on the city's extensive transit system. Dad drove a bus, but the city also had a network of trams, or light rail as it is called in many cities today. On summer weekends, when Mutti was having a *Kaffeeklatsch*— coffee talks—with her women friends, I made good use of the free pass to travel around the city. Hopping on at one stop, I rode to the end of the line and back again, standing in the large bay windows at the back of the tram and watching the city go by.

Traveling around town was one of my favorite forms of amusement because our family did not have the money for entertainment. It also gave me a lifelong love of travel. Going anywhere I wanted was exciting. Generally, I did it only in the summertime when the weather was nice and I could gaze out at the gardens, parks, and lovely neighborhoods. On Sundays, I could see people sitting at coffeehouses and parents walking with their children under sunny skies. My parents didn't have to worry about anything happening to me while taking these rides. They had taught me how to behave, be careful, and be courteous. Unlike today, crimes inflicted on kids were unheard of. The drivers and conductors recognized the employee transit pass and kept an eye on me, knowing I was the son of one of their own.

Oma, Opa, and 3-year-old Manfred.

My father did not earn much money as a driver, and Mutti worked part-time in a grocery store while I was in school. I benefited from her working in the grocery store. Every now and then, on the way home from school, I would get off at the bus stop in front of the grocery store and she would sneak me a sandwich made from a freshly baked roll filled with meats and butter, which we could not usually afford on our own. She was always afraid her boss would see her do it get her into trouble, but for me she did it anyway.

In my early years, my grandparents were my babysitters. I spent many wonderful hours with my grandfather, listening to his stories. He had been a train engineer. Hanging on the kitchen wall was a picture of him standing in front of one of his large black locomotives. As the train engineer, he had operated the massive steam engine that pulled long trains through the mountains and valleys of Austria. He told me stories of the train pushing through many feet of snow in the mountains and flowing around mountain curves. This, too, ingrained in me a deep desire to travel and have adventures. Opa, as I called him, gladly shared these stories with me while sitting on a corner nook in their kitchen. I would sit on my knees with my hands on the table, attentive to his stories. Opa always sat to my right, while my grandmother sat across from me, ready to bring us a snack, lunch, or dinner. It was a fantastic place of comfort and joy for me. Opa and I also played different board games. Of the games we played together, Chutes and Ladders was my favorite. To honor him, and to remember his childhood home, Papa replicated that corner bench at my parents' house in Benton Harbor, where it too became an important gathering place.

Inspiring Grandfathers

On March 6, 1952, I startled awake, having heard a loud thump. Next, I heard my grandmother scream for my father at the bottom of the staircase to our apartment, "Herbert, quickly, come quickly!"

Papa and Mutti sprang out of bed. Papa rushed out of the bedroom. Mutti told me to stay in bed and then quickly followed Papa down the stairs. When they got to the first floor, they found my grandfather lying on the living room floor, apparently dead of a massive heart attack. He was seventy-two. I was not allowed to see him and had to stay upstairs the entire day. I finally got a chance to say goodbye to him at his funeral as the casket passed by. He had been my friend and hero. It was difficult for me to comprehend the loss.

Thinking back, I realize now how influential my grandfathers were on me. Opa Tatzmann showed me the strength of a man. Operating those trains was a complicated task requiring skill and courage. I learned from him that you could be strong and confident, yet also kind and gentle. He looked formidable but had a heart of gold. Opa spent hours upon hours with me, taking me for walks when I was still little and letting me help him in the garden, while watching him with adoration.

Grandfather Franz Tatzmann (left) with his train engine.

Opa Lenk, my mother's father, has been my inspiration for how I have led my life. I probably spent a total of only three weeks with him over my entire life, and yet, his caring, faith, and supreme belief in people's goodness led me to follow a path of helping people. He only saw individuals, not labels. On one visit to America, he left our apartment on a Sunday morning without telling anyone, so he could seek out a church service. He spoke no English and did not know his way around town. Once we noticed he was gone, my parents and I worried but did not know where to look. Amazingly, a couple of hours later, we heard him getting out of a car in front of our apartment. A group of African American women had brought him home after he had worshipped in their Black congregation. Watching them, you'd have thought he had been a parishioner for years! He believed in God in a pure sense, which I have never seen since. More on the grace, goodness, and life of this man can be found in the Helga's memoir, *Growing Up under the Third Reich.*

I was about ten when Mutti sat me down to explain that we were moving to America, following two of her sisters. Life was beginning to improve for my parents; nevertheless, they knew a better life was possible in America. Her sisters sent pictures of their cars and homes and expressed the joy of purchasing whatever they wanted. They promised to have a job waiting for my dad when we arrived. My mother explained how we would have to leave our stuff behind, but once in America, I could get new toys and we would live in a nice place. I paid little attention to what I might leave behind, for my mind was racing with thoughts of new things and new places—all in America!

I learned about America from reading Disney magazines. It was a wonderful place: cowboys and Indians lived there. My favorite toys were a set of clay cowboy and Indian figures, including horses and other wild animals. I could not wait to see real cowboys. Excited, I immediately wanted to go and tell my friends about the trip. I was going to do something they would not be able to do!

The excitement lasted over the next few months as I watched my parents prepare for the move. That excitement ended abruptly on the day Mutti told me to start packing and sorting out the things I would leave behind. That's when it hit me: I was leaving behind not just my things, but also my friends and the only life I had known. Sadness came over me, and it stayed, no matter how hard my parents tried to evoke the excitement again.

The Party Ends

A loud voice from the going-away party brought me back from my reminiscences. Not yet paved, the road in front of our house was overgrown with grass because it saw so little traffic. A single rut, barely noticeable, served as the official street and the occasional motorcycle or bicycle passing by. On weekends, the area in front of the house became the neighborhood recreation area, with pickup soccer games or ping-pong on the neighborhood's table. For tonight's festivities, the ping-pong table served as a bar and banquet table.

Shouting from below caught my attention. I tried to make out whose angry voice it was, but the voices were difficult to recognize after hours of drink and talk. Then, I heard my father's voice rise, and other voices—men's and women's—replied in anxious and concerned shouts. I strained to make out the words, leaning as far out as I could between the balcony slats without being noticed or falling through.

Suddenly, my mother's voice cried out, and she sounded afraid. I stood up to get a view over the top of the balcony slats and spied my dad and my oldest cousin, Ernst—a large man in his mid-twenties—facing off and shoving each other. Before that picture could sink in, they had raised fits and were hitting each other. My parents and uncle had said that Ernst tended to get into fights if he had too much to drink. Most likely, I assumed, this had happened again tonight. Dad had tried to break things up, and instead, my cousin attacked him. Dad, having been an amateur boxer in his youth, was capable of handling himself, and the fight ended quickly. Tears streamed down my face as I watched the groups splinter and leave in anger. *Why tonight? Why, when after tomorrow, we will never see each other again?* I thought.

I felt overwhelmed with sadness, resentment, and even anger. What should have been a joyful farewell event had turned into a tragedy. I turned and raced back to bed, knowing my mother would come to check on me and not wanting her to see my despair. As soon as I slipped under the covers, the tears that had been rolling down my cheeks became uncontrollable sobs. I thought I had already cried myself out about leaving. The way my parents had acted in the last few weeks, I could tell that they, too, were excited about their new life in America. But the fight took the last ounce of joy out of me. I did not want to leave the only safe place I had ever known. I knew I would miss my friends, especially Werner Murko. I turned my face to the wall, sobbing into the pillow and hoping that by the time my mother came to check on me, I would be asleep. I did not want her to know what I had witnessed.

I was still weeping and unable to sleep when I heard my dad walk into the bedroom. Peeking out from under the covers, I saw my father's nose bloodied, his left cheek swollen and starting to discolor. Mutti came to kiss me good night and consoled me, "Dad will be all right. Your cousin Ernst just had too much to drink."

Knowing the obvious didn't help me a bit! Mutti turned out the light, and she and Papa retreated to the kitchen, from where I could hear the angry, muffled voice of my father and my mother trying to soothe him. Knowing that all their bags were already packed, not even this fight would change what would happen in a few hours. Through my tears I thought, *Life is good here; why do we have to leave?*

The Trip Begins

Saying goodbye on train platform.

At seven thirty the next morning I stood, looking sullen, tired, and sad, on the train platform alongside my grandmother, my aunt and her husband. The morning air was cool on my face, even though it was mid-August, until I stepped out into the sunshine and felt the heat. The smell of the steam trains on nearby tracks and the wafting aromas of coffee and fresh-baked rolls from a nearby café entered my head, clearing away the anxiety of the moment. The steam engines reminded me of my grandfather. Looking across the tracks, I saw the sun glowing on the mountains that I had seen from our bedroom window my entire life. At my left, where the family stood, were the iron pillars that held up the platform's roof. To the right were the steps leading to the tunnels underneath the railway tracks. I heard a flutter, looked up, and saw a group of pigeons take flight as a steam locomotive screeched into the station. The startled birds left their marks on the floor, and I scrambled not to become a target.

I glanced again at the mountains that we would have to cross in a short time. There would be tunnels, and beyond those tunnels, a new life and new world would open for my parents and me. I understood that my life would be changed forever. What awaited me? New places, new people, new customs, and a new language?

Reading my anxiety, Papa said, "Don't worry, we will come back." He put his large hand on my shoulder. "We are not leaving forever; we will come back for visits often!" I didn't know then that it would be many years before I would return, and never again with him—a joy refused to me.

The conductor blew a whistle, signaling it was time to say our goodbyes. We all hugged and said goodbye to each other. Oddly, no one cried. I can only guess that we had all cried ourselves out.

Mutti, Papa, and I boarded the train and looked for our compartment. On this day, we did not have to sit in the coach section. This time, Papa had paid for a compartment.

As soon as we got into the compartment, I threw my satchel on the seat and rushed to open the window. Family and friends hurried up and stretched out their arms for one last touch of goodbye. Mutti and Papa pushed themselves out the window to take a loved one's hand that one last time. My grandmother, the shortest of all, reached as high as she could, but my father's fingers missed her and her face sagged in disappointment as she turned away. I was squeezed between my parents on either side, the windowsill pressed against my chest.

The train whistle blew, steam billowed out from underneath the carriage—a sure sign that the train was about to pull out of the station—and we felt the train begin to move. Our family walked alongside the slowly rolling train until the end of the platform. Mutti and Papa shouted their last goodbyes and then sat down on benches on either side of the compartment. I craned my neck out the window, looking back while taking in the smell of smoke coming from the locomotive, amazed at how quickly the train picked up speed once clear of the terminal. The wind rushed by my face as the engineer pushed the train out of the city. Looking back, I saw the Bahnhof disappearing in the distance. Family and friends were still standing there, waving, but growing smaller with each second. Screeching noise from the rails told me the train had turned into a sharp left curve, leaving me with a view of a few distant mountains and the outskirts of the city.

I pulled the window up and sat down next to my father. None of us spoke; we just sat there, deep in our own thoughts.

After a while—I can't remember how long—my mother broke the silence, suggesting we unpack and make ourselves comfortable. I saw tears in my dad's eyes, but he refused to acknowledge his feelings. Wiping away the tears, he turned away and busied himself with storing the suitcases in the spaces above our seats.

The compartment had a large window over a small fold-up table. Armrests that divided each bench into two lounger seats folded into the back to make comfortable beds in the evening. Another small bed could be pulled down from the ceiling. Opposite the ceiling bed was the luggage area and storage for pillows and sheets, much like the overhead bins of today's airlines, but with more room. I slept in the overhead bed that night. The door that swung out into the railcar walkway had a window and roll-down shade to provide privacy. The floors had soft padding, and light-brown flocked wallpaper covered the walls. These decorative touches helped to dampen the train wheels' rhythmic rumble.

At the end of each train car was a bathroom with a small sink and mirror for the passengers. I enjoyed going to the bathroom. When you flushed, the bottom of the bowl opened and everything dropped onto the railbed below while a rush of air flooded into the toilet from the moving train. When I peed, I found that I could hold the toilet's handle down and watch the ground rush by below.

Fatefully, one of the first stops after departing Graz was Knittelfeld, the city where my aunt and uncle lived and where my grandfather had grown up. As the train pulled into the station, we could see my aunt's house. She and her husband had been on the platform in Graz to see us off, and they had remained there to console my grandmother before returning home on the same train line. Many years later, I would get off at this train station and find my aunt waiting for me.

As the train moved on, we took in Austria's beauty, so well described on many travel shows and in the famous movie *The Sound of Music*. Lush green pastures sloped upward from the railbed toward green forests high above us. The train shared the lower slopes of the mountainside with precariously narrow roads that clung to the mountainsides. Now and again, to our left, I looked into a steep gorge in which raced a torrential river coming off the mountains, white foam and froth bubbling over large boulders and water-smoothed rocks. In places where the slope spread out less steeply, brown and white cows grazed lazily in the sunshine. When the valleys became narrow, tunnels appeared out of almost nowhere. Within a few minutes of darkness, we were transported from one picturesque scene to another as if traveling through a time warp.

Late that evening the train pulled into Essen, a short distance from my maternal grandparents' home in Gelsenkirchen-Horst. As a family we had not been there previously; only my mother and I had gone in 1951 to see my Aunt Frieda and Uncle Helmut off to America. That time we had to sneak ourselves across a closed border between Germany and Austria. The scene brought up my memories of a previous trip, which had been very different.

It was a dark night in early spring 1951. I held tightly to my mother's hand, trying not to trip over the roots protruding from the pine-needle-strewn mountain path we were climbing in the middle of the night. In the darkness, I could barely see the path. Black branches surrounded us and blocked moon- and starlight from showing our way. Every now and then, when I stubbed a toe on one of the roots, I'd let out a little whimper and Mutti would lean close to my ear to say, "Shh, remember, Manfred, we have to be very quiet while we are walking." With only my short black lederhosen on, I was afraid that I might trip and skin my knees. This small mountain separated Bavaria and Austria. We were smuggling ourselves into Germany near a Russian occupied zone so that my mother could say goodbye to her sister and husband before they emigrated to America.

My heart beat fast, from excitement as much as the exertion of going up the steep slope. Late that afternoon I had slept on the train that delivered us to a small village at the foot of the mountains. My four-year-old mind did not fully comprehend the risks of this trip. I knew only that this was important to my mother, so my job was to do as she asked. As we began our hike up the mountain, she had told me that if "soldiers stopped us," I should cry as loud and as long as I could. Mutti warned me that they might take everything we carried, so I had to let the soldiers know I was afraid. That frightened me because I was carrying my little rucksack with my favorite pillow, two apples, some bread, a small knife, and my teddy bear. I was determined not to let anyone have my teddy bear.

Thankfully, we made it safely across, and the rest of the visit went well. Mom had a wonderful time reuniting with her family and seeing her sister Frieda off to America.

On the return, we made it across the mountain just as daylight was beginning to break when, close to the railway station, I heard a booming voice call out from behind some trees. "Halt" was all I was able to understand. Three men sprang from the woods and surrounded us, taking my mother by the elbow. On cue, I started to scream and cry as they led us into a building near the train depot. They brought us into a room full of soldiers, desks, and chairs. A well-dressed soldier came up to talk to my mother. I was too scared and busy crying to understand anything that was being said. It was clear from their soothing tones that they wanted me to stop crying.

Looking around the room, I saw a large, dark-skinned figure wearing a green uniform approaching. That really scared me, and I increased the volume of my screaming. I had never seen a Black person before, much less someone so large! He bent down and, speaking soothingly, produced something from his chest pocket covered with a green wrapper. He unwrapped it, broke off a piece, and ate it, and then offered me the remaining unwrapped portion. Even though my tears, I could see and smell that it was chocolate, good chocolate. Chocolate was not something easily obtained at home. Savoring the chocolate made me stop crying, and between gasps of air, I managed to gobble down the entire bar.

Meanwhile, my mother had been talking to one of the soldiers. Two American soldiers then escorted us to the train station within short order, but not without loading my rucksack with four more chocolate bars. The next time I saw that kind of chocolate was in 1957, on my first shopping experience in America with my parents.

This Time the Leaving Is Real

Once again, I watched as loved ones waved us goodbye from a train platform. Mutti cried, saying farewell to her parents once more. The first time, she had been sent away to work at the boys' camp, while her parents remained in their home in Germany's largest industrial area, the Ruhrgebieht, because Opa worked in a coal mine. She did not see her parents or siblings for most of the war, and then, within a year of war's end, she left her family again to set up a life with my dad and start our family. Leaving this time—for faraway America—was more difficult. Tears flowed down her cheeks in big rivulets as the train pulled away. I hugged her as she looked out the window, and we waved goodbye together. My father, too, was overcome with emotion.

There were no lush mountains, flowing rivers, or content brown cows grazing on this segment of the trip. Traveling from central Germany to Holland, we only saw flat farmlands, industrial areas, and cities being rebuilt. There was no black steam engine belching smelly coal smoke behind it. (Austria's abundant coal reserves made it a cheap power source there.) Now we traveled on smooth rails behind a speeding diesel locomotive. The railcars were decorated in new, gleaming steel and bright colors with that new-paint smell. Our second-class seats, covered in plush blue cloth, reclined and had leg rests, allowing passengers to stretch out and put their feet up. The aisles were wide, and the interior was a combination of light-caramel-colored walls and a vanilla-colored ceiling. Light bounced around the car as the shadows of exterior trees, houses, or bridges flashed through the spacious windows. The wheels' noise was a hum, not a rhythmic *thumpity, thumpity, thumpity.*

About four hours later, I saw a cityscape appear, replacing Holland's farmlands and dikes. It was late afternoon when the train pulled into Rotterdam, one of the largest and oldest seaports on the Atlantic Ocean. Papa had made a reservation at a small hotel where the people spoke

German, within walking distance of the train station and the waterfront from which we would depart the next morning.

Mutti and Papa chatted excitedly as we got off the train, the recent traumatic separations now seemingly behind them. Mutti and Papa seemed young and alive. It's strange to say this about a thirty-two-year-old and a thirty-six-year-old, respectively, but the years after the war had been hard on them. I could not recall ever seeing them so thrilled or excited.

After checking into the hotel and freshening up, we ventured into the city to find a place to eat dinner. Mutti persuaded Papa that we should not venture far from the hotel, not knowing the Dutch language. In broken German, the front desk man gave Papa directions and the names of several nearby restaurants. When we stepped out into the street, Mutti insisted that I hold her hand tight; I wanted to run along the sidewalk, check out the shop windows, and take in all the new sights and sounds. The people looked different; they were blond with ruddy faces. The city smelled different. It was busy with people, cars, and sales carts everywhere.

As we walked along, we came upon a food vendor selling something that smelled delicious. A couple had just walked away from the cart, holding something in a white paper cone. The contents smelled sweet and somehow familiar, but neither my parents nor I could place the aroma. We could not read Dutch, so the signs on the cart were no help. Regardless, I wanted to try it. As I watched, people lined up at the cart, made a purchase, and walked away with paper cones stuffed with golden strips of this strange food. I begged my dad to buy me a cone so I could find out what it was. Papa laughed and agreed, which was a sign that he was in a good mood, and he got in line. Seeing my parents happy and experiencing new sights and sounds also helped me forget about the pain of leaving. When he reached the vendor, Papa pointed to the cones and asked what kind of food it was.

"Pommes frites," exclaimed the vendor. In halting German he explained, "Freshly fried potatoes made every few minutes. Here, try some." He handed each of us a couple of fries.

We had never had potatoes cut and fried in that manner. Mutti's potatoes were a staple with many meals. As she was a professional cook, they were always tasty, but these tasted deliciously different. Papa broke down and bought a cone, which we shared on the way to the restaurant. On the way back, I saw another vendor and begged Papa for another ten cents to buy another *Tütte,* or cone, of this newly discovered treat. He indulged me, and I let his good mood and the excitement of these new sights, sounds, and foods ease the pain of leaving.

By the time we got back to our room, the sun was setting over the ocean. The sky was bright orange and red, the upper atmosphere slowly fading into darkness. Standing on our balcony, I spied two white streaks across the colorful sky. Excitedly, I called out to my dad to come see this mystery in the sky. Papa patiently explained that it was a jet in the sky. I had seen pictures of jets in magazines but had never seen one fly across a sunset. Austria's army had only just received its first three fighters, purchased from the British, the year before we left. They caused a great stir every time they flew over our hometown. I watched until the contrails disappeared into the sunset. Exhausted from everything that had happened in the last twenty-four hours, I went to bed. This night there was no pain or trauma, no crying myself to sleep, only the jet trails and the glowing sunset remaining in my mind's eye.

We woke early the next morning because we had to report to the ship by 7:00 a.m. In the hotel's lobby, we ate a quick buffet breakfast of croissants with butter and jelly, grabbed our belongings, and then took a taxi to the harbor. After checking in we were directed through a building toward the ship.

Our ship, Johan van Oldenbarnevelt.

We stepped out from that dark hallway into the sunlight, and before us was a large ship with a black hull and white superstructure. I had never before seen an oceangoing ship up close. I was amazed. I craned my neck all the way back to look to the top of the black smokestacks, or funnels, as they are officially called. The ship was older than it looked and no comparison to the luxury cruise liners plying the oceans today with several thousand passengers. According to Wikipedia, the *Johan van Oldenbarnevelt* was built in Amsterdam for the Nederland Line and launched on March 8, 1929. She was a 19,787 gross ton ship—no comparison to today's cruise ships, which can reach 220,000 tons, or eleven times bigger.

Never having been this close to a ship before, I thought she was huge. She was 609 feet long and almost 74 feet wide, with two funnels, two masts, twin screws, and a top speed of 19 knots. From 1940 to 1945 she was used as an Allied troopship; after the war she was refitted for passengers. Six years after our trip, on December 22, 1963, she was destroyed by fire 200 miles north-northeast of Madeira, with the loss of 128 lives.

As we stepped up to the ship that day, the salty, fishy smell of the harbor enveloped us. I wanted to hold my nose but knew better. Men were moving carts loaded with luggage, boxes, and crates. Cranes lifted pallets of supplies into the sky, swiveled, and then deposited them into the ship's hold. All this was going on around us while we were waiting in line with other passengers. At the bottom of the gangplank, four men in crisp white uniforms flanked an official-looking man with decorations on his chest, dark bars on his shoulders, and a clipboard with many sheets of paper on it. As families approached him, he politely asked their names, found their names on one of the sheets of paper, and made a checkmark. He then directed one of the other men to carry the luggage up the gangplank. As we walked up the gangplank behind one muscular young man, another one, also dressed in a white uniform, took his place at the bottom.

As we boarded, I realized that the ship was even bigger than I first imagined. From where I was standing on the deck, I could not make out people's faces at the other end; far below us, the man at the bottom of the gangway now looked small.

A second crewmember greeted us at the top of the gangway, checked our identification, and gave Papa a set of cabin keys drawn from big wooden chest full of keys. Crew members positioned along the way guided us to our cabin. Eagerly, we walked along the gray-carpeted hallway, following a track worn in the center by many who had taken this path before us. The hallway was not big. Had I not been carrying my knapsack and a small suitcase, I could have reached my arms out and touched the walls on either side. Had I jumped, I thought, I could have touched the ceiling, filled with pipes and wires. The air was dense, scented with a mix of diesel fumes and the saltiness of the sea, leaving no doubt in our minds and senses that we were now on a ship.

After a few more turns, we climbed down another set of stairs, turned right down a new hallway, and reached our cabin. Mutti let out a sigh of relief. I'm sure she thought we'd be sleeping in the bowels of the ship.

Papa used the skeleton key to unlock the door. It swung inward into a bright room with two bunk beds on the right side, past a small sink, mirror, and cabinet. On the left, a door led to a simple but clean bathroom with a basic shower stall and toilet. Opposite the door was the bright white metal bulkhead of the ship. Surprisingly, a large round porthole in the middle of the wall provided most of the room's light. Across from the bunk beds stood a single twin bed, a nightstand, two blue, padded chairs, and a small desk with a reading lamp. The room smelled clean, with none of the diesel smell so pervasive to us on the way down here. Mutti took the lower bunk, and Dad commandeered the twin bed. I climbed up to the top bunk, claiming it as my own—not that either of my parents would have chosen to climb into it every night. Stretching out on my belly, I could see straight out the porthole. This bunk would be the play area for myself and the friends I made onboard.

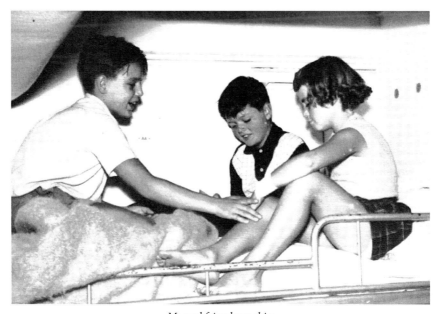

Me and friends on ship.

Once settled in, we went exploring, having never before experienced anything like this. We were overwhelmed by what we found. As we walked into the ship's dining room, I was awestruck! Like in the movies, everyone entered the room at the top of a large staircase, making an entrance as if into a grand ballroom. Paintings of hunting and wildlife scenes decorated the ceiling and walls. Under the pictures, the walls were paneled in rich red mahogany. Long tables covered with white tablecloths filled the room. High-backed chairs at each table were covered with velvety red material. We had seen such luxury in the castles back home, but we never expected anything like this on a ship—our ship! One side of the room was against the outside bulkhead. Through round portholes along the wall, we could see the sky. Later in the journey, on stormy days, we were surprised by the sight of flying fish or waves passing the porthole as we ate.

At dinner that very evening, I found the tables set with beautiful dishes and silverware. I wondered, *Who has to wash all those dishes?* In the morning there were trays filled with jars of jelly—strawberry and orange— as well as honey and peanut butter. Peanut butter was not something I had ever tasted before, and although others seem to enjoy it, I could not get used to the taste. Perhaps it was the stickiness of the peanut butter on the gums, or maybe it was the aroma—the smell was noticeable as you entered the room each morning. For me, at least, any possibility of enjoying peanut butter in the future ended one particularly stormy day when several people became seasick while eating peanut butter. It is a smell and vision that I shall never forget.

At every meal, the scent of coffee and baskets full of freshly baked rolls and loaves of bread invited you to sit and enjoy. With each service, waiters brought out shiny pots of tea and coffee in addition to large cut-glass pitchers of orange, tomato, and grape juice. A beautiful card at each place setting let passengers know what the service of the day would be. Breakfast and dinner typically had three fixed items. Lunch generally consisted of two lunch entrées, supplemented by a grand buffet of salad greens and other vegetables and sandwich makings including ham, roast beef, a choice of cold cuts, and a variety of cheeses, along with several different soups.

On our fourth day, the seas were rough and my parents, feeling the effects of seasickness, stayed in their beds. I set out to explore the ship.

Meandering through the empty hallways, I felt the ship sway from side to side and up and down as its crested waves. As the ship rose up on a wave, my legs compressed as if they were pushed into my chest; then, as the ship slid down the other side of the wave, my legs would stretch. It made me think of standing in front of a funhouse mirror at a fair or amusement park. I had always wondered what something like that would feel like. The roller coaster feeling was fun. To increase the pleasure, I started jogging through the ship, anticipating each rise and fall. After some time, I found myself near the indoor swimming pool. I thought this might be a good day for me to take a swim with no one else about. I loved to swim, but the pool was small and usually occupied by adults who frowned on the kind of frol-icking that kids enjoyed. Today, probably because of the rough seas, I had the pool all to myself. I raced back to our cabin and begged my parents to let me go swimming. They agreed, confident in their knowledge that I was a good swimmer. Most likely, they were just pleased to have me out of the way while they dealt with their own misery.

As the ship rocked from side to side and up and down, I walked to the end of a long passageway and down two flights of stairs, finally reach-ing a wooden door with large white letters *POOL* painted on it. I opened a door that led me down another hallway, against which on either side were the men's and women's dressing rooms. I could smell both chlorine and the sea and noticed moisture hanging in the air as I got closer to the pool. Reaching the end of the hallway, I pushed open a second door made of thick glass and stepped through into the pool area. It was empty except for me. As I walked toward the edge of the deep end of the pool, moisture covered the tile floor, and I had to be careful not to slip as the ship rocked. Looking into the pool, I noticed that the ship's swaying motion was creat-ing small waves in the pool. *This is going to be fun*, I thought.

Without thinking, I jumped off the edge of the pool, legs tucked under my chest in the cannonball position. As soon as I was airborne, though, I realized the ship had hit a valley in the waves, pushing the ship's front down. I hit what little water was left at my end of the pool hard, even though I had quickly extended my legs to catch myself. Landing at the bottom of the pool, I looked up, realizing that the ship had now gone up the crest of the wave. All the water that had rushed to the other side of the pool was now coming back toward me. I had barely enough time to gulp air into my lungs before the tsunami hit me, forcing me hard against the pool wall. Fortunately, the water also crested the rim of the pool, raising me up with it. I grasped the edge of the pool and held on tight, afraid I might be pulled back into the pool as the wave receded again. Once the water pulled back, I scrambled out of the pool, coughing out saltwater and gasping for air, grabbed my shirt and towel, and ran to the door and out into the hallway.

There I found myself sloshing through water that had pushed its way past the glass door as the wave crested the pool. Wet, cold, and scared, I ran back to the cabin to tell my parents. Papa found the event hilarious and laughed at me. Mutti, concerned that I could have drowned, scolded me for not knowing better than to try jumping into the pool during such conditions. This disciplinary process would prevail for the rest of my life. My father generally took a hands-off approach, while my mother spoiled and corrected me as necessary.

Parents and I enjoying the passage.

Late in the afternoon of the fifth day of the journey, the ship glided through slight swells as the sun ended its daily journey over North America on the horizon. While the ocean was tranquil, there was much activity aboard the ship. All afternoon, passengers gathered at the ship's rails, anticipating the sights of America coming into view. For most of the 680 passengers, it was the first glimpse of America, and each wanted to be the first to see the lights of their new home. Agonizingly slowly, darkness fell, and the warm breeze blew over the side of the ship, making women's dresses and long hair billow in the wind. The gentle sea and warm air made it an enjoyable viewing event. Gradually, like distant stars twinkling on the evening sky, lights began to appear on the far western horizon, and whispers among the passengers stationed along the railing turned to excited chatter. Many pointed toward the horizon, trying to identify specific points of light.

For the last couple of hours, I had run back and forth from the deck to our cabin, keeping my parents informed of our progress. Listening to other adults on the deck amplified my anxiety. Some, with utter confidence, claimed that the distant light they were seeing was the Statue of Liberty or Empire State building. Never mind that no one standing around us had ever seen either of these landmarks from the ocean. In fact, the ship was still too far at sea to recognize anything but light sources.

Displaying our own excitement, Mutti, Papa, and I staked out a space on the port side railing. As we stood there, I saw Papa gently put his arm around Mutti's waist and pull her close to him in a gentle caress. The sight made me feel secure and protected, knowing that my parents genuinely loved each other and were both very happy. Before long, the orange of the setting sun gave way to darkness, clearing the way for the moon and the stars to appear and blend with the distant city lights. The outlines of large buildings and skyscrapers became visible on the horizon as the ship progressed toward land. Rumors spread among the passengers lining the railing that the Statue of Liberty would come into view within the hour. The warm breeze slipping alongside the ship soon brought with it warm, thick, and pungent air mixed with the sea breeze. It was a different mix than what we had breathed for the last few days. Now it had tinges of city smells.

In various languages, adults called out to each other, beckoning friends and family members to see the view. Shortly before eleven o'clock, in awe, we beheld Lady Liberty coming into view in the distance. Soon we realized that lights glowed in her crown and the flame. Simultaneously, the full skyline of New York came into view. The thousands of city lights made it seem like we were staring into another universe—silent, yet bright and sparkling, blending into the cloudless sky until they competed with the stars themselves. Looking down through the railing, I saw the sleek water gliding past as the ship moved closer and closer to our dreams and our future.

"Look, Mutti! Over there! Papa, look at that building," I cried out as more of the city came into view. "Look how tall that one over there is!" As we entered the harbor, an uncountable number of lights from thousands of buildings: Staten Island to our left, and lower Brooklyn to our right.

"Oh, look, look," passengers cried out is what I assumed from the different languages. The anticipation was catching. People scurried from one side of the ship to the other to see the sights. After entering the outer harbor, the ship began to slow down. Soon, an announcement was made that the ship would not dock tonight but would remain at the mouth of the harbor for the night and dock early in the morning. The hour was late, but a loud cheer rose from everyone on deck when the anchor dropped. As the passengers went to their cabins, I could feel and hear their delight, their growing anticipation for the next day. I had a hard time going to sleep with these astonishing views and thoughts of the new life before me swirling in my mind. I laid my head on the pillow and looked out the porthole at the end of my bunk. In the distance I saw the lights of our future.

The next morning, I awoke to strange vibrations within the ship, a lot of clatters, and my parents busily talking to each other. Papa, always an anxious man, was telling my mother to hurry and get our things together.

He came over and shook me awake. "Manfred, wake up, we are in America," he said, a broad smile on his face. It did not take much to get me moving. In a flash, I was out of the bunk. Quickly, I rinsed my face, combed my hair, jumped into my clothes, and headed out the door.

"Hold on," my mother yelled at me. "Pack up your stuff and bags. You, too, have to carry your load." What? I was ready for America! Who cares about clothes and such stuff! Let's go, let's go!

It was 6:55 a.m., September 7, 1957, and the sun was shining brightly through the porthole. Dad answered a knock on the door, and a ship officer handed him a card that read "9:35," our time to depart the ship. Departure procedures had been distributed the previous night, which explained that the stewards would be coming around to pick up the luggage before breakfast; we should eat, debark at our assigned time, and proceed to immigration.

This morning, breakfast was abbreviated to a simple self-serve buffet. I really did not care to think about food, being too excited to consider eating. I wanted to go topside to see America. Mutti and Papa finished packing the bags and set them out in the hallway as instructed before we headed to the dining room one last time. At the top of the stairs, I took a moment to pause and remember the wonderful aromas that had welcomed us during this trip. I wanted to remember the people and the fun we had, to never forget the beauty of the room. Each of us quickly grabbed a roll and some coffee or milk and then headed topside, not wanting to miss out on extra seconds of seeing America.

As I opened the door to the deck, I was hit by an unexpected heatwave. My body felt surrounded by the moisture of the Hudson River, along with the aroma of the city. More than that, though, there was the noise, a rushing sound that froze me in the doorway until I realized it was the sound of rushing traffic, people, and whatever else makes noise in a big, big city. I stepped onto the deck as the combination of a sunny, bright day and cloudless blue sky overwhelmed me. While we slept, the ship had reached the dock. The shuddering I'd felt earlier in the morning was the ship being pushed against the dock by a ship tender and tied to big metal stanchions embedded into concrete. People lined the railings, chatting in an array of languages, craning their necks to see the skyline and perhaps searching the shoreline for friends or relatives whom they expected to meet. The ship rested against thick timbers tied together in sets of three and cushioned with tires. In between the ship and the dock, we could see water and flotsam, the source of the musty smell in the warm summer air. Large seagulls dashed in and out of the water and scurried across the dock, picking up scraps while trying to avoid being hit by carts or people.

Across the dock was a huge two-story building that ran the entire length of the pier. The bottom floor was a warehouse-like structure with many doors; the second floor had offices and an open walkway crowded with people. Passengers had been instructed to depart the ship at the assigned time and walk across a gangway toward the building; once there, immigration officers would screen us. Then we could proceed to the first floor to pick up our belongings. Below us, small tractor-like trucks were bringing large, flat carts up next to the ship.

Everyone watched with fascination as, above us, large nets swept across the ship, dipped into a ship's hold, and rose a few minutes later filled with steamer trunks, suitcases, and boxes. The nets rose high above the dock and then, at some unseen signal, were slowly lowered dockside. Men grabbed the net with wooden poles that had metal hooks at the end; they gently spread the net open and moved the trunks and luggage onto the waiting carts, much as airplanes are loaded today. The carts were then either driven off or pushed into the building. We watched this dance repeating itself again and again.

My parents had packed the essentials we needed to start a new life in the United States into three trunks. The trunks had been shipped ahead weeks earlier and placed in the hold of the ship before boarding. Looking up as another set of nets swung above us, I saw our trunks. Papa had built two of the trunks himself, while the third was an old classic steamer trunk that had been in the family forever. Each had to conform to the shipping line and customs standards, measuring about three feet high, four feet long, and three feet wide. Both were painted with a waterproof navy gray paint, and, using his superb handwriting skill, Papa had labeled each with black paint. The old steamer trunk was black, and he had used bright white paint to inscribe our names and final destination, as instructed by the shipping company. Indeed, all our worldly possessions were now clearly visible in one of the nets coming out of the ship's hold. Papa had taken special care to make sure the two trunks were sturdy, with handles to lift them on either end.

"Mutti, there is our stuff," I shouted, pointing up to a net swinging above the ship.

As we followed the nets containing our belongings toward the dock, we smiled at each other, happily looking forward to our new life before us. A loud seagull's screech made me look up again, and I noticed that one side of the net—our net!—had opened, allowing part of its contents to tumble into the chasm between the ship and the dock. We watched in horror as our trunks, along with others, crashed into the water. Craning to look over the side of the ship, we saw them floating in the narrow gap between the ship and the pier. Dread replaced our joy. Mutti grabbed Papa's shoulder and right arm—whether in panic or fear, I couldn't tell.

With obvious skill and speed, the stevedores sprang into action. Several secured the loose edge of the net with their long hooks, while others rushed to collect the trunks now wedged between the ship's hull and the dock. Luckily, the net had not fully opened, thus preventing all the trunks from falling out. But ours, we saw in horror, floated on top of the water. It left me with the impression this kind of accident was not unusual. The stevedores teamed up to pull the trunks out of the water by their handles. Noticing how the stevedores grabbed the trunks, Dad thought aloud, "So that's why the instructions for the placement and size of the handles were so precise." When the dripping-wet trunks containing all our worldly belongings had been securely guided onto the dock, Papa proudly reassured Mutti, saying, "I made the trunk just in case something like this would happen." As if he'd had any idea that it would happen! Mutti just rolled her eyes. I smiled, proud of my dad.

Welcome to America

After clearing immigration, we went down to claim our luggage. Then we were shown where we could inspect our trunks. Mutti carefully checked each trunk's exterior; inside was all we owned—sheets, pillows, towels, clothing, and personal effects. The trunks were wet, but it was clear they had not been in the water long enough for the contents to be damaged. Mutti had to be satisfied with this cursory inspection because she could not open the trunks yet. By prearrangement, once immigration officials were satisfied that the seals put on at departure had not been broken, the trunks were immediately transferred to a delivery agent. Inspection finished, we took our suitcases to the reception area, which was the size of an airplane hangar. It had well-worn, dirty cement floors and drab gray walls from which the paint was peeling. After the luxury we had enjoyed for the last seven days, the strong smell of people, grease, and exhaust from the cars and trucks was a blow to our senses.

From our left, a deep voice called out, "Trautchen," as my mother's younger brother, Fritz, came running up. He and his wife Renate lived in New Jersey, across the river from where we had arrived. My uncle was pastor of a small, German-speaking Evangelical Lutheran congregation. Mutti fell into her brother's arms with exuberant hugs and greetings. After a round of introductions, my uncle looked me over and said, "My, look how big you have gotten!" and rubbed my hair while my aunt gave me a warm but reserved hug. The last time she had seen me, I was four years old.

We walked along a hallway and down a couple of flights of stairs to the ground floor, at last stepping out into the warm sun and a slight breeze. I took my first deep breath on American soil. It smelled exotic. This is the way I had always imagined what my first day in the United States would be like. Sunny! Fantastic!

As we walked across a huge parking lot, I was surrounded by the large, shiny cars that I had only seen in magazines or movies. I was mesmerized. Uncle Fritz stopped at a large green car, unlocked the driver's side door, reached in, and pulled the button to open the back door. Mutti opened the door, and I dodged around her and jumped up onto the large back seat, bouncing on it and petting the soft upholstery like a dog. I couldn't believe it; I was actually sitting in a large American car. Mutti scolded me for being so impatient and impolite and pulled me back out of the car.

Meanwhile, my uncle had stepped to the back of the car and opened the trunk. He and Papa placed the suitcases in it. Peeking around the corner of the car, I was amazed at how big the trunk was; for a moment, I thought, *What fun it must be to ride in there.*

Mutti pulled me back again and told me to get into the car, which I found silly because she had just pulled me out a few minutes earlier. Joyfully, I hopped back in and slid across the seat to be next to the window. Mutti then climbed in, followed by my aunt. Dad sat up front with my uncle.

Uncle Fritz started the car, and it moved smoothly across the parking lot and pulled out onto the busy street. As we drove, I stared out the window, my mind spinning as I tried to take in the view of all the large buildings swiftly moving past. My head swiveled from side to side as I looked at buildings on the left, then the right, and cars whizzing by; I peered up toward the tops of the skyscrapers. "Look, Mutti! Look, Papa!" was all they heard while trying to carry on their own conversations.

My uncle's house was on a quiet residential street of older homes that looked very much alike. He took us upstairs and showed us into a guest room where bright sunshine poured in through lace curtains. The room had old but nice furniture, a plush green carpet, and yellow print wallpaper. It was the largest bedroom I had ever seen, much larger than our bedroom back home. In the middle of the room was a round table with a single glass bowl sitting on a beautifully crocheted white tablecloth. In it were half dozen packages of assorted flavors of gum. I had never seen such riches! Back home, I had been able to buy only one pack of gum on rare occasions, and now, here, I had a bowl full of gum, and chocolate too.

Yes, I thought, *Mutti and Papa were right. America is a great place!*

It was a sunny midmorning as we pulled into the Greyhound bus station in South Bend, Indiana, next to four other buses. As the bus had made its various stops throughout the night, we slept, knowing our stop was many hours away. Afraid to leave the bus at any of the stops, Mutti brought sandwiches, a thermos of coffee for the adults, and juice for me. As soon as the bus stopped in its designated slot, Mutti pressed her face to the bus window, looking for her brother Manfred, who was supposed to pick us up. He had arrived a few years earlier with Mutti's sister Elsbeth—or Elschen, as the family called her—and her husband, Gunther.

"There they are!" she exclaimed. Manfred, after whom I was named, was standing next to Elschen by one of the doors. Mutti quickly packed up the thermos, food, and other items that had comforted us during the fourteen hours since we left New Jersey. A hissing noise told us that the bus door was now open. The driver, an older man with a big belly and gray hair, stood up, turned toward us, and exclaimed, "Luggage can be picked up in a few minutes on the right side of the bus. Please take your belongings so others getting on can place their belongings into the baggage hold. Thank you!" And with that, he stepped outside.

Next, I heard a latch open. Out the window, I could see two African American porters come up and pull luggage out of the bus's hold. Passengers stood around us, crouching beneath the inside luggage rack, waiting to exit the bus, while others remained seated. Most passengers seemed to be getting off the bus here. My dad rose from his aisle seat, and Mutti handed him our bags. Papa told me to sit and wait until they organized everything. That gave me time to look out the window and watch the people and see America's many new faces. There were people of all ages, colors, sizes, and shapes. The boredom of the long road trip disappeared as I realized my new life was just ahead for real!

As the queue of people waiting to get off the bus began to move, Mutti stepped into the aisle to lead the way. When she stepped through the bus door, Manfred came up and threw himself into her arms, followed by Elschen. My uncle was good looking, with a tanned complexion, brown hair, and a strong build, which came from handling bricks each day as a bricklayer. Although only nineteen, he had started his own business already. The three of us stepped off the bus into a big group hug, blocking the way for the remaining passengers. Embarrassed but not concerned, we finally moved onto the sidewalk, allowing others to get by.

After a few minutes of excited chatter, Papa and Uncle Manfred grabbed our suitcases, which the porters had placed on the curb next to the bus. Our group set off through the terminal building to my uncle's car parked out front.

I was in awe of what I saw. My uncle had a shiny, four-door, dark maroon 1954 Pontiac, with big whitewall tires, a beige vinyl top, and some of the largest chrome bumpers I had ever seen. Elschen gave me a warm hug on the way to the parking lot and commented on how I had grown since we last saw each other five years earlier. My uncle opened the back door of the Pontiac and told me to hop in, which is exactly what I did. Loaded with excitement, I hopped onto the bench, and just like with my Uncle Fritz's car, caressed the smooth, velvety fabric of the car seat as if I were petting a cat. Papa sat up front with Uncle Manfred, and Mutti and Aunt Elschen got into the back with me.

Fascinated, I watched my uncle start the car. Then he turned backward, his right hand draped over the front seat, and maneuvered the car out of the parking space and out onto the street. It was a warm day, so I grabbed the silver handle and rolled down the window. The wind cooled my face as I watched cars and trucks whizzing by. I had never seen so many of each at one time.

I loved the whooshing sound each truck made as it passed by us in the opposite direction. Some trucks roared loudly, almost like a train; others flew by in near silence. Riding in their wind was the intoxicating smell of diesel and gas exhaust that reminded me of riding with my dad in his diesel truck when I was little. He would take me to pick up big blocks of granite from a quarry in the mountains.

The forty-minute ride to our new home, Benton Harbor, was much better than the last fourteen hours on the bus. The adults were busy talking. Aunt Elschen explained that others had wanted to come to greet us, but they could not take time off from work. My parents regaled Uncle Manfred and Aunt Elschen about the bus trip and the voyage's excitement. I eavesdropped as I watched the scenery as if at the movies. First, there were the big buildings, people, cars, and trucks of the city of South Bend. The buildings here were different from those I had known in Graz. Those buildings, in some cases, were hundreds of years old; here, most buildings, even the factories, looked new. Before long, the cityscape became countryside, with green fields and trees all around us. I had never seen such wide-open spaces before. I was surprised not to see any mountains nearby.

Our New Home

Upon our arrival in Benton Harbor, Michigan, on September 20, 1957, we moved in with my aunt Frieda, or Friedchen, as the family and friends called her. Thankfully, a few weeks later my parents found an apartment on the upper floor of a large older house on the east side of the city. It had white siding and a black roof, surrounded by mature chestnut trees on a corner lot; a narrow strip of grass between the garage and the back door was the backyard. At one time, the area had been the location of stately homes, most now converted to apartments. The neighborhood was changing from an upper middle-class neighborhood of stately homes to a working-class area with single-family residences converted to apartments. Trees with canopies that had seen many years grew large on one side of the house, shielding it from the hot summer sun and breaking up the harsh winter winds. The apartment consisted of two small bedrooms, a living room, a bathroom, and a small kitchen with a table and four chairs. Uncle Manfred occupied one of the bedrooms, helping us to pay the rent.

The house was owned by a couple with a daughter who was a senior in high school. Knowing that we were new immigrants, and wanting to help our family, they offered the apartment at a reasonable price. Each Wednesday evening I was invited downstairs to watch the popular TV series *Wagon Train*. This was a family event for them. The wife made a big bowl of popcorn from which we each filled our own smaller bowls, and then we sat back and watched. Sitting there with them made me feel at home. I realized that this was my new life: TV, cars, popcorn. All these things I did not have in Austria, and more, would now be part of my life.

Popcorn, for example, was new to me, and I loved the smell of the freshly popped corn, which I had never had before. All TVs at that time were in black and white. Television provided me with an opportunity to learn English. Today, as I teach new immigrants, I encourage them to watch family-oriented TV to learn the language, just like I did.

Uncle Manfred lived with us to help us adjust. He took us grocery shopping, and on weekends he showed us around the area. It amazed us; everything was so large compared to back home.

Not knowing the language created unexpected problems. Unlike at the small corner grocery store near our home in Graz, where you had to request everything, National was a large, sumptuous chain store where you could help yourself. On one of the first shopping trips, Papa found what looked like hard salami, just like he ate back home. Smoked hard salami had always been one of his guilty pleasures. He would sit down at the kitchen table, get out a magazine to read, and take a couple of slices of fresh bread, a beer, and a chunk of hard salami; with this, he was content. Therefore, it was with great delight that he saw a firm, brownish-orange sausage wrapped in plastic in the meat counter. Dad told my mother he could not wait to get home and sink his teeth into that salami. It had been weeks since we had left, and Papa was having salami withdrawal. Once home, Papa pulled back the plastic wrapping and bit into the sausage with great gusto. It came out of his mouth no sooner than it had gone in, along with some curses!

"Verdammt! What kind of salami do they make here? Don't they know how to make salami? This is awful!" His mouth was burning. We later learned that he had just bitten into a chunk of spicy pepperoni sausage.

Every day was a new and exciting experience for me. It was like living in a movie, having a new scene before me every minute of the day. One of my favorite new pleasures was Honey Nut Cheerios. I could not understand why my mother would not let me eat them three times a day.

On weekends when he was not working, Uncle Manfred took us on outings to Lake Michigan's beaches. He showed us the extensive fruit farms that dominated the area's economy and took us to Chicago a few times.

US-12, a two-lane highway, was the main road between Chicago and Detroit. Once in LaPorte, Indiana, we got on the Indiana Toll Road, the first interstate in the area. I had never seen such a large highway, with two wide lanes each way and cars moving fast. Every few miles we had to stop at a tollbooth and drop twenty-five cents into a sliding down a funnel, triggering the gate to open. Later, when we had our own car and traveled the same road, Papa would get a kick out of tossing the quarter in close to the end of the funnel to see if the gate would open sooner. He also tested the system by using twenty-five pennies instead of a quarter coin. It was all very funny. Secretly, I hoped he would drop a penny so that he would have to get out and pick it up. We went on these excursions to learn more about our new country and because my dad loved driving. Mutti enjoyed getting out in farm areas to select fresh fruits and vegetables from farm stands.

These trips were special occasions, and we dressed appropriately. Mutti wore a nice dress and shoes with heels; Papa wore a suit and tie. Mutti always made sure I, too, was dressed in my best clothing. Although we did not have much, we all had at least one set of Sunday clothes, worn only on that day and special occasions. We were not church people like the rest of Mutti's family, so these trips were our main dress-up occasions. Eventually, Mutti joined a Lutheran church, and I was confirmed there to please Mutti. Even at the age of fourteen, I could not blindly accept the faith aspect of religion. Papa had little use for organized religion. He, like almost all Austrians, had grown up Catholic. At age nine, for some reason that remains murky, he was beaten by a priest. He vowed then never to participate in regular church activities again.

Dad, unable to speak English, took a job working for my uncle Manfred in his bricklaying business. Hauling bricks was not the job my dad had been trained to do or hoped to have in America, but he knew that he needed to earn a living for our family. Like most immigrants, he had to start off somewhere.

Papa had been trained as a mechanical draftsman and was proud of his drafting skills. Back home, in trade school, he was first in his class and excelled when it came to mechanical drawing. In America, he hoped to use his skills to get a job with a large automotive company. In European fashion, he had also learned a trade as an auto body mechanic. That was his fallback job in case he could not find work as a draftsman. Drafting, though, was his first choice. After about a year of helping Uncle Manfred, Papa got a job at the Laboratory Equipment Company (LECO), a local manufacturer of laboratory test equipment. Papa started in the company's plating section, where they made metal cabinets to house the test equipment. He had to lower metal parts into the acid baths used in the plating process. This was a time before the worksite safety regulations we have today. Dad came home almost daily with acid burns on his skin and coughing up blood from breathing the acids. I believe that experience, along with his smoking, may have led to his throat cancer and removal of a vocal cord later in life. After a while, he was moved to the ceramics division, where they made high-temperature ceramic test equipment. Still, daily, he breathed in dust from the ceramic powders.

The owners took advantage of the European immigrants, not paying them much but knowing they were dedicated and skilled workers who needed the jobs. Despite the dirty and dangerous nature of the work, it provided our family with a steady income.

Mutti stayed home at first, trying to accustom herself to a new life. Eventually, she got work cleaning houses and then became a cook at

Whirlpool Corporation headquarters and the Lake Michigan Community College cafeteria. In both jobs, she was one of the lead cooks—this was what she had been trained to do in Germany. Mutti enjoyed the work, and she was loved by her employers.

CHAPTER 2

SCHOOL DAYS

Octber 6, 1957, exactly twenty-nine days since I'd first set foot on US soil, was a day I dreaded, though I knew I couldn't avoid it. On that day, Aunt Frieda came to take me to my first day of school in America. I was scared and excited at the same time. The elementary school, Seely McCord, was only three blocks from our apartment. On a couple of weekends, Mutti, Papa, and I had walked past the school to check it out. We peeked into classroom windows and walked around the grounds. We were impressed with the school's size and the colorful paintings and interesting objects we saw in the classrooms. Obviously, the school was well funded, and teachers seemed to work well with the kids.

That morning, Mutti decided not to go along, claiming it was because she could not speak the language. However, I believe she had a hard time letting me go and did not want to embarrass herself in front of strangers. Mutti had always been very protective of me—whether because I was the only child or because of my childhood accidents, I wasn't sure—and I had been spoiled. Whatever may have been the case, now I was on my own.

In Austria, I had ridden the city bus for several miles to and from grade school. My parents were not concerned. Here, where Mutti did not know what to expect, I could see the worry on her face. She had made sure I was dressed in black slacks, a nice white shirt, and a sweater she had knitted herself. Knitting was a passion Mutti enjoyed until the very end of her life.

The morning was splendid—a bright, pleasant fall day. I excitedly chatted with Aunt Frieda in German as we walked toward the school, asking her questions about the school and the students— all questions she could not answer. Trees had begun to show signs of red, yellow, and orange leaves. We went down Britain Avenue and crossed the bridge over a creek. I looked down at the creek and the railroad track that ran below it. Weeds had begun to grow between the rails, making me think that the tracks were used less than they had once been.

A block away, around some trees, I could now see the corner of the school building. Fear grew in me as the school came into sight. There were no other students to be seen. We crossed in the middle of the block at a pedestrian crossing where, later on, I would be a school safety officer, wearing my white belt and stopping traffic so students could safely cross. Aunt Frieda had been asked to bring me at midmorning, after classes had started. As we got closer, I realized the school had two buildings, not just the single-story one my parents and I had peeked into. The other was a larger, red, two-story building with a small courtyard and large playground behind it. I saw swings and slides and thought, *Oh, what fun!* In Austria, schools were all business; we had no slides or swings. In nice weather the monkey bars, which doubled as exercise equipment during gym class, were the only play equipment we had.

We walked up to the single-story building, my heart beating fast. Opening one of the two large wooden doors, we looked into a long hallway. The floor was gray marble, smoothed by all the children's shoes that had polished it over the years. To our left was a large office with glass panels extending up to the ceiling. I could see chairs placed around the office's edges and a woman sitting behind a counter, working on her typewriter.

As we walked in, the woman turned, smiled, and greeted my aunt. Although I had tried to learn English, I still did not understand everything. Back in Austria, I had taken one English class in school. But that was limited to singing songs like "My Bonnie Lies Over the Ocean" from a very British sounding teacher. Watching TV for a month and communicating with our landlord's family had helped a lot. My aunt told me, in

German, to sit in one of the chairs while she filled out paperwork the secretary had given her. Listening, I found the school surprisingly quiet.

I had expected to hear the chatter of children's voices, but the only
sounds came from other typewriters in the office. Looking at the walls, I
saw pictures that students must have made, plus a couple of official-looking
photographs of men. I had no clue who they were, nor was I interested in
finding out. After completing more paperwork, the secretary walked to a
door behind her, leaned in, and spoke to someone. A man appeared, and
the secretary introduced my aunt to the principal. Then he came up to me
and shook my hand. He was big, and his hand was warm. I let my hand go
limp, allowing him to squeeze it hard. He looked at me and said, "Come
on," and we walked out of the office. Walking down the hallway, past classrooms, he said, "I'll take you to meet your new friends," which my aunt
translated into German, although I understood some. The hallway smelled
of people. All these years later, I still remember it: I can't describe the smell,
but it was a distinctive odor that will somehow always be the essence of a
school to me

We crossed a courtyard and entered the old red-brick building. As
soon as we walked in, a musty odor confirmed the building's age. Looking
around, I guessed that probably thousands of children had passed over the
same threshold I just crossed. The inside of the building was not as well-
lit as the building with the principal's office. Unlike the fluorescent lights
there, large bulbs here hung suspended on long wires underneath round
shades. On this sunny day, the tall windows let in most of the light.

I followed the adults up wooden stairs that creaked with each step.
I saw that kids' feet had worn down the center of each step over the years.
The further we went, the more my stomach began to tighten. I was aching
to tell my aunt that we should go home, thinking, *What am I doing? Why
did my parents put me in this position? I'm scared!* Reaching the second
floor, I was sure that I should run back down those wooden stairs, out
the door, across the bridge, and back home—it wasn't that far, I could do

it! Fear almost got the best of me. I even worried that I might not be able to hold my bowels and embarrass myself in front of everyone . . . that had happened once back home when I did not want to go to school.

Sixth grade. Ernie Hudson, top row, sixth from left. "Angels," second row, fifth – Julie P., next Maxine C. Bottom row, third from left, Michael G. Eight place, Earline G., last seat Manfred.

I came back to reality when the principal knocked on the first door to our left. Excited voices of children rose in response to the knock. Next, a man with a firm voice called out, "Come in!" followed by what sounded like a warning aimed at the children in the classroom. They instantly quieted. The door opened, and a large man wearing a gray suit, white shirt, and dark tie appeared. He swung the door open wide and beckoned the three of us in. I looked around and found myself staring at a room filled with more young Black faces than I had ever seen in my life. Unlike back home, girls and boys were together in the same class here. Moving further into the room, the principal stepped aside and spoke to the teacher. As soon as their backs were turned, I heard whispers and an occasional girly giggle from the students.

My aunt joined the conversation between the teacher and principal, leaving me standing by myself near the door. Fully dressed, I nevertheless felt naked and exposed, all eyes focused on me. The three adults talked a bit longer and then shook hands. My aunt came over, hugged me, and, in

German, assured me that everything would be OK, saying, "God will protect you." With that, she and the principal left the room.

Wait a minute! Protect me from what? I thought. As if coming here today were not enough, now she had added to my anxiety, expecting something bad enough that God would need to protect me. Why did she think I needed God's protection? In what kind of place was she leaving me? Before these questions could be answered, the teacher took my hand and walked me to a seat near a window in the back of the room. Then he returned to the front of the class.

"Class, this is Manfred," the teacher said, drawing the attention of the students who had been staring at me. He pointed to me with his right hand. "He is a new student at our school and country. This is his first day here. I want you to welcome him."

A chorus of "Hi" and "Hey" went up from the students. Girls waved, while boys made weak efforts at showing interest. The teacher continued, "Manfred came to us from Austria, which is a country far from here, and he does not speak English well, so I want you all to be nice to him and help him out. OK?" Much of this conversation was later related to me by my classmates.

A hand shot up from one of the boys near the front of the room. "Ask him if he had any kangaroos."

A gaggle of laughter erupted from the other kids. The teacher explained the difference between Austria and Australia and that "No, there are no kangaroos in Austria."

"So, what do they have there?" asked Michael, with whom I would later become friends.

From above the blackboard the teacher pulled down a map of the world and explained where Austria was located and how it was different from Australia. At least, that is what I assumed the teacher was saying, as I was still insecure about my language skills. Seeing the map helped me catch on to some of his explanations. Several students turned to me, some looking in awe while others—mostly the girls—giggled.

My aunt had given me some paper, and I had brought ink pens and colored pencils from my school in Austria. All my pens and pencils were contained in a beautiful leather pouch that closed with a zipper. I was very proud of my pencil case, which I had used for the last two years in my former school. As students heard me unzip the case, several craned their necks to look at my writing instruments. From their expressions, I assumed they had never seen anything like it. Anyone would have thought it was brand new by how clean I kept it. I lifted the desktop, placed my things in the desk, and then sat back, ink pen in front of me. Later, I found out that pencil and paper were the norm here, not ink pens. The teacher, Mr. Sibley, continued the lesson while I took in the classroom and my fellow students.

Two of the walls were covered with pictures and writings by the students. In front of the room, behind the teacher's desk, was the blackboard with writing on it in white chalk. There were bookcases along the wall, and closest to the door to the hallway were square cubbies for students to keep coats, hats, and other things.

Three very tall windows, almost reaching the ceiling, let in a lot of light. Fresh air came in from smaller open windows at the top. The room was warm for a fall morning, with the easterly sun streaming in. The sun's warmth, combined with the students' bodies, gave the classroom a slight gym locker odor—not unpleasant, but clearly noticeable.

I was listening to the teacher, trying to understand what he was teaching when suddenly a loud bell rang out. My new classmates jumped up from their desks and ran for the door. The teacher said something, and three Black girls stopped, turned, and came up to me. From their gestures, I realized that they wanted me to follow them. All three had very dark skin. I had never seen girls like this before, or any girls in my class at all, and here these girls were asking me to join them. That was strange.

They led me out of the room, down the same stairs I had just come up earlier, and out onto a large playground. Once we got out into the sunshine, other kids came around and started pelting me with questions. My three new guardian angels responded with what I could only assume was something like, "Leave him alone; he's new here." The other kids started backing away.

Maxine Cox, Earlene Guidry, and Julie Perry would become my mentors and guardians, teaching me English and African American culture. We would remain friends all the way through my turbulent high school years.

After recess, I looked at the class and realized that I was a minority member of this class. During recess, it dawned on me that I was one of only six white students in the entire class. The school was in the low-income section of town, and even the white kids in the school, like me, came from impoverished homes. Many of the Black kids came from single-parent households.

At the end of the day, my guardian angels walked me home back across the bridge. Meanwhile, I thought back over every minute of my first day of school, the principal, the teacher, the students. Halfway across the bridge, I saw my mother coming toward me. I'm sure she must have been sitting on pins and needles all day. As we got close, she put her arms out and I ran toward her, slowing down only upon hearing the giggling of my angels. The three passed us, smiling and waving as they walked to their own homes nearby. Mom asked me if I knew them, and I excitedly told her that they were my new friends and had taken care of me that day. Somewhat astonished, she said, "Oh, that's nice," in puzzled German. As the school year went on, my grasp of the English language grew rapidly—or, at least, so I thought.

In spring, the warm sun streamed in the large windows, and Mr. Sibley used a large stick with a metal hook at the end to open the upper window to let fresh air in and cool the room while pulling down shades on the lower half of the windows. One morning, Mr. Sibley had left the shades up so we could bask in the glory of the spring day. We were eager to head out to the playground and watched the clock, high up on the wall, slowly ticking closer and closer to 11:25, lunchtime. The large round timepiece must have been there for many years. The dust on top of it was visible even from the back of the room. When the class was quiet, which was not often, you could hear its *ticktock* sound. Although electric, the sweep of the second's hand provided a constant aural marker of the passing of time. Caught up in my thoughts about the clock, I was startled when the bell rang for the start of the lunch hour. Kids ran out of the classroom after grabbing their lunches from the cubbies along the wall. Mr. Sibley's warning of "No running, walk down the stairs!" was drowned out by the squealing and laughter of students racing down the stairs and dashing toward the playground.

When the bell rang to end recess, I called out to Michael, urging him to come back inside with a phrase I had heard other kids use. Michael had become a friend with whom I spent a lot of time on the playground. In response, Michael got in my face and demanded, "What did you just call me?"

I repeated what I said: "Hey, n****r, let's get back into class." Angry, Michael disappeared into the building, shouting back at me, "You'll pay for that!"

By the time I got back into the classroom, Julie, Maxine, and Earlene had alerted the teacher to a potential problem between Michael and me. Michael sat in his seat at the front of the room, glaring at me. As the other students walked back into the classroom, Mr. Sibley quieted everyone, walked up to me, and asked, "Manfred, what did you say to Michael?" With the entire class staring at me, I innocently repeated what I had said.

Hearing both gasps and giggles from the students, Mr. Sibley calmly asks if I knew what the word n****r meant.

"No," I replied honestly, but I now felt certain, based on the response of the students and Mr. Sibley's voice, that I had done something wrong.

"Where did you hear that word?" he asked.

I explained that one of the other kids had said that Michael wanted to be called that. "He told me it was a funny name," I explained to Mr. Sibley.

With both concern and a barely hidden smile on his face, Mr. Sibley went on to explain, in a voice loud enough for everyone to hear, that that word was a bad word and should not be used. He asked me to apologize to Michael. Embarrassed, I apologized to Michael, even though deep inside, I didn't quite understand why a word could have such powerful repercussions. Michael was my best friend and someone I had fun with. The other students' reactions and Mr. Sibley's words made me realize my friend had been hurt by something I said. I felt bad. Not only did I feel bad, but I was worried about some kind of retribution. I sensed that some of the boys had not taken my apology as sincerely as I meant it. In later school years, some of the students who were in the class that day would remind me of the incident as a good school-age prank at my expense. Michael had been in on it all along.

In 2019 our graduating class had its fifty-five-year high school reunion. I had great hopes of seeing some of my friends from high school and sixth grade. I asked one of our other sixth-grade classmates, Ernie, if he knew how to get a hold of Michael, presuming he still lived in Michigan. I had not heard from him since our forty-fifth-class reunion. I got his number and tried to call him. Unfortunately, I learned that he was hospitalized with heart problems and unable to attend the reunion. I took some pictures and sent them to him. Shortly after that, I got a call from him, apologizing that he could not come because of his health but sharing how much he appreciated my thinking of him. He went on to say that he had considered me his lifelong friend, and followed it with a text that read, "Thank you for being you! I love you and am so proud to have been your friend. You will always be my Human Brother." It is a sentiment I will always carry with me.

Although Michael was my playground buddy, one of the other boys in the class Ernie had also caught my attention on the first day. He sat in the front row and made a real effort to look back at me, with great curiosity. I saw him staring at me and noticed that this boy was already larger than some of the other kids. Over time, "Poochie" and I became friends. His given name is actually Ernie Hudson. Our friendship lasted through junior high and on to high school, and it has grown stronger in our waning years.

Junior High

In between sixth and seventh grade, we moved from our first apartment to a new one owned by Uncle Manfred's in-laws. He had gotten married that summer to Christa, who came from a German-speaking Ukrainian immigrant family. Our new apartment was only a ten-minute walk to downtown, and getting to school for seventh and eighth grades was a breeze: I simply crossed the street to the junior high school! It was good for my parents, too, because I could come home right after school while my parents worked. I was a latchkey kid before the term became popular and accepted. I'd come home, pull out a big bag of Be-Mo potato chips, and hit the couch. Cartoons and Westerns kept me occupied until one of my parents got home, after I had polished off half a bag of potato chips. Why I didn't weigh four hundred pounds or die from all the salt intake, I still don't know.

The apartment was on the second floor of another older home. We had a kitchen, living room, and two small bedrooms. A large Congregational church sat kitty-corner from us. Across from the church was a pharmacy, which was my hangout. There, I bought candy and read magazines that I could not afford to buy. The pharmacy staff allowed me to sit in front of the magazine rack and look through the magazines as long as I wanted. Main Street—aptly named—was the center of town and ran about seven blocks north of us. In those days, Main Street was where all the businesses were located, long before malls became the rage. Banks, Sears, grocery chains, and movie theaters all were located on Main Street. It was convenient for us. On one corner of Main Street, straight down from our apartment, was a bakery where I would get fresh rolls and other baked goods. Fresh-baked goods gave my parents and me a feeling of being back home in Austria again.

I was adapting well. My language skills had improved dramatically, and I had done well enough in sixth grade to move up to junior high. In the spring of seventh grade, the school held its annual spelling bee. Each grade would crown a champion. My competitive nature clicked in, and I was determined to win that spelling contest to show the rest of the kids that I was just as good as they. Winning became my quest.

Each day, the words for the next day's competition were handed out. As soon as school was over, I went home to study the words. As the finals drew close, I was still in the competition, I kicked up my study habit up to a new level. On weekends, I asked my mother if I could sit in the bathtub to study. I would fill the tub with warm water, take my spelling words, and sit in the bathtub for two hours, learning the words and spelling them over and over. Finally, the day of the competition came. Three finalists from each class were selected. All the seventh-grade students gathered in the auditorium, with the competitors seated on the stage.

The principal announced each student's name, and cheers went up from the classmates. As if simply being on the auditorium stage was not frightening enough, I had to sit in front of all my classmates. One by one, the competitors were asked to repeat a word given by one of the teachers acting as a judge. In addition to spelling it, each student had to place it in a sentence. It was intimidating!

The challenge of what I was doing never occurred to me. I had only been in the country for eighteen months; my competitors were born here. I should have been scared, but except for some stage fright, I was confident I could win. If you missed a word, you were summarily dismissed. I did not know how the other students felt, but it seemed that whenever a student missed a word, a large, dark hole opened in the stage, and they fell down into it. Of course, in reality, they walked off stage left, but the feeling of dread was there. Finally, it was down to a girl from another seventh-grade class and me.

My name was called, and I slowly went up to the microphone and stood there, looking not out at the students but only the teacher judges directly in front of me on the stage. I was afraid that if I looked at one of my classmates, I might chicken out and run off the stage. I was sure the students were waiting for me to bomb out.

Slowly, I repeated the word I was given, spelled it out, and then gave its definition or meaning. "Correct," the principal, as chief judge, affirmed. I sat down and stared at the audience; a few girls from my class giggled. The tension in the auditorium was beginning to be palpable, and the usually noisy student body was hushed. The girl from the other seventh-grade class stepped up to the microphone for her second word. She repeated her word to herself. Then, slowly, and haltingly, she again repeated the word. She looked at her shoes, balled up her fists at the sides of her dress, and began.

"I-M-P-O-S-S-I-A-B-E-L . . . IMPOSSIABLE. Not being able to do something."

A gasp went up throughout the student body. "No, I'm sorry," said the principal, "that is not correct." She turned and walked back to her chair, barely able to withhold her tears.

"Mr. Tatzmann, would you please step up to the microphone," said the principal.

I got up, feeling like my shoes had been nailed to the hardwood floor of the stage. I could no longer see anyone out there; the entire audience had become a blur. "Your word," the principal intoned, is *reticent*."

I focused, hearing only the word. *Reticent, reticent,* the word was turning over in my head. Throughout the process of learning the words, I had felt that I had an advantage over the other kids because of my language background. My trick to learning to spell was being able to decipher each word into its German sounds. Using the phonic method, I was able to decipher most words easily. "Reh-tee-cent," the voice in my head spoke to me.

I cleared my throat, clutched my sweaty palm shut, looked straight at the principal, and said, "R-E-T-I-C-E-N-T . . . RETICENT. Being reluctant to do something."

"That is correct!" I heard the principal say over the cheers of the student body. "Mr. Tatzmann, you are the new Benton Harbor Junior High seventh-grade spelling champion. Congratulations!"

Students cheered and yelled out my name. Competitors on the stage came over to congratulate me. After the competition, students were dismissed, and we went back to our classroom on the second floor. Once we were all seated, the teacher asked me to come up and again congratulated me in front of the class. He explained to the class that I had not known any English about eighteen months ago, but today I had won the seventh-grade spelling championship. One of the boys in the back of the class called out, "How did you do it?" I responded by saying that I had sat in a bathtub. Not fully understanding what I meant, the class broke out in laughter, and the teacher sent me back to my seat. I was happy, joyful, and amazed. I do not remember much more of that day except being proud of my accomplishment, which I feel every time I think back on it.

Eighth grade was my favorite year. I was not sure why, but it may be because I was becoming a teenager and growing more confident in my knowledge of the English language. I also developed my first crush on a girl, Barbara. While there had been other crushes—Shirley, for instance, in seventh grade—I was really hooked on Barbara. Nothing ever came of it; she just considered me a silly boy she could toy around with and on whom she could test her flirtatious teenage wings. For me, though, she will forever be my first heartthrob.

My eighth-grade homeroom and social studies teacher, Mrs. Reinhardt, will forever be my favorite teacher. She was supportive, allowing me to do lots of independent studies. Based on my earlier education in Austria, Mrs. Reinhardt recognized my academic maturity. I had not been able to apply my skills here until my language had improved.

Ironically, even though my mother never met Mrs. Reinhardt during my school years, Mutti met her late in her life at a ladies' garden club and they ended up being good friends. Over coffee and cake visits, Mrs. Reinhardt filled my mom in on all my exploits while Mutti proudly listened.

Because of their limited English language skills, Mutti and Papa felt insecure, shy, and afraid to participate in school functions. They trusted me to get my homework done. I could not get much help from them due to the language barrier, except for in math, at which my father was exceptionally good. Otherwise, I knew that I would have to struggle through on my own. Later, my mother would recall how impressed she was with the one and only Parent Night she ever attended while I was in ninth grade.

When we walked into the gym that night, Mutti was surprised how large it was. As I took her around the gym, she was anxious and reluctant. I showed her where the teachers had tables set up. The bleachers had been put away. The upstairs balcony, normally used for gymnastics, was lit, making the gym look large and very tall. At the first table not occupied by other parents was my homeroom teacher, who also taught music. He was a tall man with wavy black hair and a big black mustache. As we got close, he rose, recognized me, and greeted us with "Guten Abend, Frau Tatzmann." Mutti, surprised at hearing the German greeting, could not respond immediately. In an astonished voice, she asked, "You speak German?"

"Only a little bit," was the teacher's reply, but those few words were enough to make her feel comfortable. He invited us to sit on the two folding metal chairs in front of the table. "I'm originally from England, and we were taught some German in school. I'm sorry, but that's all I can remember," he said with a chuckle.

Mutti sat down, and he told her what a good student I was. After listening intently, beaming at what she heard, Mutti thanked him, and we went home. Both of us walked out on clouds, glowing with pride, each for our own reasons. Many years later, upon the retelling of the story, friends would ask, "Well, did you speak to any of the other teachers?"

"No," she'd reply, "I didn't want to take a chance on the news getting any worse."

In her final months, as she was dying of cancer, Mutti recalled these conversations and apologized that she was not more supportive during my school years. "I hope you know we tried, your father and I," she said plaintively. "We always knew you were a good student, but we were afraid to go there with our bad English." I never doubted their support and told her that I knew how much they both loved and cared for me. I only wished I could have been more understanding of their problems.

"Nazi, Nazi . . ."

By ninth grade, we had moved again to an apartment about three miles north of town, requiring me to ride a bus to school. To get to the bus, I had to cross the playground of an elementary school. The buses were parked there overnight. Once it got cold, and throughout the winter, the bus drivers would start the buses, unlock the doors, and retire to have a cup of coffee in the school while the bus warmed up. As students arrived, we would push against the door and let ourselves into the bus. At the required time, the drivers would board, and the buses would start their runs. If we got there early, we had about twenty minutes to ourselves.

Late one cold fall morning, as I walked up to the bus, a boy named Barry pulled down the window and called out, "Here comes the Nazi; here comes the Nazi. Hey, Nazi, hey, hey." This was not the first time Barry had harassed me. Other students on the bus began to laugh, encouraging Barry even more. The closer I got to the bus, the more Barry shouted taunts at me. He had taunted me previously, but usually only with snide comments on the bus itself. That day, I had enough.

Anger welled up inside me. I stood in front of the door and yelled, "Get out here, Barry."

"What are you going to do, Nazi, kill me?" was his sarcastic reply, still looking out the window.

"Come out here and see," I replied.

Thinking back, I realize that this was the point where logic and reason had left me. Barry was about five foot ten and heavyset; I was five foot seven and a scrawny one hundred and thirty-five pounds. The odds were not in my favor, but anger overruled reason. I stood in front of the open bus door, waiting for Barry to come out and not knowing what I was going to do next. Barry walked to the bus steps and launched himself onto me from the last step of the bus. We both tumbled to the frozen ground, Barry having already gained the upper hand by landing on top of me.

I was flat on my back. As soon as we both hit the frozen ground, Barry began beating me in the face and chest. I tried to fight back, but Barry was now sitting on my stomach, punching me. Some of the other kids began yelling out the windows for the bus driver, who just happened to be walking out of the office, a short distance away, coffee cup in hand. The driver, seeing what was happening, yelled at Barry to stop. Barry quickly got off me and stormed back onto the bus. I collected myself, grabbed my backpack, and was running for home by the time the driver got to me. I heard the bus driver yell at me to come back, but I just kept going. Halfway across the playground, tears now flowing from eyes, I looked over my shoulder to see the bus pull out. Minutes later, I walked up the steps to our apartment, realizing I had a cut lip and a slight nosebleed.

Hearing me come up the steps, Mutti opened the door. She looked at me in shock and asked me what happened as she pulled me into her arms. She guided me to the bathroom and moistened a washcloth to wipe my face and mouth while asking me what had happened. My story frightened and outraged her. She scolded me for not having said anything to her or my dad about Barry's previous bullying. I knew why I hadn't. It would not have made any difference, because neither of them would have done anything, both afraid to speak English. It would have meant them possibly embarrassing themselves to school officials. Mutti insisted that I stay home that day. The next morning, after getting dressed and having breakfast, she insisted on going to the bus with me to talk to the driver. I pleaded with her not to, presuming that having my mother going with me would only make matters worse. After further pleading, she agreed not to go if I would leave late enough that the driver would already be on the bus. I agreed, and I thought the matter was settled!

Leery of what could happen, I walked to the bus, my lips still swollen and bruised. Would Barry lay in wait for me? What did the other students on the bus think? What would the bus driver say? Would he protect me from Barry? Thoughts of turning back came to mind the closer I got to the bus, but I was determined not to let my fear show or give in to the bully. By the time I reached the bus, the driver was in his seat. He looked at me through the open door, motor running, as I approached and stepped onto the bus. Before I made it to the second step, he asked, "Manfred, do you have anything to tell me about yesterday morning?"

"No," I mumbled under my breath, simultaneously feeling the swollen lip and the cut. I looked up and saw Barry sitting in the third row, by the window, on the bus's left side. The look on my face must have given away my feelings.

The bus driver said, "It's OK. Barry won't bother you anymore. Mr. Bierman, the assistant principal [whom every student feared more than Godzilla], had a long talk with him yesterday as soon as we got to school. You just sit down, and we won't talk about it anymore. Don't let it happen again because you were also responsible for what happened." Sheepishly, I said, "Thank you, and OK!"

Looking toward the back of the bus, I realized I had to pass Barry to find a seat. As I walked by, Barry mumbled under his breath, "Sorry, Nazi," which was the end of the episode. The incident was never again discussed.

Barry and I eventually came to talking terms, and by our senior year in high school, we even went to some away football games together.

High School Years

Moving on to high school was a big deal for me, and ninth grade was an adjustment. There were many more students to deal with, including the big seniors. The school was large, with almost three thousand students. I now had to walk from one class to the other. As would happen on many occasions throughout my life, I jumped into things despite not knowing what I was getting myself into. Accordingly, I took on the challenge of running for ninth-grade class president, and somehow, I was elected by the student body. No official functions came with the job; it was the student council that had the real power in the school, and for some reason, the class president was not an automatic member of the student council until tenth grade. Nevertheless, considering I had only been in the school system since sixth grade, I took it as an honor that students voted for me. I wish I could recall my campaign platform—it must have been good!

Like teenagers probably everywhere, spring fever hit us hard come May. The sunshine coming through the windows precipitated migratory instincts, the need to be outside, to bask in the first rays of warm sunshine. This part of the state usually had wonderfully warm springs, with plenty of sunshine and blue skies. The summers could be hot, and the moisture coming off Lake Michigan made the humidity unbearable at times. Before California took the title, this area was known as the fruit-growing capital of the United States.

Lunchtime gave us a chance to escape from the warm, smelly classrooms to take in the sunshine and fresh air. The teachers' parking lot was about the size of two basketball courts, next to a chain-link fence on the school's north side. The west-facing portion of the lot overlooked a brush-covered ravine with a sharp drop-off and a view of the St. Joseph River about a half-mile away. In between were homes in what was called the "flats," a primarily African American area. Eventually, this area was torn down and replaced by businesses, a yacht basin, and now townhouse units.

The southern portion of the parking lot faced the school's tall and windowless gym wall, which blocked out the sun and threw its shadow across the pavement. Those of us not wanting to put up with the noise, crowds, and smell of the former gym turned massive lunchroom found this area a good place to relax and take in the spring air while enjoying our lunch. Teachers had their own lunchroom or ate at their desks, so rarely did a teacher or other staff member come around the side of the building to see what the kids were doing. They probably knew but chose to ignore us. Some students used the lot to smoke. Others took the opportunity for teenage romance, girls with their backs to the wall, boys leaning over them, quietly whispering in their ears, maybe brushing their lips on the girl's cheek. Others would stand at the edge of the lot, hand in hand, looking off into the distance; the blue sky above, birds chirping and flitting through the brush. I did none of this. Instead, I enjoyed the solitude, sunshine, cool shade, and fresh air, eating my lunch and watching the other students.

One nice morning, I was sitting on my haunches, my back against the wall, and eating my lunch when three white classmates came around the west side of the building. As they approached me, one said, "Hey Nazi, what are you doing here? You're not allowed here, go over there with those kids," meaning the Black students on the other side of the building. It was commonly known that I had come from the same area in town as many of the Black kids, the city's poor area, and these three, and their parents, represented the community elite.

I tried to ignore them, having heard their taunts many times before, especially during phys ed class. I also remembered my incident with Barry and did not want to have a repeat.

"Didn't you hear what I said?" yelled one of the boys, Todd, who was tall, with dark curly hair. The three of them advanced toward me. Todd and one of his friends were on the school tennis team, the elite sport. I ignored them, stood up, and turned away from their approach. Disregarding my effort to avoid a confrontation, they quickly were upon me and shoved me to the ground, yelling, "Nazi, Nazi, get out of here. Go back where you came from." They kicked and pushed me as I tried to get off the ground. I could not see what was happening, but suddenly a booming voice yelled at my attackers, "Hey, get the fuck off him! Leave him alone!"

I was lifted by the left arm and turned to see the three attackers retreating, but still hurling taunts my way. Turning all the way around, I saw that my friend and locker mate Poochie, now taller and bigger than me, had come to my rescue. His intervention ran off my assailants. Had Ernie not come around the corner, I would most likely have received a more severe beating. While I brushed myself off, Ernie just walked away, giving me no chance to thank him. At the end of the school day, he met me at our locker and I thanked him for what he had done.

"Wow, were you really going to beat the shit out of them, like you said?" I asked, considering his bigger size.

"Naw, I was just acting, bullshitting, trying to scare them away." He laughed. Little did we realize that his comment would presage his future. It may have been nothing for him, but it was an act I never forgot. The three boys also seemed to understand that they would have to deal with Ernie if they tried it again.

Later, as I thought about it, I assumed their anger with me that day was related to my background as an immigrant from a German-speaking country. It had only been seventeen years since the end of World War II. The atrocities committed by the German Nazis during the war were still very much on Americans' minds, especially those with family members who had served in the US military or died in the war, or with relatives who had been victims of the war's Holocaust atrocities. All three boys were Jewish, so possibly they were especially sensitive to the issue.

Word spread about the parking lot incident, and I was called to the assistant principal's office and questioned. The assistant principal told me to stay away from the other boys and not "bother them" again. Their parents were respected members of the community, and I was "just an immigrant." I realized at that point that I was being judged not by who I was but by my heritage. Subtle taunts and harassment, now called bullying, continued from that group of boys throughout my high school days, even when we accidentally ended up on the same tennis team. I realized then that I was an outcast, but it helped me to understand why in sixth grade, the n-word had been so hurtful to my friends.

Ernie and I went our separate ways after graduation, and I did not see or hear from him until twenty years later, in 1984, when I went to see the original *Ghostbusters* movie. He played the character of Winston Zeddemore, one of the four Ghostbusters. After leaving Benton Harbor, Ernie went to Wayne State University in Detroit and then the University of Minnesota. There, he received his Masters of Fine Arts degree, eventually ending up in California.

He became a respected actor, starring in many movies and taking a leading role in the HBO series *Oz,* and in *Frankie & Grace,* where he played Lily Tomlin's love interest. At our forty-fifth high school reunion, I had a chance to make amends and again thank Ernie, and Ernie recalled the story of the beating for my wife, Maria. That same evening, she also had a chance to meet two of my three sixth-grade angels, who laughed at recalling some of my clumsiness and attempts to adapt to a new life and culture.

Times of Change

High school years were fun and a time of growth and learning for me. Two more events occurred that shaped my life. In ninth-grade math, Mr. Rogers, the only African American instructor in the school, was adamant about students not chewing gum in class. One day he caught me chewing gum and told me to spit it out "unless I had some for everyone!" A few days later, I again was chewing gum in class, and he repeated that he did not allow gum chewing in class. I responded by asking if he had not said that it was OK if everyone had gum. He agreed. I then brought out a bag full of gum that I shared with the entire class. Against his better judgment, I'm sure, but with a broad smile on his face, he agreed to let everyone have the gum. I realize now that this was my first act of defiance against authority—a trait that has stuck with me all my life.

In tenth grade, an event occurred, that negatively impacted my life well beyond high school. Growing up, I had always been interested in science and science fiction stories, reading Jules Verne's *20,000 Leagues under the Sea* in both German and English. My goal was to become an oceanographer, to dive beneath the waves and study the oceans. Mr. Pifer taught tenth-grade advanced biology. One day in class, he asked each student to say what kind of scientist they wanted to be. When it came to me, I proudly said I wanted to be an oceanographer. He laughed and, with disdain in his voice, responded, "That won't happen, Mr. Tatzmann; you are too stupid!" For some unknown reason, I believed him.

From that moment on, I bought into what he said, believing I could not learn! I never gave one hundred percent for the rest of my time in high school and throughout college. I believed Mr. Pifer that, when it came to academics, I was "too stupid!" I wonder what I could have achieved, had I not been convinced I was stupid?

The mid-1950s was the era of the fight for civil rights. Our school district was part of a court-ordered busing program, making the community's existing racial divide even greater. Busing was intended to integrate schools so that no school was predominantly white or Black. It forced students together through education, with the intent to provide equal educational opportunities and build new friendships and respect. Some parents and other adults didn't see it that way; instead, it highlighted the differences among the races. Eventually, even students began to divide into racial groups. Old friendships experienced the divide. Cliques formed, with white and Black kids joining separate groups.

My high school years were a time of great change in this country. The Civil Rights Movement was in full swing. The Freedom Riders were a mix of Black and white anti-segregationists from the North. The group included such future famous figures as Rev. Ralph Abernathy, a good friend of Martin Luther King Jr., Stokely Carmichael, and James Farmer, who would lead the Urban League. In 1961 the Freedom Riders took a Greyhound bus tour to Jackson, Mississippi, where they were arrested and sentenced to thirty days in jail. Through the efforts of the NAACP, which took their case to the Supreme Court, their convictions were overturned, and others began Freedom Rides into the South to protest the segregationist laws. In 1963, more than two hundred thousand people participated in the March on Washington to force civil rights legislation and establish job equality for everyone.

Almost every night on television we saw protests and police attacking peaceful protestors. And on November 22, 1963, at about 2:00 p.m., the school public address system came on while I was sitting in Advanced English class and we heard Walter Cronkite, CBS news anchor, in a somber voice tell us that President John F. Kennedy had just been killed by an assassin in Dallas, Texas. We all sat in utter silence and shock, not believing it could be true. These events all occurred while the Vietnam War was being carried out. American soldiers were dying by the hundreds, and many of us feared reaching age eighteen, when we had to sign up for the draft.

In February of my senior year, 1964, the Beatles made their first trip to the United States, arriving in New York to great fanfare. Our French teacher allowed us to listen in class to a live radio broadcast of their arrival.

My American Parents

In my sophomore year I found a new friend, Jim, whose family came from Tennessee and whose parents welcomed me into their home as if I were another of their three sons. The family taught me about being a teenager in the United States, dating, and other social norms. His mom educated me about menstruation, getting me to understand why some girls sat on the other side of the gym, not participating, at certain times of the month. Mutti and Papa could not educate me on the ways of being a teenager in the United States. Jim's parents filled that role, for which I will forever be grateful.

I enjoyed being in their home and eating Jim's mother's Southern cooking, which was new to me. Jim's older brother Bill had a popular rock band that cut several records, which got some national exposure. It was fun listening to him tell tales of his touring adventures. In our senior year, on weekends, Jim and I traveled with his brother's band to a few gigs nearby. We ate up the adoration of the girl groupies, but we never interacted much with them because Jim and I had an active social life back home.

That social life consisted largely of dating other girls from school. After going to the movies, we would park in his parents' driveway during the colder months. Jim's parents believed it was better for us to make out in their driveway rather than on some dark and lonely road. His dad would bring blankets out to the car so we could cuddle with our dates. He also bought us condoms and told us that he would beat us to an inch of our lives if we ever got a girl pregnant. He was a bear of a man, well over two hundred pounds and over six feet tall. Simply the thought of him getting angry kept us in line. I'm profoundly grateful for them helping to get me through the turbulent high school years. They were my second set of parents.

Unfortunately, Jim's parents were also openly racist. Overt racism was new to me. I felt strange whenever they used the n-word around the house, which they did frequently. After my experience with Michael in sixth grade, I knew the word was hurtful and hateful. Hearing them use that word casually, I knew it wasn't right. I should have known better, based on my own experience with Barry. Sadly, my mind never connected these two sides of the same coin. I was just glad to be part of Jim's family and appreciative of everything they did for me.

I was recently asked, especially in light of the events surrounding the killing of George Floyd in May 2020, how, knowing my background, I could spend time with them. My only explanation was that Jim and his family's friendship were important to me at that stage of my life, so I chose to ignore their utterances. I still wonder about that today. Was it the fear of not fitting in that allowed me to dismiss something I did not feel good about? I am glad to have had the opportunity to see both sides. It made me much more aware of and sensitive to my own biases and prejudices, and more able to see it in others.

Today, I look back at my strange journey of learning about racism. Totally naïve, in sixth grade, I learned that a word can offend and hurt someone. Subsequently, I had to personally fight to not be called by a name; later, I was beaten for my ethnicity. Finally, while working in a liquor store as a young man, I understood that you can't judge people by their appearance, period! Mine has been a roller coaster journey of learning about racism.

Not judging or being afraid to be judged benefited me later when my friend Richard came into my life. Having spent most of his life in an institution, his social graces, demeanor, and even dress for a long time did not meet social norms. Yet, thanks to the lessons I had learned earlier, I did not care if he and I were judged by others in places like restaurants, ball games, and movie theaters. He is my friend, and if his clothing was too colorful or didn't fit well, or if he spoke too loudly, that was OK.

Life of a High School Student

Benton Harbor High School 1964.

By the end of tenth grade, I was beginning to feel like an American teenager. I still felt the angst of being different and desperately wanted to fit in and participate in school activities. In those days, high school dances were a time for teenage preening. On Friday night the school sponsored dances, which were held in the same gym where I started school in sixth grade. These dances were like tribal rituals, with each group of kids hanging out in a different area of the gym. The Black kids hung out near the front, where the band was. Yuppie white kids hung out near the back of the gym. Those of us that did not identify with any clique were relegated to the sides of the gym. Girls danced more than the guys, who came just to look cool. The movie *Grease* got a lot of it right. In an era of Elvis and other rockers, I had a flattop haircut, with the sides of my head shaved in a way that would have made the Marines proud. Whatever made me think that was cool still escapes me!

When it came to fast dancing, I felt very awkward. I had no rhythm—I still don't! I talked to the girls, but rarely would I ask a girl to dance unless it was a slow tune. Still, I always made sure to ask some girl for the last dance; it was always a slow dance, so you got to hold the girl real close. The craving of hormonal teenagers to physically bond with the opposite sex overcame the fact that everyone was hot and sweaty by the end of the evening, and the gym smelled like an unclean locker room. When I told my friend Jim at the end of the evening that the girl I danced with had a hot body, it was not a compliment but a complaint!

I didn't buy my own car until my senior year, but I was lucky to have the loan of Dad's car to go to games and dances. That put me one notch up on the high school cool meter. The car was a red and-black 1958 Mercury Monterey De Luxe, considered a luxury model. He had bought it used after it had been in a bad accident and fixed it up, so it looked brand new. The car was ahead of its time, having, among other gadgets, a push-button transmission. Five buttons on the dash—Reverse, Neutral, Low, Drive, and Park—were all you needed to put the car in gear. On the top of the dashboard was a rocket-shaped dial that moved the front bench seat up, down, forward, and back. Girls loved to sit in the car to just move the seat up or down, back, and forth. Power windows went up or down at the press of a button—very advanced for its time. My dad kept the front and back bench seats covered with clear plastic. Unlike the bucket seats of today, these benches were large enough to lie down on, very handy for a dating teenager.

After the dance, which ended at 10:00 p.m., the evening ritual continued as cars sped a couple of miles down the highway to the only McDonald's in town. The fast-food joint was the new, hot place to meet and hang out. We had to race down there because McDonald's parking lot had perhaps only two dozen parking spaces.

McDonald's in those days was nothing like today's restaurants with a play area, indoor seating, and drive-through. The only seating was a couple of plastic picnic tables in a patio area between two rows of parked cars. The Mac's front was a floor-to-ceiling glass wall, so you could see all the customers lined up and the counter behind them. Inside, it was just wide enough to hold two lines of waiting customers. During a rush, people lined up out the doors to either the right or left of the store. There was no drive-through; you had to park and go inside to get your food. At other drive-ins you parked the car next to a tray and speaker mounted on a post, and you placed your order by talking into the speaker. A girl, generally a high school student, would set your tray of food to the tray on the post and collect your money. At some fancy places, the girls worked on roller skates. They would come rolling out, tray in hand. It was always fun to watch them deliver the trays.

McDonald's promoted "fast food" because you did not have to wait for someone bring the food to you. The food there was simpler than at another drive-ins, but as they promised, it was "fast." The french fries smelled fantastic. Mac's made sure to vent the fryers into the parking lot, so as soon as you got there, the smell of those fries hit your nose and woke up your taste buds. Having experienced my first taste of fries on my way to America, I was instantly hooked on Mac's fries. The smell was greasy, yet sweet, with a strong potato aroma . . . heavenly. Sadly, Mac's fries today don't taste or smell anything like the early ones; the restaurant no longer uses beef fat for frying because of cost and health-consciousness. Today, you can stick your nose into a bag of fries and barely get the aroma of potato.

The other "fast" pitch was that Mac's made the hamburger quickly. There were only three kinds of burgers on the menu: regular hamburger, one patty of meat; the cheeseburger; and the fish burger, with a tasty tartar sauce. That was it! No double burger, chicken sandwich, or pumpkin latte mochas, like those available at MacDonald's today!

If we could not find a parking space after the rush to Mac's, we would have to drive through the lot until someone else left. On weekends, when there was no dance, it was not unusual to see a line of cars slowly circling, waiting for a parking space. On occasion, the manager would call the police because too many cars were lined up on the road, waiting, and others could not get in. Of course, driving through became a mating ritual of sorts. Girls, sometimes four or five per car, hung out car windows, urging boys to follow them. Or boys with fancy cars enticed girls to follow them, offering a ride in a hot car with the possibility of romance along the way.

At Mac's, Jim and I would order a hamburger, fries, and a Coke, all handed to us at the counter in one nice-looking white paper bag for $1.15. We'd sit in the car, munch on those fries, eat the hamburger, listen to rock 'n' roll on station WLS out of Chicago, and make the Coke last for two hours. We checked out the girls cruising by, rating them on a scale of zero to ten. On weekends, shortly before the midnight curfew, the lot cleared out. Most of the students, even the ones with the cool cars, had to be home by a certain time. Our parents strictly enforced curfew, and the police would show up at midnight to check out who was still hanging around. An hour later, Mac's closed, so the cops made sure the lot was empty by then. Jim and I rarely picked up any girls during our Mac's outings. For us, the sport of watching was generally enough. Both of us were more interested in serious dating, not just pickups.

The guys with shiny cars souped up with big engines were more interested in racing, so they didn't bother going to the dances. Drag racing—seeing who can drive the fastest quarter mile—was the time's hottest sport. Once I had my own car, a brand-new 1964 Chevy Malibu Sport SE, we would challenge other guys to drag races. We'd drive to a deserted blacktop road in Stevensville a couple of miles away. The strip was frequently used as a dragstrip, so it had *Start* and *Quarter Mile* marked on the road with white paint. Jim was the starter, standing between the two cars to signal "go," while I drove. Jim brought a slide rule along to figure out our opponents' weight ratio to determine whether we had a chance of winning. With the help of his math skills, we frequently won. Apart from the basic fact we were racing down a blacktop road at over eighty miles per hour late at night, there was also the risk of meeting oncoming cars or the police. If the police showed up, it was a mad scramble to avoid them by squealing off on one of the side roads. The cops could only follow one car, and you hoped it wasn't going to be yours.

Sandi, My Lost Love

Our high school sports teams, especially the football and basketball teams, perennially were top teams in the state. The basketball team earned two state championships during my time in high school. However, my only brush with team sports came in the eleventh grade, when I was drafted to play on the tennis team despite never having even held a tennis racket in my hands. It started when one of my good friends, Gary, who had an amazing voice, asked me to join him in the a cappella choir. The choir had a statewide reputation for excellence, and I thought joining would get me closer to a girl in the choir named Sandi, on whom I had the most incredible crush.

Six weeks after joining the choir, Mrs. Archer, the choir director, met me as I walked into rehearsal and handed me a note stating that I should see Mr. Braddock, the tennis coach. When I got there, Mr. Braddock explained that my singing was not good enough to be in the choir, but I could still qualify for the tennis team because he needed another doubles player. So, I spent my junior and senior years on the tennis team. I wasn't particularly good, but my partner was a state-ranked singles player, so he kept us in our games. Meanwhile, I had to find new ways to stay in contact with Sandi, knowing I could never impress her with my tennis playing.

I'm not sure when my crush for Sandi started, but it was probably in Mrs. Laity's tenth-grade Advanced English class. Oddly, I was promoted into the advanced class because I was doing poorly in regular English class, which focused a lot on grammar and vocabulary. Today, I'm still not sure what a gerund is. Who knows how that decision was made? Advanced English focused a lot on reading, interpreting what was read, and writing book reports. We used the *Atlantic Monthly* magazine as one of our sources for reports and read it every month. I did extremely well in that class, getting A's on most assignments. Sandi hung out with girls from other well-to-do families like hers. In class, though, she would frequently look back at me and smile. She became my dream girl.

Like in the Billy Joel song, she was an "Uptown Girl," and I was a "downtown" kind of guy. Her dad was a prominent optometrist in town. They belonged to the area's most exclusive, all-white, non-Jewish country club. She lived in a nice large house and had all the benefits of privilege. In our junior year we dated for some time, but her parents broke it up because I wasn't the right kind of guy for her. We started dating again in our senior year. Her parents gradually accepted me, and even allowed me to spend time with her at her house.

We went to the senior prom together. Sandi wore a long, straight, white silk dress that shone like a polished pearl. With long matching gloves and perfectly matched white heeled shoes she wore a yellow rose boutonniere on her right shoulder strap that matched the yellow carnation in my lapel. Her long, dark brown hair hung down to her shoulders, and one wisp coyly hung over her right brow. I wore a tuxedo with a white jacket and black slacks and a black bow tie over a starched white shirt. All evening we danced, holding each other close, her head on my shoulder. Although there were probably a hundred other students and their dates on the dance floor, it was

Senior Prom picture of Sandi and I

just us as far as we were concerned. I could feel her warmth as she pressed into me, mingling with the warmth of my own body generated by an evening of dancing. We were in a cocoon of our own making. I can still see how she looked at me and feel her love for me. Sandi held my hand tightly and pressed against my chest as we flowed across the dance floor. That evening cemented our love for each other.

Later in August, after graduation, we further explored our love when Sandi was invited to be in one of her friends' weddings. The wedding was in a city two hours east. Sandi had arranged to stay with another friend— or at least that's what we told her parents. I told my parents that Sandi and I would be staying together in a motel. Mutti did not really like it, but she knew how much we loved and cared for each other, so she reluctantly agreed. She loved Sandi too, and Sandi really liked my parents.

We were excited as we drove east on I-94 on a sunny and warm Saturday morning. Sandi's head was on my shoulder, her dark brown hair against my cheek, her sweet perfume captivating me. She wore a special scent, one I had never noticed on any other girls. It captured me. Every now and then, we'd look at each other, our brown eyes meeting. Sandi would smile and squeeze my arm tightly, making my heart melt. I don't recall much of the traffic, conversation, or anything else about the drive except for how much we were in love with each other. I stayed at the motel watching TV while she went to the wedding. Later in the evening, friends dropped her off. It was an unforgettable night. Although I have not looked at it in years, I still have the motel receipt, a remembrance of a very loving, meaningful, and important point in my life.

Throughout the summer we dated. Sandi's job as a server at her parents' country club meant she had to work some evenings and weekends. Sometimes we would meet up after she finished work for the evening. During the day, whenever we could, we would go to the beach. We loved laying on a blanket, sometimes just staring at each other. When we got too hot, we dashed into Lake Michigan and splashed each other with the warm water. It felt great to share our joy. On other dates, we went to see movies. The M-39 Drive-In Theatre was our favorite.

Drive-in theaters were big at that time. There were no seats; instead, you drove into the theatre grounds, parked your car, and watched the movie. The movies started after sunset, when it got fully dark. I say movies because you got to see three movies for the cost of one admission ticket if you wanted to stay until after 1:00 a.m. For poor high school students, three for the price of one was a deal.

The movie was projected on a huge white screen at one end of the lot. On warm nights we'd roll down the window and hook the speaker to the door, and Sandi would slide across the bench seat and snuggle up close to me.

One evening, at the end of August, just before she was to head off to college, I got a call from her. We had not spoken for a couple of weeks because she had told me that she and her parents were going on a brief vacation, shopping for school, and getting packed up. One of our two house phones was on the wall right next to the kitchen table. The phone rang as we were having dinner, so Mutti answered the phone and passed it on to me once she recognized Sandi. I got up from the table and went to the basement to talk privately on the second phone. As soon as I picked up the phone, I noticed Sandi sounded upset; she was crying. Collecting herself, she told me that I could never see her again. Never again!

"What? Why?" was all that I could blurt out at the moment.

With tears in her voice, Sandi explained why I had not heard from her. She had not been on vacation; her parents had taken her to Chicago to have an abortion. Through tears, she told me that she loved me but asked me to please not ever call or see her again. Her father had threatened that if I ever saw her again, he would call the police and have me charged with rape. She told me she loved me and was deeply sorry, but that's how it had to be, and hung up. I rushed upstairs; my mother, still sitting at the kitchen table, saw how upset I was. Knowing I had talked to Sandi, she asked what was wrong. In tears, I simply blurted out that Sandi had broken up with me. I rushed to my room, closed the door, and slammed myself unto my bed. I had never ever felt such pain before. I wanted to jump into a deep dark hole and pull the world in over my head. I cried all night, thinking about what life could have been for the two of us. My mother, thinking it was only a breakup, tried to console me, without success. Looking back on it now, I know Sandi's parents did the right thing, but it still doesn't erase the pain of that day or its memory.

I never told Mutti or Papa, or anyone else, about the real reason for the breakup. Sandi went on to study at Michigan State University while I attended the local community college. Later that year, despite her warning, I drove to MSU to look her up. We went for coffee, chatted, and agreed to remain friends. She needed and wanted to get on with her life. During our college years, I saw her occasionally for coffee. Eventually, she fixed me up with her roommate Lil, whom I dated for a couple of years after that. Several times, Lil and I double-dated with Sandi and her new boyfriend, who eventually became her husband. Over the years, I went to high school reunions simply to see her again. I admired her from a distance, always afraid to speak to her unless she initiated the conversation, which she did every time. Though the pain never left me, I kept our conversations casual and to a minimum.

Many years later, I received a call from her husband informing me that she had died in her sleep of unknown causes. He said, "I knew you two were close, so I thought you'd like to know." I was amazed at his kind gesture and sad for the passing of an incredibly special person in my life.

CHAPTER 3

LATE-NIGHT LESSONS OF TOLERANCE AND UNDERSTANDING

After I graduated from high school, I needed a job to have money to go on to college. My grades had not been good enough to earn a scholarship, and my parents did not have the money to pay for my education. During the last couple of years of high school, I had part-time jobs after school and on weekends, but those barely paid for my car loan and maintenance. So I attended Lake Michigan Community College, which allowed me to bring my grades up to transfer to a four-year university. It also saved me money because I could live at home. Consequently, I had to find a job that allowed me to go to classes during the day.

I found one at a rundown liquor store downtown, two blocks south of the Benton Harbor city dump. My shift started at 5:00 p.m. and ran until closing at 11:00 p.m., Monday through Saturday. Although I was not yet of legal drinking age, with my almost-shaved head I looked older. The liquor store owner, of questionable reputation, had asked if I met the state legal requirement to sell alcohol. I said, "Of course!" I needed the job, and I suspected he needed any warm body, considering the store's location. Proof of my actual age never came up again. The owner was one of several brothers who ran businesses in town and were reputed to have connections to the Chicago mobsters. I'm sure that skirting the law was nothing new to the owner.

Located one block north of Main Street, it was the only liquor store in the most rundown and seedy section of town. The store had no air conditioning, only an old wooden screen door that let fresh air into the store.

In the summer, two antique wood-bladed ceiling fans slowly moved the muggy air around the store but did little to make it feel more comfortable. At one time, this had been the finest part of town, housing a couple of large hotels, office buildings, and many businesses. The main post office was still at the end of the street.

The city dump, a block away, was a relic. Environmental rules had finally caught up with the city and required that the dump be shut down. However, it was not yet closed because the city was granted five years to phase out the existing dump and build a new "waste management facility" located away from the city center.

The dump was home to many homeless and destitute people who scraped out their survival from the junk and garbage dropped off by others. Rats, mud, and dirt made up most of the dump. It was understood that people who had no other income would scavenge the dump for odds and ends, either for personal use or to sell. For many, the dump was their only way to make any money. Some people had built shelters there out of discarded cardboard or wood. The city allowed them to eke out their survival there. During spring and fall rains, the foul smell of the dump would drift across the city. To keep the stink from entering the store, we closed the door.

At one time, Benton Harbor had been a flourishing resort and manufacturing community located in the southwest corner of Michigan. In the 1920s it was known worldwide for the baseball team from the House of David, a commune located at the eastern edge of town. The commune also had a small park with kiddy rides and a small train that looped around their grounds. While I was young, my parents took me there on our Sunday afternoon excursions to ride the train and eat their delicious homemade ice cream. Strawberry was my favorite, with chunks of frozen strawberries in each scoop.

White flight and the downturn in manufacturing exacerbated the decay of Benton Harbor, like many other American downtown areas. Now the area surrounding the liquor store had turned into a skid row. Rooms in the formerly elegant hotels down the block were rented by the hour or used by individuals too poor to find other housing. During the day the area saw some commercial traffic, but after eight o'clock at night it came alive with people looking for ways to forget their sorrow: to find love for a short time or gamble meager savings on a fast game in a backroom or alley.

The store was not large, perhaps the size of a classroom. A doorway jutting across the northeast corner of the building was the only entrance. As you entered the store, to the right was a large plateglass window that may have been a display window at one time. It faced the street. Along the left wall were shelves with bottles of liquor and wine. The bare bricks of the right wall made up the exterior wall of the building. The two sets of fluorescent lights and the fans hung from the high ceiling. Its old, metallic tiles had been painted over so often that the original design had disappeared. Indeed, the only word to describe the ceiling was *dingy*. The wood floorboards were black, except for the gray valleys where an untold number of shoes had worn down the paint. I never discovered whether the black was paint or just dirt, ground in over years of use. The wood floor gave off a smell that was somewhere between moldy and very stale. In front of the wines and liquor was a low wooden counter running the store's length to the back storeroom door. In the back section of the store was the cooler, an ancient thing with four heavy wood doors, each two feet by two, with thick glass panes facing the store's interior. A simple chrome handle allowed access to racks of refrigerated beer, wine, pop, milk, eggs, and cheese. A few metal racks in the store's center held meager groceries, such as white bread, sweets, and a few shelves of canned goods.

During each evening shift we routinely sold over 500 dollars' worth of the store's top sellers, Alta Red and Alta White wine, at seventy-nine cents each. It was the drink of choice for our customers off the city dump. White Horse whisky was the hard liquor of choice, going for $2.49 a pint. Cigarette prices ranged from twenty to thirty-two cents a pack, and a folder of book matches sold for a penny. Our "fine wines," which in any other liquor establishment would be considered low quality, gathered dust on the top shelves until Friday and Saturday evenings, when well-dressed men would come in to purchase higher-end bottles. We suspected that those purchases went to the hotel, to impress whomever the buyer shared the room-by-the-hour with.

Most memorable were the customers from the city dump. These folks were noticeable by their smell—generally putrid, as you'd expect from someone who had no access to washing or laundry facilities—as they entered the store. Keeping money while living there could be dangerous; thus, they would hide their meager funds in strange and disgusting places. Many tried to intimidate me, threatening harm if I did not give them a "loan" to get their daily supply of cheap wine. After some cursing, sometimes spitting and swearing, they would reach into their crotch or socks to pull out a smelly, moist, one-dollar bill to pay for their bottle. In the case of one of the few couples living there, the woman kept their joint resources inside her bra. More than one time, I saw her companion reach into the woman's dress with astonishing deftness, without even looking at her, and pull out a smelly dollar bill. His artistry was astonishing. She never complained or prevented his move. Today, looking back on handling this money and knowing where it came from, I would have killed to have a bottle of Purell to kill the germs on my hands. I just made sure my hands did not go near my mouth or nose until after I gave them a good soaking wash at the end of the evening.

Early one afternoon, a young, respectable-looking man, wearing clean clothing, walked up to the counter. He took a minute to look at me and then said, "You don't recognize me, do you?" He looked familiar, but I could not place the face. Delighted by my confusion, he said, "I'm pint of Seven Crown and Winstons," with a grin on his face.

"Really, it's you!" I replied. "I didn't recognize you. What happened to you?" As was the case of other customers, I did not know him by name, only by what he purchased.

"I dried out for a few days. I'm trying to get a job, so just Winston's today."

"Hey, congratulations," I replied. "No, I did not recognize you; that's great. Keep it up." I felt tempted to give him the cigarettes as encouragement. I had seen this customer almost daily, a scruffy, dirty, smelly guy from the dump. Now, in front of me stood a nice-looking young man. I was stunned. I gave him the cigarettes and wished him well. With a broad smile and a step of confidence, he left the store.

Ten days later, he was back again, dirty, smelly, and unshaven. I did not have the heart to ask him what had happened. He just said, "You know what," while I reached for the Seven Crown and Winstons. Without a word, he paid, picked up his bottle and cigarettes, and headed out the door, shoulders drooping this time, with the shuffle of feet accustomed to being drunk.

He taught me another life-altering lesson: life is fragile, and your fate can change quickly. No matter how smelly, vulgar, or unkempt, our customers were individuals, each with their own story of success and tragedy. It convinced me to treat every person I met in life as an individual. Don't judge a book by its cover!

"Hands up!"

One summer evening, after the initial rush of customers, things began to slow down around eight o'clock. This gave me time to restock shelves before the last-minute rush around ten. The heat of the day had crept into the store, which was now extremely uncomfortable. The exterior glass door was propped open in hopes that an evening breeze would bring some cool air into the store. That left only the screen door separating me from the outside. The glass door had a bell at the top to alert me if anyone came into the store. The screen door had no such bell.

Working with my back to the counter and the radio on the wall blaring out the latest rock 'n' roll hits, I did not hear anyone walk into the store. Still, I felt a presence and slowly turned, expecting to see a customer. Instead, two guys were standing there, wearing sweatshirts with hoods up around their heads, which at first glance struck me as odd on a hot summer day. I looked down and noticed the barrel of a small gun pointed at me.

"Give us all your fucking money," said the hooded man on my left. It took a bit to realized they were not men but teenage boys, looking frightened. The one on my left was screaming at me, while the one on the right, closer, nervously held a small pistol in his hand. Scared though they might have been, they had planned well. They had probably watched the store from the other side of the street and seen the brisk business earlier in the evening. It was simple enough for them to hang out just outside the store, as many of our customers did, until everyone left.

A loaded shotgun lay on a shelf just below the cash register; a pistol, loaded and ready to use, lay on a shelf below that. In the cooler was a rifle. The assumption was that if a robbery occurred, the robbers would want to lock the store clerk into the cooler to make their getaway. The rifle could be used in self-defense. By opening one of the small the cooler doors facing the storefront, I could either detain the culprits or shoot them as they exited the store.

It only took an instant for me to figure out what to do. Without any other overt moves, I hit the open button on the register and said, "Help yourself." Simultaneously, I raised my hands and took a step back toward the liquor shelves, thinking that someone going by on the street might see me with my hands up and call the police.

The robber without the gun quickly reached into the till and grabbed all the cash from the money tray. Then he ripped out the drawer and gathered up the checks and additional cash, which made me think they must have watched me put checks beneath the drawer. My heart raced as the other robber pointed the small revolver at me. Time seemed to stand still as we eyed each other, trying to read each other's thoughts. *What will his next move be?* I wondered. *Will he shoot? Will they run?* The one with the gun pointed to the door, yelling, "Let's get the fuck out of here!" Both fled. Briefly, it occurred to me to grab the pistol under the counter and run after them. However, just as quickly, I realized that they had me at a disadvantage since I had no idea in which direction they had gone. Stepping out of the store, I would be exposed, backlit and vulnerable. Instead, I paused to make sure they were gone, took a minute to catch my breath, and reached for the phone to call the police.

Per store policy, I had been putting twenty-dollar bills and other large denominations in a plain brown paper bag under the counter behind some cleaning cloths. The robbers made off with only the $123 in bills that had been in the register, a small portion of our usual take.

I had just begun to catch my breath when I heard someone say, "What the fuck are they running out of here so fast for?" My heart made a giant leap. Looking up, I saw one of my regulars, a very athletic middle-aged African American man, walk into the store. My heart pounded like crazy; I told him what had happened and that needed to close the store to prepare for the police.

"That's bullshit, doing that to you," the customer exploded. "Those fucking punks, messin' with you; I'm gonna put the word out on them. Let me grab a couple of things and then I'll be outta' here."

He picked up a few groceries, asked for a bottle of Scotch, and handed me some money, before leaving. I locked the door behind him and called the police and my boss. Within a few minutes, the city police, whose station was only two blocks away, came and took a statement from me. My boss, Mike, showed up about twenty minutes later.

"Those dumb fucks!" my boss yelled to no one in particular while pacing the floor. "Don't they know that we are their only business around here? If this keeps up, I'm going to close this place; to hell with them!" *Them* referring pejoratively to the predominantly African American customers.

The people from the city dump were, to him, invisible nobodies who did not count.

The owner's indignation aside, the police and I knew that this store was a goldmine for the owner. The minimal overhead and elevated prices on outdated groceries brought in cash aplenty for him. The police took only a cursory report. Never having experienced anything like this, I could not believe their response. I thought the police gave the incident as much attention as they might give to a lost pet call—I had the impression of *What do you expect, doing business in this area?* In retrospect I'm not surprised, considering the store's location and the loss of a mere $123. My description of the robbers did not help since it could fit any number of young African American men living in the surrounding area. Though I tried, I had not noticed any distinguishing features, nor could I recall seeing them in the store previously. Thus, without much further ado, the police finished their report and left. Seeing I was still upset, the boss suggested I head home; he would lock up the store.

The next day, Saturday, I went to work as usual since it was the store's busiest day. Word about the robbery had spread, and customers came in to talk to me because they were upset that "their" establishment had been robbed. I learned that the store was part of the community's fabric, and the robbery was an insult to the community. It was gratifying to see the community pull together and be concerned over my safety. Their supportive response provided me with another unexpected lesson in life. Then, three days after the robbery, the man who had come in right after the robbery walked into the store and placed forty-six cents on the counter. I looked at the money and asked, "What can I get for you?" assuming he wanted to purchase something.

"I owe you this," he said. "The other night, you were upset, so you didn't charge me enough for what I got. Here is what I still owe you." With that, he turned and walked out of the store.

I was flabbergasted. I didn't know what to think! I knew this man did not own a car, did not have a job, and was barely able to get along, yet he felt obligated to pay back what he owed . . . and had walked a distance to pay his debt. I was certain that the forty-six cents would never be missed by the store. I also knew that this small amount was the equivalent of a pack of cigarettes. That simple act is something I have remembered for the rest of my life, a reminder that you can't assume anything about an individual.

Civil Rights Protests Arrive

Late that August, on my way to work, I noticed more than the usual number of people out on the streets. It had been another hot summer day, the kind that kept people who did not have air conditioning outside in the evening, trying to stay cool. Rumors of racial strife had been circulating in the community for several days. The disparity between the town's white power base and the African American community had become more obvious over the last few years. The white flight across the river to St. Joseph, Michigan, was only one sign. The African American community had asked for improvements in Benton Harbor's schools, more jobs, and better treatment by local law enforcement. The disparity reached a point that it became the basis of a book by *Wall Street Journal* Chicago reporter Alex Kotlowitz, entitled *The Other Side of the River: A Story of Two Towns, a Death, and America's Dilemma.* The book describes the racism and segregation of the two cities and suspicious death of a young African American male found in the St. Joseph River. The population of Benton Harbor was over 90 percent African American, while St. Joseph was, and still is, over 90 percent white. The book's title comes from the fact that the two cities are separated only by the St. Joseph River.

To get to work, I had to drive through the predominantly Black section of town. My car had no air conditioning, so I had lowered all the windows to keep cool. As I drove, people saw my white face going by and started hurling taunts at me. It made me wonder what might be in store for the city and me tonight.

Anyone sensitive to issues of race knew that tension in the community had been festering for some time. African Americans were denied opportunities for steady employment. Ongoing social inequality, combined with racism and police brutality, had sparked a series of riots in cities across the country, including Chicago, Detroit, Newark, and Los Angeles. Our community was not immune to that civil unrest. Riots occurred in our town in August 1966 and again in 1967.

Shortly after I got to work, a Michigan State Police sergeant came into the store and told me that there was a probability of trouble later that night. He said, "We can't force you to close up, but we believe your store may be in danger if the rioters come down this way. We will not be able to protect you."

Two large, middle-aged Black men, regular customers, were there and heard this warning. Both enjoyed hanging out in the store, talking with other customers and me. John, in his mid-forties, with short-cropped hair and a dark complexion, was tall and had the athletic build of a tight end, if slightly overweight. Bob, of a lighter complexion, was a bit shorter, with a round waist due to hard work involving a lot of lifting. He could have passed for a center on a football team. This evening, his pants were held up with large blue suspenders, and he wore a bright red short-sleeved shirt. They usually came in together to buy bottles of pop, which they drank while hanging out in the store. They discussed sports, weather, and politics and commented on the customers that came and went. Eventually, both would buy their liquor and cigarettes and leave. I loved shooting the breeze with them. Listening and learning, they taught me more about African American culture and experiences of the time.

"What you going to do?" John asked after the officer left.

"Well, I better call the boss and find out if he wants me to close up," I said.

"Wait until we come back before you close," said John, giving Bob a nod toward the door.

"OK," I said, not thinking much about their comments. I was focused on staying open, which meant more money for the store and my paycheck. Closing meant fewer hours for me. I called my boss, who grumbled at losing money on the most lucrative day of the week. Nevertheless, he agreed it would be safer to close and show local law enforcement that he, the owner, was a good citizen. I prepared the store for closing, but shortly before 11:00 p.m., as I was about to lock the door, John and Bob returned, each with a shotgun in hand.

"Wait," said John. "Nobody is going to mess with this store. You folks treat us right, and we're going to take care of you." With that, they grabbed a couple of folding chairs they had brought and sat themselves down in the large display window, visibly demonstrating their intention to guard the store. Not sure what to think, I decided to trust their judgment, locked the store door, brought some beers from the cooler, took some chips off the shelf, and joined them, making sure I sat behind them, hidden from view. About an hour later, we saw National Guard trucks rumble by, followed by a sheriff's deputy, who stopped his car in front of the store, got out, and came to the door. As he crossed the sidewalk he noticed the two men sitting in the display window, shotguns across their laps, and quickly sized up the situation. I went to the door and identified myself as the store employee.

"Everything OK here?" the officer asked with a knowing grin and a nod toward the two men with the shotguns. I assured him that everything was under control. "Good, I thought so. You folks take care, and don't do anything stupid," he said, still grinning, and walked back to his squad car. He pulled out onto the street and turned on his lights before hightailing it after the National Guard convoy.

My protectors and I stayed until shortly after 4:00 a.m., when we agreed that it was safe for me to leave, as the city had become quiet. Only a few small groups of young people had come by all night, and seeing the guardians in the window, they'd kept going. As we left the store, I thanked Bob and John as they walked out of the store. "No problem, man," and "Just taking care of business," they said, and with that, they walked off toward their homes as I got in my car. It was unlikely that the store would be damaged during daylight hours with a large contingent of National Guard troops patrolling the city.

Driving home through empty and quiet streets, I realized the evening's events had intensified the confusion that had been growing in me since starting this job. A completely new world opened up to me. I was now seeing and participating in a part of society to which I had been oblivious.

My personal life was spent in the white world where racism and racist remarks were common among friends, colleagues, and even my extended family members. I always found it ironic how my relatives preached love and understanding, citing biblical passages at the drop of a hat, and yet didn't see how antithetical their own comments were to religious teachings of tolerance and goodwill. It made me indifferent to them and their religious beliefs. The evening's events, plus the support I had been given after the robbery, changed my thinking and viewpoint on people of color. There was no way that I could again look at African Americans or other people of color the same way. These events burned into my soul a determination to not judge a person by their skin color, sexual preferences, or any other intrinsic quality—a belief I still hold very dear and have tried to instill in my own children.

CHAPTER 4

1968: THE YEAR WE MET

"Hello," Maria said, her tone more of inquiry than greeting, as she stuck her head through the doorway of the language lab, on the ground floor of Lake Superior Hall. She walked into the small room, which was located under a set of stairs and had a sharp angle to the right, impeding anyone from seeing both ends of the room at the same time. Glossy, industrial-white-painted brick walls gave the room a stark appearance, especially under the fluorescent lights. Voice tape reels and cassette tapes crowded shelves and tables in the small space. Anyone could probably touch the walls on both sides at once with outstretched arms. Watching her approach, I could tell she was nervous.

Maria needed a job to support herself. Her parents helped to pay for the tuition, but she had to find the money for living expenses. At the time, work-study programs allowed students to hold campus jobs in support of, or instead of, regular employees, while working around their class schedules. Work-study students saved the college money because the program was funded by a government grant. Maria had been recommended for the job in the language lab, but beyond that, she had no idea what she was getting into.

As she tells it, she turned the corner, and before her stood a young man dressed in a nice shirt and tie, surprising and impressing her. Since she had arrived at the school less than a month earlier, the only people she had seen wearing ties were a few faculty and administrators. After all, this was the late sixties, and blue jeans, long hair, and an unkempt appearance—the counterculture uniform—were in fashion. Nevertheless, before her was a young man whose initial appearance left her speechless. He seemed to be a bit taller than she was, with deep, dark brown eyes that were bright and felt as if they looked right into her soul. She felt instantly naked in his presence. His face was handsome, and his movements were graceful and smooth, with no hesitation.

"Hi, are you Maria?" I asked, extending my hand to her.

Years later, she told me she had been instantly drawn to me, the blood rushing through her body. She attempted to recover but could only stammer, "Yes, that's me," suddenly aware of her Latin accent and feeling embarrassed. *Oh God, how stupid do I look? Nice first impression*, Maria thought. *This is not going to go well!*

I didn't see it the same way. I recall that I quickly covered the space between us, reaching out to shake her hand. Maria took a couple of steps toward me before taking my hand. Although plain-looking at first glance and slightly overweight, Maria had long dark locks of hair that bounced as she moved her head and beautiful brown eyes: she had that classic Latin beauty about her.

Laughing slightly because I saw no reason for her to be embarrassed, I said, "Maria, right? Come on in, let me show you around." I introduced Maria to a student seated at one of the desks with an array of buttons and a microphone in front of him and a set of large earphones on his head.

Students working in A-V lab.

"This is Leon," I said, and Leon turned and gave a slight wave. "He will be one of your coworkers." I guided her past him to a chair at the end of the room. After a brief interview, which seemed to take only a few minutes, I shook her hand and said, "Welcome to the Language Lab." Little did Maria realize the lasting impact that those few words would have on both of our lives. Still uncertain of what she had gotten herself into, Maria accepted the offer of the much-needed job. We sat down at one of the other desks to fill out some paperwork, and then Maria left without any further discussion.

Maria was now the new student assistant in the AudioVisuals Language Laboratory, generally called the A-V Lab. The language lab had state-of-the-art foreign-language teaching technology of its time, possessed by only a few colleges. On a floor above the lab, students sat at carrels, which were small desks with two side partitions to keep sound isolated. Using a rotary dial phone, the student called into the lab to request a specific tape, which had been assigned by the language instructor, to be inserted in the machine. The student then would use earphones to practice the language lesson. Student assistants in the lab were responsible for setting up the tapes and monitoring that students were doing their lessons by listening in on them. Consider it the 1960s version of distance learning!

After Maria walked out the door, I smiled. An immigrant myself, I instantly recognized her vulnerability and naïveté, trying to fit into a new culture and environment. It is generally tough, when coming from a foreign country, to blend in with the predominant culture. Arriving at that time, when the United States was questioning its own direction and values, made the transition even harder. Fortunately, she had been an exchange student in a nearby town during high school, so she had some idea of what she would encounter. Still, I vowed to keep an eye on her.

Maria recalls that, after leaving the interview, she thought that I seemed more mature than she, and worldlier, which fascinated her. Once she started working, it did not take long before she felt attracted to me. At first, she was unsure if it was romantic or just the feeling one gets for a caring big brother. I, however, was all business, making sure everything ran like clockwork in the lab. I was precise and punctual to a fault and expected the same from the student workers. I came to work every day wearing the shirt and tie, in contrast to the other students' casual clothing and long hair. As time went on, Maria and I spent more time together, which only confused her emerging feelings about me. Later, she wondered how it was possible she could have feelings for such a straitlaced individual, especially one who did not share her belief system and laid-back ways. I was not aware of her family's long history of political activism. Protests against the Vietnam War really resounded with her. I was the opposite of what she had always imagined in a man, except for my looks. I was regimented and disciplined, the opposite of her.

Taking Care of My Little Sister

Every week, Sunday through Thursday, promptly at 6:00 p.m., I picked Maria up and took her to the library to study. We appropriated a small third-floor study room as ours. During every study session I insisted on taking only one fifteen-minute break, so we would finish promptly by 9:00 p.m. Time was not the driver of Maria's life, and my exactitude drove her nuts, yet she could not say no to me. Once we had established our study routine, she convinced other students working in the language lab to join us. Having others present allowed Maria to watch me without my noticing. Now, she tells me that the longer she watched, the more she began to admire me.

Study evenings.

She would spend long minutes just staring at me, her romantic feelings beginning to grow, but I remained oblivious. Maria was puzzled: why I was spending so much time with her? Why was I so concerned? In her eyes, she was a plump ugly duckling not worthy of someone as handsome as me. Nevertheless, her mind played pictures of the two of us together, of taking me home and introducing this dashing gringo to her parents and friends. She could show her mother that she, too, could find an elegant husband like her dad.

But I was engaged to Judy, my future wife, and saw no reason to be romantically interested in someone else. Judy was executive secretary to the dean of students. Her office was down the hall from the language lab, so we interacted daily. Maria knew that, yet still felt she could compete romantically with Judy.

Grand Valley State College, as it was known then, was brand new. Built by conservative visionaries in western Michigan to provide students from its quickly growing west coast access to quality education without having to move far away from their cultural and religious identity. People in that part of the state felt that premier universities in larger cities did not match the Christian beliefs, moral values, and standards so prominent in this part of the state. One nearby community still banned dancing altogether, and businesses were required to be closed on Sunday. The college founders felt they could establish a Princeton of the Midwest, small, with a high quality of academic training and positive core values.

Maria and I had been brought up with different values from those that shaped the institution. The college's brand-new buildings, with white columns and white-brick facades, made it look like an ancient Greek city sprouting out of the middle of former cornfields. Although the college was barely tolerated by the very conservative community nearby, they accepted it because the students, staff, and faculty represented visions of profit. In that part of the state, most of its residents placed profit somewhere between God and family.

Maria had enrolled at Thomas Jefferson College (TJC), an experimental school within the college where only pass or fail grades were given. Students of all cultures, races, and socioeconomic classes flocked to it. The students who enrolled in this college believed that they could change the world and make an impact. One of Maria's classmates was an artist who displayed works that elicited either disgust or avant-garde emotions, depending on your perspective. There were openly gay and lesbian students, along with those who had not yet decided or declared their gender preferences, at a time when discussing sexual identity was taboo. Free spirits found this college a safe place to express their lifestyles. Weed was a favorite form of relaxation. Maria delights in recalling how she and others laid on a living room floor after smoking, stereo speakers blasting out Tchaikovsky's Manfred Symphony and other classical pieces.

TJC was a haven of academic freedom and expression. Students designed classes by simply posting an interesting area of study on a three-by-five-inch card on a bulletin board. If at least five other students agreed, a class was established. Even the regular college students, seen as liberal by the surrounding community, looked with disdain upon these hippies—their disregard heightened by the fact that many of these countercultural kids did not feel that cleanliness was next to godliness. Drugs, while illegal, were no strangers to stimulating conversations or augmenting the development of academic discussions. The administrators did not always approve of the programs or students in this radical college. Yet they knew it attracted many brilliant students and educators who were not satisfied in a traditional university setting and understood that having this school would help them foster the larger college's growth. Still, their own values and upbringing made them shudder at what they saw.

The students and faculty of this school were, not surprisingly, leaders of the campus anti-Vietnam war protest movements. I did not agree with Maria's participation in campus protests because I was concerned for her safety. I was concerned that she might be caught up in things beyond her ability to control, whether drugs or highly radicalized activities. Although

I never shared it with her, I believed just as fervently in the antiwar movement as she did. I believed that I could influence the decision-makers
from inside the building, rather than protesting and being locked out and
kept away by police. I was concerned that Maria might get caught up in
a raid, knowing that law enforcement organizations had planted under-
cover agents in protest groups. Her arrest would have probably meant jail,
or worse, deportation. I assumed Maria's participation in protests was her
search for something, finding her own identity and how she could fit into
this strange American culture. Little did I know then of her family's history
of protests and fight for justice in Chile.

The Argument

On May 3, 1970, Maria came to the lab and told me that she would not be
coming to work the next day. I assumed she had an exam or a special test
for which she had to study. No, she said, May 4, 1970, had been declared a
national moratorium day against the Vietnam War. Maria explained that
across the country, students were planning on boycotting classes to protest
the war. She, too, planned to honor the day by not coming to work and
instead joining the campus protest.

It was common knowledge that the war in Vietnam had been going
on officially since 1965, when 150,000 Marines went ashore in Da Nang.
But more than 23,000 "advisers" had unofficially been fighting there since
the late 1950s. A draft had been instituted to supply the required military
manpower, meaning that every male, once they reached the age of eighteen, had to sign up for the military. A lottery system selected those who
would most likely be shipped off to the war zone. The American public
had little understanding of or love for fighting a bloody war in another
part of the world. Protest and anger had been growing as more and more
families lost their sons in the war. (Women were not eligible for the draft.)
President Nixon had announced that although he was planning to pull
troops out, more men would be sent there in the interim. On some college

campuses, the protests had turned violent, with the firebombing of campus buildings and protestors being killed by riot police. Kent State University became one of the most tragic examples when police arbitrarily shot and killed four student protestors.

Although I sympathized with the protestors and opposed the war, I also had a responsibility to my job. I informed Maria that she needed to show up the next day for work or she would be fired. She became truly angry and felt I was unreasonable. She came to work the next day, but that would be the last time I saw her for the next thirty-five years and fourteen days.

When she left, I felt betrayed because we had been an essential part of each other's lives for almost two years, working together and studying together. She seemed to have forgotten it, over some political event that mattered less to me than it did to Maria. Despite my feelings of anger, I continued on. I was anxious about graduating in a few weeks and my upcoming marriage to Judy in September. I had also been given an opportunity to travel back to Austria to meet with friends and family I had not seen since leaving with my parents in 1957. I could not allow my quarrel with Maria to delay my plans.

Ironically, many years later, after Maria and I had been married for some time, we tried to remember the reason for the fight that caused our estrangement. Neither of us could recall until one day, when we were in the car listening to Hillary Clinton's biography. When Clinton described the events at Kent State and the moratorium, suddenly, Maria smacked me with her left hand and shouted out, "That's it! That's what our fight was all about!" We both instantly recalled the argument that had caused our separation almost four decades earlier. And, despite the passage of time, we still each justified the positions we had taken at the time.

Fickle Fate Works Its Magic

The day Maria walked out of the Language Lab, it put us both on very separate tracks. Maria went her way, and I went my way. Yet, without either of us ever being aware, over the next thirty-five years, our lives would be intertwined like a DNA helix. The fates, it appeared, meant to keep us in the same universe. Although we did not know it, for the next thirty-five years our lives would circle around each other like the strands of a helix in DNA.

For example, a few years after I graduated from college, Maria and I both worked in downtown Lansing for about eighteen months. We spent each day within three blocks of each other yet did not meet. Later, I attended meetings with Maria's first husband, never knowing that she was his wife. After divorcing him, Maria worked at an agency that I visited many times but never saw her nor realized she worked there. Subsequently, Maria took a job at the Hannahville Bay De Noc Indian Reservation while I lived in Marquette, fifty-four miles away. I had meetings with tribal leaders in Escanaba, close to the reservation, without ever knowing of her presence. She came to Marquette occasionally to shop and socialize with friends. Still, our paths never crossed.

CHAPTER 5

IT NEVER HAPPENED

Sunday afternoon, snowflakes are whirling past our bedroom window. Maria's head is on my left chest, our skin touching as we watch what we hope is the last snowstorm of the season fly by outside.

"I'm excited," she whispers.

"About what?" I reply.

"Our trip."

"Yeah, it'll be nice," I reply in a casual tone.

We were going to Lisbon, Portugal, to attend the Annual Rotary International Conference. As president of the Anoka Rotary Club, I had received a stipend to attend the conference to represent our club. With my expenses covered, we could both afford to go. While I was at the conference, Maria could do some sightseeing, and afterward we would continue on to Barcelona and then to Austria to visit my family. We would fly home out of Frankfurt after spending a few days with my childhood friend Werner and his wife, Gudrun.

"Aren't you excited too?" she asks.

"Yes, I am," I say pensively.

"What are you thinking about? You seem far away."

I pause before answering, "Oh, just my previous trips to Europe."

"How often have you been back?"

"The last time was just before we met—after the divorce. Before that, it was in 1996, with my mom and Steve, and prior to that in 1970."

"Did you go with Judy? Was that your honeymoon?"

"No, I went by myself," I replied, sinking further into thought.

"You went back to Austria, where you were born, and did not take Judy along? Why didn't you?" said Maria, pulling away from me in surprise and leaning her head on her raised hand. I stared off into space, looking for a way to change the subject.

"I'm excited too," I said, hoping to avoid further discussion of my past. "I'm excited to show you around Graz and a lot of my beautiful country. Hopefully, seeing where I came from will give you a chance to get to know me better." Then, I closed my eyes and pretended to drift off to sleep.

My mind was on a beautiful, sunny, warm autumn Saturday afternoon. Knowing that the gray depths of October and November were closing in, I had opened the sliding patio door of the apartment I shared with four other guys, allowing the fresh air to flow in. The record player blared out the hit "You Were on My Mind," by the We Five. The lyrics took me back to when I was madly in love with my high school sweetheart, Sandi. The song was an anthem to me, about a love lost but not forgotten. It always made me feel good. Mellow days easily brought memories of her back to me: beach days and warm summer nights at the drive-in.

My roommates had either gone home for the weekend or were off doing their own thing. Three of them were jocks. I shared one of the apartment's two bedrooms with Jimmy, a basketball player, and Phil, a student athletic trainer who resembled a huge character out of a Marvel comics movie. We had divided up the cleaning duties. Jimmy and I handled vacuuming and dusting. The other two guys—another basketball player and a member of the tennis team—had kitchen duty, and Phil had volunteered for bathroom duty. No one wanted to incur the wrath of Phil, so we made his job easy by keeping the bathroom clean—unusual for a group of young men!

I had just finished dusting and vacuuming the carpets and was about to put the vacuum away when my attention was drawn to the noise of people below. In the parking lot and the grassy area by the street, music was blaring from car radios as others took advantage of the nice weather to clean or work on their cars. Across the street, several of the co-eds who lived in the building next to ours were playing volleyball against their male counterparts. My eyes were drawn to Edith's long, flowing brown hair whipping in the wind as she played. I had dated Edith a couple of times and found her looks to be almost overwhelming.

A knock on the door brought me out of my daydreams. Not expecting anyone, I put the cleaning cloth down on the coffee table, turned the stereo down, and went to the door. I was startled to see two men in suits standing in front of the door.

"Are you Mr. Tatzmann?" one of the men asked.

Both were slightly taller than I and in good physical shape. I tried to assess why these men were at my door. Their gray suits were pressed but not expensive; it looked as if each had bought them off the same rack.

Being a college community in the sixties, I immediately suspected that they were the police of some kind, but not the local police because of the suits. Local police would harass the students, demonstrating their authority by showing off their masculinity and all the military gadgets that they could attach to their belts. The next thought that went through my mind was, *Oh shit, is one of my roommates a suspect in some drug-related issue?* I didn't think any of my roommates were involved in drugs; I simply did not trust cops! Instead of panicking, I decided to play dumb and find out what these guys wanted.

"That's me," I replied. The two men almost simultaneously pulled badges out of their pockets and flipped them open and closed so fast that it would have taken Superman-like vision to read who they represented. Still, the quick glance I got, combined with their appearance and demeanor, convinced me that they were probably legitimate. Reading their faces, I could see they would not entertain questions from me.

On college campuses in those days, the only thing more hated than drug cops and narcs were the draft boys, the Selective Service people who sent boys off to fight in the ugly war in Vietnam. "Can we come in and talk with you?" one of the men asked politely.

"Sure," I answered, thinking, *As if I have an option.* I stepped aside to let them in. As both men walked past the dining table, they scanned the kitchen alcove and looked down the hall past the two bedrooms and into the bathroom.

"Nice apartment you have here," said the taller of the two men, "I don't think during my college days, my apartment ever looked this nice."

"No kidding," the second man responded, "my house doesn't look this nice now!"

I felt surprisingly at ease. My overwhelming sense of curiosity, which had gotten me in trouble throughout my life, was controlling any fear or apprehension that I should have had about these strangers. They seemed to sense that they did not intimidate me.

"Please, sit down," I said, pointing to the couch and bending down to sweep the latest issue of *Playboy* magazine from the coffee table to a side table. I crossed the room to lift the tonearm off the record and place it into the cradle, stopping the music. Out of the corner of my eye, I caught the men giving each other a quick glance and brief smiles crossing their faces.

"Are any of your roommates here?" asked the taller of the two.

"No," I replied. "They are all gone for the afternoon, possibly the weekend."

"Good. Do you have the time to talk with us?" asked the other man. *Stupid question*, I thought, *as if I have a choice!* I knew I would end up talking to them whether I wanted to or not.

"Let us introduce ourselves again," said the taller one. "I'm Smith, and this is Mr. Jones." I almost broke out laughing at the absurdity of that, knowing full well that neither was a real name. "Smith" went on to say that they represented a government agency associated with the Selective Service. *Oh shit, my ass is grass*, I thought. *I'm going to be drafted.*

"Do you recall filling out certain forms at the draft physical in Detroit?" asked Smith, phrasing it less as a question than a statement. Frankly, I could recall little about that entire episode, except that it was one of the drunkest nights I had ever experienced. Thinking back, I could remember the events of the evening but almost nothing about the physical itself.

A year earlier, I had been called up to go for my Selective Service physical. All men over the age of eighteen had to go through the draft physical unless excused for medical or religious reasons. Eligibility and call-up for military service was then based on your age and outcome of the Selective Service physical. On the arranged day, thirty-eight other boys and I got on a rickety government-owned bus for a four-hour trip from Benton Harbor to Fort Wayne in Detroit, where the Selective Service held all physicals for men in Michigan. We were put up in a decrepit hotel downtown. The evening was ours, but, we had been warned, at five thirty in the morning we would be transported to Fort Wayne for our physical. Our group was divided into those who chose to enter the military and those, like me, who wanted to avoid going to Vietnam but couldn't avoid this mandatory trip.

Once checked into the hotel and assigned rooms, several of us decided to explore the city. We jumped in a cab, asking the cabbie to get us to "where the action is." The cabbie, obviously having done this before, took off without any further ado and a few minutes later dropped us off near the Detroit riverfront. All along the street were bars with various come-on signs inviting the innocent in for a good time. My new friends and I wandered into one of the closest places, sat down, and ordered hamburgers and beers.

The place was tiny and dark, and it reeked of stale beer and smoke. The bar went around the room in a J shape. The bottom end of the bar was wider than the rest and appeared to double as a stage. The waitress who brought us the beers never bothered to check if we were of legal age to drink. I asked her about the bar top's strange shape, and the waitress told me that there would be an exotic dancer performing at that end of the bar in about another hour. For four young men with raging hormones and nothing better to do, this was manna from heaven, so we decided to enjoy our food and drink and stay for the show. The waitress agreed to tip us off before the show started so we could get good seats in front of the action. We got the signal from the waitress shortly after finishing our hamburgers. After ordering another round of drinks, we moved to the end of the bar. I decided to demonstrate my manhood by ordering a Manhattan. No sooner had my drink arrived when loud recorded music started up. Surprisingly, our waitress stepped out from behind a curtain at the end of the bar, dressed now in an outfit that left little to the imagination. She began dancing and gyrating to the sound of Mitch Ryder's "Devil with a Blue Dress On."

Never having experienced anything like it, I was transfixed. By evening's end, at 2:00 a.m., we had sat through four sets, each becoming more erotic as guys bought more drinks. The dancer's gyrations came closer and closer to our faces, encouraged by five-dollar bills stuffed into her panties and bra. I cannot remember how many Manhattans I drank that night or how much money I spent. All I know is that it was at least one for each set she danced. By the time the bar closed, my head was throbbing to the sound of "Devil with a Blue Dress On." A taxi took us back to the hotel. I vaguely recalled falling into the bed, and the next thing I remembered was being shoved out the door with my companions to board the bus for our draft physical and being pushed around with several hundred other young men in their underwear.

"Listen, guys," I said to the two suits, "in all honesty, I can barely remember anything except feeling very lousy. I had way too many drinks that night. Did I sign some paperwork? Yes, I probably did. Can I tell you what I signed? Impossible!" The men chuckled, and Smith said, "We understand. Nevertheless, there are some questions we have for you."

Mr. Jones, who had been sitting quietly until now, moved forward in his seat, making a loud squeaking noise on the plastic sofa cushion. He looked me in the eye and asked, "Mr. Tatzmann, what do you think about the war in Vietnam?"

Oh no, my goose is cooked now, I thought. This was one of those no-right-answer questions. My heart sank, and for the first time, I felt uncomfortable and nervous about these two guys. I did not believe the war in Vietnam was just. One of my friends had come back from the war, and I saw how it had changed him. Many of my high school classmates had been killed or injured over there.

The peacetime conscription process, initiated in 1947, was no longer providing enough men for the war. I had a high draft number, so I felt it was probably only a matter of time before I would be called up too. One time, when a demonstration got rowdy in front of the college's administration building, the police were called and all the doors were sealed. Demonstrators stood in front of the building, hurling epithets at police and administrators. Meanwhile, I had been inside, talking to the administrators, trying to get them to see the demonstrators' point. I felt I could be more productive inside the system than being locked out and dismissed out of hand.

Taking a deep breath, I decided to risk it, assuming I had nothing to lose; if they wanted, they could send me to Vietnam tomorrow, so they might as well know where I stood.

"I think the war is unjust, and we are killing a lot of people on both sides—and for what?" I asked. *There*, I thought, *it's out now, what are they going to say? Your move!*

Without blinking or changing expression, Mr. Jones asked, "What do you think about America?"

"Huh," is what I wanted to say. The question threw me off guard even more than the previous question. Instead I managed, "What do you mean?"

"We'd like to hear your thoughts about America, Mr. Tatzmann," Smith replied, sounding serious.

"Well, I think America, as fucked up as it is, is a great country. It has its faults—the war, the discrimination against Black people, poverty, and so on—but overall, it's a great place." Anger crept into my voice.

"How strongly do you feel about that?" Jones asked the question this time.

Uh-oh, I thought, having no idea where their questioning was going.

"Would you guys like something to drink—pop, water, a beer?" I asked, stalling for time to think about how to answer these questions while trying to figure out what it was they really wanted.

"No, thank you," Smith replied for both of them.

"We know that you are an immigrant, Mr. Tatzmann, from the information you completed for the Selective Service. We are curious how you feel about this country and living here," Jones asked.

I'd hidden my anxiety up to this point, but all my confidence went out the window with these questions. *How do I feel about the country? What are they after, and what do they want?* were the thoughts racing through my head.

As if reading my mind, Smith said, "Look, we are not here to arrest you or cart you off to Vietnam. In the forms you completed at your physical, you provided some information that came to our attention, and we would like to explore it further. Can you tell us a little bit about how you came to this country and where you lived before that? By the way, your English is particularly good; are you still fluent in your native language, German?" Before I could answer, both pulled notepads from their coat pocket as if they had done this a hundred times.

Recognizing defeat when I saw it, I spent the next hour explaining where I came from, my family, and the family that had been left behind. I made a point of telling them that although I was not yet a naturalized citizen, I felt fully American. I hoped that would quiet any concerns they had about my loyalty. They listened intently, taking notes on occasion, and asking questions as follow ups to some of my explanations.

"Thank you, this was helpful," said Smith, abruptly standing up, putting away his notebook, and reaching out for a handshake while thanking me for my time. Then he and Jones headed for the door.

"Wait a minute," I said, with more anger in my voice than I had intended. "What the hell is this all about? You come in here, say you're from the government; you have some information about me. You ask me some more questions and then get up and leave, without any further explanation?"

"Mr. Tatzmann," Smith said, turning toward me, "we are not at liberty to tell you why we came, only that you are not in any kind of trouble. One of us may be back in touch with you again. At that time, we can explain why we need your assistance."

"Assistance? Doing what?" I blurted out as both men left, closing the door behind them. For a minute I stood there, baffled, and then I walked to the balcony and watched them leave the building. I noticed they had parked not in the building's parking lot, but across the street, where they entered a nondescript dark green sedan. When they pulled out on the street, Jones looked back. I just stood there, trying to look more confident than I really was.

What was that all about? I thought.

An Offer Too Good to Be True

A few weeks later, the fleeting warmth of Indian summer was gone. A cold wind whipped across the former cornfields upon which the college had risen. It had not snowed yet, but the ground was frozen, and the windchill matched the ground temperature. Looking out the windows of the building where I worked, I saw students walking across campus bundled in coats, collars up and hats on, looking down to minimize exposing their faces to the wind.

I buttoned up my camel-hair winter coat, ready to leave the building. Fortunately, my car was in the parking lot adjacent to the building, so I did not have to confront the wind for too long. As I stepped outside, my head down against the chill, I heard a voice call out, "Mr. Tatzmann, could I have a minute of your time?" Startled, I turned and saw Smith standing a few yards to my left. Before I could respond, he said, "Mind if I walk to the car with you?"

"Sure," I said offhandedly, uncertain of how to respond. How did he know that I would be coming out of the building? Scary! Obviously, Smith had learned my schedule in order to be waiting for me at this particular time and place.

We got to my car without speaking. I unlocked my door and looked over the top of the car as Smith asked, "Could I ride with you?"

I couldn't let the man freeze and doubted I had any choice anyway. I got in, reached across the front seat, and pulled up the knob to unlock the passenger door. Maybe it was his winter coat, but Smith was a larger man than I remembered; he had to squeeze himself into the seat, taking off his hat so it would not get crushed on the car liner.

"What's this all about?" I asked once we were both settled. I started the car and turned on the heater but did not put the car into gear.

"If you'll give me a ride, I'll explain."

Startled at the request, I asked, "Where to?"

"Mr. Tatzmann—by the way, may I call you Manfred? I really hate formalities," Smith said.

"Whatever." I probably sounded surly, not sure yet what to make of all this. It was midafternoon; I had hoped to go home and make myself lunch. I had worked since seven in the morning, including two classes. I was hungry, had homework to do, and really did not feel like talking to this man right now. I get cranky when I'm hungry!

Apparently reading my thoughts, Smith asked if I had eaten lunch yet. At my reply, of course, he suggested we go somewhere quiet where we could talk for a bit; he would buy. Not many college students turn down the offer of a free lunch! I considered the offer and situation and agreed, thinking, *What do I have to lose?*

"Do you know the Embassy?" he asked. "If it's not too far for you, let's head there. It should be quiet at this time of the afternoon." Yes, I knew the Embassy, but how did he? The Embassy was a local watering hole that had served the area since 1951. It was a few miles west, past the dry and deeply religious little hamlet that hosted the campus. It had been a rural farming community where most residents were members of the conservative Dutch Christian Reform movement. Everything was closed on Sunday, no alcohol was sold in stores, and there were no restaurants or bars in town.

Light snow began to fall as we drove. It whipped across the road and the cornfields, which, denuded of the crop, were no match for the wind. We drove west on M-45. Smith asked me how classes were going and made other small talk along the way. In turn, I asked Smith why Jones was not with him today. Smith replied that Jones had been reassigned. I had no time to follow up as we pulled into the bar's parking lot, which held only two other cars, a good sign.

Co-eds, if asked, might describe the Embassy as "disgusting," while male students called it "a great guy's bar." The parking lot was not paved, but the cold kept the dirt and gravel as hard as cement, and the snow just blew across it. I pulled right up to the front of the building, a two-story 1920s-era home with the lower floor converted into a bar. The front door, split with a screen on top and the bottom in old wood the color of dried blood, creaked open, setting off the tinkle of a small bell mounted over it, and banged shut behind us. It reminded me of the doorway in the liquor store where I had worked for one summer.

Smith led the way. The place was dimly lit, its primary illumination coming from a Miller High Life sign on the wall and the backlit shelf of liquor bottles behind the bar. The few light bulbs hanging from the tin-plated ceiling weren't much help. Beer and vodka signs hung all around the walls. The bar took up the entire left side of the room, and the pool table, pinball machine, jukebox, darts, and eight tables with four old wooden chairs each filled the rest of the space. The place had a classic bar smell, which in this case was not all bad—a mixture of beefy hamburger with onions, stale beer, and a hint of smoke.

Only two other students were there this early, sitting near the dart game and drinking beer. An older man, who looked like he spent many afternoons sitting on a bar stool, nursed a beer at the bar. Smith and I moved to a table away from the students. We placed our coats over chairs at the next table over, signaling that we wanted some space, though I doubted that there would be a rush of patrons on a cold midweek afternoon. Few students had cars, and those who did were mostly commuters and tended to head in the opposite direction, east toward Grand Rapids. I got the bartender's attention, and she came over to ask, without any other introduction, what we wanted to drink.

Smith asked if we could still get lunch. She said yes, she could still make sandwiches, but it might take a bit since she was the only person working.

"What do you think?" Smith asked.

"Sure, I'm always hungry when someone else is buying," I answered, allowing a mischievous smile to cross my face.

"How about drinks to get you started?" she asked. I ordered a draft, sixteen ounces. Smith ordered a Coke. The bartender turned and said, "I'll be right back with menus, boys."

Turning to Smith, I said, "OK, I'm listening. What's this all about? I haven't heard from you in a couple of months, and now you show up and buy me lunch. What gives?"

"It's my understanding that you will graduate next spring or summer, depending on when you can get one last credit that you need. Correct?"

Before I could answer, the bartender appeared with the drinks and two menus. "Here you go, gents; I'll be back in a minute to get your order."

Neither of us spoke while we glanced over the plastic-covered one-sheet menu. I moved the beer closer and took a long pull from it. Having wetted my throat, which had gone dry from the drive and nerves, I decided that I needed to get some answers.

"OK, Smith"—I emphasized his name, making it clear that I did not believe it was really his—"who are you, and what do you want? Obviously, you have checked with the college to find out my class standing. You and

Jones had information about me and my background, and now you're my buddy, buying a poor college student lunch. Honestly, I don't really like this."

The bartender appeared, order pad in hand. Then the door opened, and a couple of students walked in and seated themselves near the other students. "I'll be with you in a minute," the bartender yelled at them across the room. "OK, what can I get you boys today?" she asked, looking back at us somewhat impatiently. I ordered the house hamburger special with fries, and Smith ordered a grilled cheese sandwich with fries.

After she left, Smith turned around to see that no one was within earshot and said, "Jones and I work for a government agency that is associated with the military. He is no longer my partner—he's been transferred. We use the Selective Service system to find and select candidates to help us. That's how we got your name."

"OK, just which government agency are you with, and what do you want with me?" I asked suspiciously.

"I'm sorry, I can't give you any more information than that right now. If you accept our offer to help us, then I can go into more specifics and details."

I looked at Smith. I had no idea how to reply or what question to ask, so I simply said, "Tell me more," and took another big swig of my beer.

"Like I said, our agency scans Selective Service records to see if individuals come through the process with special skills or background that may be of help to the government. Your record was flagged because of your nationality and ability to speak German and English fluently."

"Thank you," I said.

"You do still know the language, I hope," he said, almost as an afterthought, as the waitress put the sandwiches in front of us.

"You asked me that the first time you came to my apartment," I responded. I stuffed my mouth full of hamburger.

Recognizing he would not get much cooperation out of me, Smith asked, "How long has it been since you were back home in Austria?" He took a big bite out of his grilled cheese sandwich, demonstrating that two could play this game.

Startled, I swallowed and said, "You know everything about me! You'd know if I had a passport or if I had left the country."

"Yes, I do," Smith said, a slight grin crossing his face and not at all reticent about admitting it. "But I wanted to hear it from you. It is my understanding you still have family there, and an Austrian passport. Am I correct?" Seeing the frustration grow on my face, he put down his sandwich and wiped his mouth on the paper napkin. "Let me get to the point."

I gave Smith a look that was a mixture of exasperation and incredulity.

"OK," he said. "The government is willing to pay for you to take a trip back home, and while there, we ask you to help us out. In exchange, we make your high draft number go away, and if you are successful in helping us, we will make sure you have a job when you get back. We can't pay you except to arrange your travel. Once there, you will be on your own. The government will not employ you. Lastly, no one—and I mean *no one,* not even your fiancée—must know of this arrangement. Is that clear?"

I put my hamburger down, not knowing how to respond. After what seemed like a long time, I blurted out, louder than I had intended, "Are you kidding me?" Smith immediately looked around the room, but the other students were busy in conversation and the man at the bar was taking a long sip from his beer. The bartender was nowhere to be seen, so one had noticed my outburst. Quickly, I drew back and whispered across the table, "Are you for real?" anger entering my voice.

"The US government does not waste its time on wild goose chases," he said sharply. "I understand this may be unexpected, but I want you to take my proposal seriously. I will call you in two days, and you can tell me your decision. If you agree, then we can make further arrangements to get together and go over the details. By the way, how are the wedding plans coming? Judy is a beautiful woman; bright and pretty."

His reference to my fiancée just made me angrier; I wanted to ask him more questions. Still, it was clear that Smith had cut off the conversation and I might as well not try to take it any further.

Smith took one more large bite from his sandwich, wiped his mouth, got up, and put a twenty-dollar bill on the table, saying, "That should cover everything!" He walked toward the door, and the man from the bar met him there. I watched the two walk out together, still stupefied by what had just happened. This had all been a setup. Smith had planned all this out. . . . I was angry!

I grabbed my coat off the chair next to me and sidled up to the barstool abandoned by Smith's friend. His beer had hardly been touched. I called out to the bartender through the service window into the kitchen, showed her the twenty-dollar bill, and placed it on the bar.

"OK, thanks! Have a great day!" was all I heard in response.

Outside, I started my car and pulled out onto the road, which was now covered with a light layer of snow. My mind swirled with what just transpired. Never in my wildest imagination had I expected to be asked to help the government. Staying far from the notice of any government agency had been more in keeping with my plans. Half of me wanted to focus on what just occurred; the other half was full of excitement about going back home for the first time to see my family.

I thought about walking again on the soil of a place I loved so much and being with the childhood friends who had meant everything to me. Could it really be? My parents had been back, but as much as I had wanted to, I could not go with them. They could barely afford their own trip, and I had to stay to earn money for my education. This offer, if real, would be my opportunity to make it back "home" again.

As I drove back to my apartment, excitement began to overcome my fear of what I might be getting myself into. My education so far had been financed by student loans, money I'd saved by working full time for two years after high school, and now working at the college. I had no money for a vacation to Europe. In fact, I spent many weekends at home to have my mother's great meals and take leftovers back to school. I never left home without a supply of food that would last me most of the next week or more. Many a week went by with no more than two dollars to last the entire week until the university's paycheck came in, and the home-cooked supply came in handy. Thus, the possibility of a paid trip to Austria was overwhelmingly tempting.

Still, my thrill was overshadowed by the reality of what had been proposed and what might be expected. *Why me? What do they want? What are these "certain things to help us" that Smith wants from me?* As I pulled into the parking lot of my apartment, Smith's warning, "No one—and I mean *no one,* not even your fiancée—must know of this arrangement," rang in my ears and produced sudden pangs of guilt. The thought of hiding something from my fiancée and my parents was inconceivable. However, Smith was adamant. *How will I handle that?* I thought. *Judy will know when I leave; what if she wants to go along? Can I tell my parents? Surely they will ask how I got the money for the trip. They will be excited and want to alert family and friends about my pending arrival. How do I lie to them?*

Turning off the engine, I sat in the parking lot, deep in thought. Then a sudden gust of cold wind shook the car, pulling me back to reality and waking me from my deep thoughts.

Two days later, I received the promised call from Smith. "Have you decided?" he asked. I said that I still had some concerns and many questions but was willing to listen further.

"If you had no concerns or questions, I'd be worried" was his reply. He said that he was putting a confidentiality agreement in the mail that needed a signature before we proceeded any further and hung up. When the agreement arrived, with a Selective Service return address, I carefully read both pages. I had expected a long document in government legalese, but to my surprise it simply said that I would never disclose to anyone any information or facts that I might learn or be exposed to while assisting the "US Government." Not who, when, or where, just the "US Government."

Heaving a big sigh, I got my pen out and signed. I folded the document, stuck it into the prepaid envelope, and carried it downstairs to the mailbox, where it would be picked up by the mail carrier the next day.

Training for What?

A couple of weeks later, my education started at the Federal Building downtown. There, I was given many intelligence, personality, and stress tests to see how I would react to certain conditions. These tests were followed by intensive interviews under the direction of Smith. Amazingly, I passed all the tests. Smith seemed to be impressed with my ability to handle stressful situations and to prioritize, not letting emotions distract me. I told him about the stress of working evenings at the liquor store. Along the way, Smith gave me more hints about the "certain things" expected of me in return for the vacation. I spent some weekends at a former military base turned into a National Guard base, which now was in the process of being converted into an industrial park. There, I was trained on using a weapon, self-defense, surveillance, and being vigilant of my surroundings. When the weapons instructor handed me a weapon, my skepticism must have been obvious. He said, "Don't worry, it's just part of the training routine; you'll probably never have to use it!" *Probably just enough training to be dangerous to only myself,* I thought.

Based on the testing and training, it was obvious that this "vacation" included some risk. Each time I ask Smith for more details, he responded, "You'll find out soon enough." I realized that backing out was not an option.

One day, sitting in my apartment, I wondered what I had gotten myself into. It had been a few months since I started meeting with Smith on and off. How did I end up in this? Would it have been better to say no to Smith and walk away? I was too far into it now to say no or back out.

Sure, I felt excited about what I was doing, knowing that I had skills and knowledge that others did not have. On the other hand, I worried about never being able to talk about it.

I dreaded telling lies to Judy and my parents. I'd already lied to Judy about why I was gone on some weekends. Moreover, while Smith had trained and tested my ability to conceal information when needed, lying to my parents was another matter. It bothered me a lot! As a family, we had gone through a lot so far. They had always been there for me, caring and protecting me. Keeping such a big secret from them did not feel good.

Smith and other interviewers kept asking me about the Soviet Union, the Cold War, and what I thought about people's oppression in Eastern Europe. "Do you think the Soviet Union is a threat to the West?" was one of Smith's favorite openers in the questioning process. Growing up with British and Russian troops in my hometown, I had little love for the Soviet Union or its regime. Although I had been young, I distinctly remembered May 5, 1955, when Austria had kicked out the Soviet occupiers. There was cheering and stone-throwing as the troops pulled out. Then came the Hungarian Revolt in October 1956, when Soviet troops and tanks rolled into Budapest, the Hungarian capital, and Russian troops came within miles of Austria's border. Those events fortified my negative feelings about the communist regime.

In keeping with his promise, Smith arranged for me to interview for an internship position that would lead to a permanent job after I got back. The firm was a small five-man partnership that provided retirement insurance for small to medium-size firms throughout the state. With the college instructors' approval, the internship gave the firm a chance to see how I would work out. My employers wanted me to develop a preretirement training program that could be marketed to existing clients. Once back from my "vacation," I would have a full-time job. I knew that this was my opportunity to move into a promising career, allowing Judy and me to get married in the fall, while many of my peers would still be busy writing resumes and looking for jobs. I graduated in April and began my new job.

Shortly before graduation, Smith's staff made arrangements for my trip to Europe. I told my parents and Judy that I had received a starting bonus from the new job, part of which I planned to use to take this trip. Overjoyed to hear that I could see my homeland again, Mutti and Papa did not question it any further. Although our wedding was planned for September, Judy understood that I wanted to see family and friends again. She agreed that with me starting a new job and us getting married, it was very unlikely that I would have another such opportunity. I was grateful for her understanding. Sadly, of course, I could not let on how the vacation was really financed.

My training with Smith had been scaled back. At one of our meetings downtown, Smith showed me newspaper clippings about new and secret military equipment being stolen from German military bases, presumably to end up behind the Iron Curtain. It was embarrassing to the US military, but it also gave the Soviet Union access to some of America's newest weapons technology.

About a month before leaving, at another training session. Smith walked in and asked, "You ever read *Playboy*?"

My simple reply was, "Doesn't everyone?"

"No, I mean it; how much do you know about *Playboy* magazine and what it is all about?"

I explained that yes, I actually read the articles monthly. I knew that it was published in Chicago and that Hugh Hefner, its publisher, had a late-night show, *Playboy's Penthouse,* on a Chicago TV station. During my teenage summers, when my hormones were beginning to kick into full gear and it was too hot to sleep, I snuck into the living room while my parents were in bed, turned the sound down on the TV, and watched the show late into the night. Seeing the scantily dressed Bunnies and celebrities was thrilling. Before Smith had a chance to explain more, a good-looking woman, who I judged to be about fifteen years older than me, walked into the room and introduced herself as Sally.

"He's all yours," said Smith as he left the room.

Sally walked over to a movie projector that had been set up in the corner of the meeting room and said, "I'm here to teach you a few things you will need to know." I had been through all kinds of training in the last few months, so I didn't give this moment much thought. Sally hit the switch on the projector, and a movie of a nude woman appeared on the screen. Her hands began to rove over her entire body, finally ending in her pubic area, where she proceeded to pleasure herself. I was dumbfounded and embarrassed. I could not keep my  eyes off the screen yet felt guilty for being a voyeur in front of this woman. A second scene showed in detail a man making love to a woman.

Once the film stopped, she asked, sounding totally nonplussed, "Have you ever heard of a honey trap?"

"No," I responded honestly, still staggered by what I had just witnessed on the screen.

"A honey trap is where someone, usually a male, is enticed by a woman to do something in return for sex or passion. One of the parties usually feels that they have a relationship with the other party based on their sexual encounters. We believe that you may need to use this device in your assignment."

I had been told on occasions that I was good looking and women were attracted to me. Yet I had never taken such comments seriously. Sally went on to describe, in graphic detail, how women achieve sexual pleasure and what a man could do to seduce a woman. The next two hours were a blur for me, not just because of the sexual content but also because it was the first time I had heard the word *assignment* associated with my trip.

I walked out of the building afterward, still in a daze, seeing erotica displayed on the back of my mind. A cold wind blew through my hair and jacket. *Who was she?* my mind kept playing over and over.

Her delivery had been clinical and matter of fact. She had a slender body and long, dark brown hair that fell lazily to her shoulders. Her deep brown eyes projected an attitude of practical experience in the subject matter. I stood at the crosswalk, waiting for the light to change, so I could retrieve my car from the parking ramp. As the light turned, other people stepped into the crosswalk while I stood there in a trance, still transfixed with visions of "Sally," whoever she really was.

"Damn," I said to myself aloud, anger in my voice. Sally never even asked me what kind of sexual experiences I'd had; she just assumed I needed to learn. Suddenly, I felt offended that she had not been curious or courteous enough to ask. The anger woke me up, and I crossed with the next light.

I got into my car, started the engine, and pulled out of the parking ramp, no longer in reverie but pissed at the assumptions that had just been made about my manhood. On the way back to my apartment, I figured out another piece of the puzzle. Whatever it was that they wanted me to do, it involved a woman. What other reason would I have received today's lesson? Surely it was not to help me in my upcoming nuptials to Judy! Right!

Touchdown

My heart beat fast as the plane touched down at the Frankfurt airport, midmorning, under a gray and cloudy sky. I couldn't believe that I would be stepping off the plane, onto home soil, in a few minutes. Even though I was not yet in Graz, my true hometown, this was close enough. They spoke

German here, and it was the country of my mother's birth. Emotionally, I was home.

The plane taxied to the terminal and came to a stop about thirty yards from the terminal doors. I watched through the window as the crew rolled a large set of stairs up to the front of the plane. I was anxious to get out and get some fresh air. It had been a long overnight flight from New York. Although I and most other passengers had slept for the duration, the nervous ones had kept their cigarettes going most of the night, and the superstitious ones lit up just before landing. The cabin and my clothes reeked of cigarette smoke. Foul air aside, the rest of the flight had been enjoyable. Lufthansa, the German airline, provided excellent service: free wine, excellent fresh food, white linen napkins, and beautifully engraved steel cutlery with every meal that passengers could take as a souvenir, promoting the airline. I kept a dessert spoon.

I knew that someone was waiting for me, although not who. I went through customs, showing my Austrian passport. When asked by the customs official about the nature of my visit, I said, "Coming home to visit family." That put a smile on his face, and he waved me through. I followed the crowd of fellow passengers down the hall, noticing the open windows on each side where people leaned out, gazing at the arriving and departing planes. Some even called out to passengers as they walked up to the steps of the plane. At the end of the corridor was a large hall filled with people, some seeking out deplaning passengers, others rushing to gates, and many just milling about. Light from huge windows at the roofline lit the hall. The tumult was mixed with the aroma of fresh coffee, baked goods, and other delicious smells emanating from restaurants nearby.

"Manfred," I heard a male voice call out above the din of the crowd. Listening to find the source, I wondered, *Is someone calling me or someone else with that name?* After all, the name was not that uncommon here. I looked over my left shoulder and saw "Jones" striding toward me, the same man who had sat in my apartment with Smith during our first encounter. Jones came up to me and gave me a gregarious handshake.

"Glad to see you. How was your flight?"

"Good, good," I stammered, surprised to see him again—a fact that did not escape Jones's notice.

"Here, let me help you with that," he said, grabbing my suitcase; then he turned and walked away. Looking over his right shoulder, he said, "I have a car waiting outside. We should be out of here in a minute, then we can talk."

At the curb, a black Mercedes sedan idled. A tall, muscular man with a military bearing, clothed in a gray suit, stood next to it, clearly waiting for us to appear. I was impressed momentarily by this VIP treatment, but then I looked around and realized most of the taxis were the same model and color. The man moved to the back of the car and opened the trunk as soon as he saw Jones. He easily hefted my suitcase and carry-on into the trunk. Jones opened the car's back door and beckoned me to get in while himself opening the front door and sliding into the passenger seat. I wasn't really ready to get into the car. I wanted to stay there, look around, and breathe in some of the local air. Just a few minutes ago I had just stepped out of one sardine can. I was not sure if I wanted to be cooped up again, no matter how luxurious the surroundings. Jones closed my door. The other man got into the driver's seat and, without any delay, pulled out into the terminal traffic.

"I take it you did not expect to see me here, based on that shocked look on your face back there," said Jones. "I'm stationed in Germany, and when we first met, I was back home for only a short time to set this whole thing up. I will be the person you will work with while here. Right now we are heading to your hotel. I'll give you a few hours to rest up, and then we can talk and fill you in further on what your vacation is all about. How does that sound?"

"Sure, no problem!" I said. I was still dazed, distracted by the plush leather seats and the smooth ride, watching the city zipping by, not really focused on what Jones was telling me. "I'm not feeling too tired, but it may help if I get some food in me and rest up for a bit. Maybe then I'll be able to pay attention to you." I'm sure I sounded more distracted than I had intended.

My hotel was located in an older section of the town filled with shops and restaurants. Jones looked at me and said, "You look exhausted. Why don't I catch up with you early tomorrow morning? This is Tom." He pointed to the driver, who smiled back at me through the rearview mirror. "He will pick you up at eight tomorrow morning. The registration is in your name, and here is your identification." With that, Jones handed me an American passport. I flipped it open to see it made out in my name, picture, and even signature. It looked used, even though it had never touched my fingers until this minute. Before I could ask any questions, Jones said, "That should get you registered, and we'll talk further tomorrow morning. Stay out of trouble tonight!"

Jones opened the door for me while Tom got out, opened the trunk, and deposited my luggage on the sidewalk, never saying a word.

It was now slightly after noon, and pedestrians filled the sidewalks, so I hurriedly grabbed my bags and stepped into the hotel through a revolving door. The lobby's décor was nothing fancy, but it instantly made visitors realize they were in Germany: beer steins, floral designs, and hunting scenery covered the walls, with a massive wooden front desk that just looked old. Although it was busy on the sidewalk and street, the lobby was serene and quiet. I walked up to the desk, behind which stood a young man with rimless round glasses and blond hair combed over from left to right.

"Good day, Mein Herr," he said in German-accented English, "May I help you? Do you have a reservation?" Did I really look that touristy or American? How did he know to address me in English?

"Yes," I answered, stammering a bit. "A reservation was made for me." I gave the clerk my last name.

"Ah, yes, it is right here," the young man said after looking through a box of index cards. "How was your flight from America?" he inquired, businesslike.

"Fine," I said. All of this was becoming even more unreal while it was happening.

"May I see your passport please?"

I reached for my jacket pocket to get my Austrian passport. Then I realized that along with my carry-on bag, I was still holding the American passport Jones had given me in my right hand, so I handed that one over. The man took a cursory glance at it, compared the picture to the man standing in front of him, and then wrote down the passport number. Lesson number one: this dual identity vacation would not be simple.

"Is this your first trip to Germany?"

Although I was tired, my training kicked in and I answered, "Yes, I'm here on vacation." I added, "I did not realize how tiring the flights are. I can't wait to get into my room to get some sleep," hoping to break off the conversation and get away from more prying questions.

"Understandable, sir." With that, the desk clerk handed me a card to sign then exchanged it for an old-fashioned key with an attached round wood piece with the number nine on it.

Pointing to the number, the clerk said, "That will be your room. It is upstairs, at the end of the hallway, the very last room, nice and quiet."

"Danke schön," I responded in my absolute best German.

"Ja, danke," the desk clerk answered with a pleased smile.

I walked up the single flight of stairs, which was covered in thick, old carpet in a regal red tone that spread into the hallway, worn looking but exceptionally clean. At either end of the hallway were highly polished wooden benches beneath windows overlooking the street below. The hall smelled old but not musty—a pleasant antique smell. I walked past five other doors on the way to my room, inserted the key into the lock, and with a twist, unlocked the door before pushing it open with my right shoulder. Light beamed into the room through one very large window, which had been cracked open a bit to let fresh air in. I wondered if this building had survived the bombings in the war or been renovated. Both, I suspected— the structure having survived the bombings and been refurbished.

To my left was a large bed with tall bedposts at all four corners but no canopy. On top of the bed lay a down-filled duvet and four large down-filled pillows that looked inviting. A small bathroom across the room, opposite the bed, was all white tiles, with an old claw-footed metal bathtub with a shower on a large wand above the handles. A basic black telephone sat on the nightstand next to the bed; it had no numbers on it, so I assumed I would have to ask the clerk to dial a number for me.

A bit inconvenient, I thought. I put my bags down on what appeared to be an upholstered trunk in front of the window and opened the large armoire, thinking I would unpack. Then I decided instead to clean up after the long flight, hoping to get rid of the smell of smoke and not to transfer it to the bed. When I came out of the bathroom, wearing only my T-shirt and shorts, the duvet beckoned me like a moth to the light. I laid down on the bed, and my head sank into the down pillows, making me wonder if this is what it might be like to sleep on a cloud.

A loud, ringing noise startled me awake. My eyes tried to orient themselves to the dimmed room where dying slivers of light peeked around the corners of the curtains. With a jump, I sat up on the side of the bed and picked up the phone.

"Hello," I said in groggy English.

"It sounds like I woke you up," said Jones on the other end of the line.

"Oh shit, what time is it?"

"It's about six p.m."

"Damn, I just laid on the bed for a minute. Hell, I didn't even unpack my bags yet!"

Laughing, Jones said, "Let it go, it's no big deal. Take it easy tonight. I just wanted to remind you that Tom will pick you up at eight tomorrow morning; by then, your body should be adjusted. Have a good night."

"You sure?" I felt guilty about having screwed up already.

"Yeah, no problem. I've gone back and forth to the States often enough to know how jet lag can hit you."

I hung up the phone, sat there, trying to clear my head, and then headed to the bathroom to wash my face with cold water. Slightly less groggy, I walked back into the bedroom to unpack my suitcase, wondering how I could have been so exhausted. I unpacked, wondering if it were necessary since Jones had not told me how long I would be here, and decided to get some food. My last meal had been breakfast on the plane. I pulled back the curtains and saw that the hotel was located on a small square surrounded by old buildings. Each building's façade was white or a muted color with long brown or black beams of wood crisscrossing each. Green or black shutters flanked windows, and peaked gables of red clay tile accented the matching roof. The scene was like a picture postcard of the Old World—although I doubted its authenticity because much of Frankfurt was bombed heavily during the war. Many cities had rebuilt their towns in the old style, and I suspected that was the case here. Either way, it was comforting to see such a familiar sight. With a smile, I dressed.

Relaxed but now very hungry, I stepped out of the hotel. The young man was still behind the reception counter, looking down and busily shuffling through some papers. A few guests sat in the lobby's spacious chairs, talking or reading newspapers. The sun had broken through the clouds, and the sky was a beautiful combination of blue, orange, and red, with puffy clouds hiding the setting sun. It was still bright enough that the streetlights were not illuminated, yet the shadows were long in the narrow streets. The sidewalks were again busy, not with the rush of workers going to and from their offices, but with a mix of people out for an evening stroll or looking for a place to eat, just like me. Looking up and down the street, I saw young people, elderly couples, and families; some people had long hair, most were casually dressed, and a few families were outfitted in traditional clothes. Some men wore suits and ties, while women wore summer dresses. In my jeans and a nice short-sleeved shirt, I was not as well dressed as the older men, yet not as outlandish as a few of the hippies around me.

"Fit in with the crowd," is what Smith had taught me. I wandered for a few blocks, taking in the atmosphere and feeling very at home, yet strangely also like a voyeur, looking in on a scene where I really did not belong. My plan had been to walk some distance, check out various places to eat, and then settle on one in which to enjoy German *Gemütlichkeit*, relax, and linger over a few beers and some good food. Led by my nose and stomach, however, my legs abandoned my well-laid plan. After walking past three Bavarian-looking restaurants from which the aroma of good food and fresh beer wafted out the door, I lost my willpower and walked into the next restaurant I came to.

The restaurant was busy but not crowded. I found a table away from other patrons, hearing in my head Smith's reminder to always stay vigilant of my surroundings. Right now, I didn't care! I was so damn happy to be back in this atmosphere that I wanted to drink in all of the sights and sounds from every vantage possible. The tables were made of sturdy wood, with the tops almost two inches thick covered with a healthy layer of lacquer. The four chairs surrounding each table were equally sturdy, not easily moved by a child. The restaurant had at least three rooms that I could see.

I was seated in a room with beige walls with wood shelving running near the ceiling around the perimeter of the room. The shelves were loaded with beer steins in a variety of Bavarian styles. Hunting scenes showing woods and valleys adorned the walls, giving the impression that you were sitting on a patio. It was "gemütlich"—relaxing—no doubt about it! Large wrought-iron chandeliers with electric candles provided a subdued glow through the room. Patrons were a mix of families and adult diners clearly enjoying themselves on an evening out. The chatter of people was loud, yet not overwhelming. Every now and then, I'd pick up a German phrase or word followed by hearty laughter or the clicking of beer mugs.

A decidedly German-looking server, blond and big boned, approached with a welcoming smile on her face. She wore a dark skirt and a white blouse that barely contained her ample bosom, and a sleeveless black vest hung loosely on her shoulders. I froze, not because of the server's looks, but because I did not know who I was supposed to be, an American tourist or a tourist from my own country. Should I respond in German or in English? *This dual-persona thing is going to be tricky to pull off*, I thought. The server most likely understood English. Was my German really still good enough? New doubts about my language skills suddenly hit me.

"Guten Abend, mein Herr," she said, smiling and placing a menu card on the table.

"Guten Abend. Wie geht's?" I replied, thinking it was no use giving away that I was American while watching her reaction to my German. Although most Americans consider German to be a single language, in fact, there are great regional differences in dialect. The range can be as different as the dialect of a southerner versus a New Englander in the United States, or the variety of accents in the United Kingdom. I wanted to read the waitress's reaction to see if, by chance, she would identify me based on my pronunciation.

"Can I bring you a beer or something else?" she asked with a hint of a Bavarian accent. This being Frankfurt, the regional dialect was closer to *Hochdeutsch*, or high German, than Bavarian, which seemed to be her native dialect. The further north in Germany one traveled, the more formal the dialect became, the German equivalent of Oxford English.

"Yes, a large pilsner please," I replied in Hochdeutsch, rather than the Austrian accent I grew up with, which was the German equivalent of a Texan drawl.

"Ja, mein Herr," she responded, and she turned and walked away, not showing any further interest in me.

I was still trying to figure out the language dilemma when she returned with a large stein of beer. Sizing up the glassware, it dawned on me that the beers here were larger than those served back home in the college bars; I'd have to specify the size the next time. I asked for a few minutes to enjoy the beer before ordering, to which she replied, "Natürlich! (Of course!)" and departed.

I took a long sip of the cool, refreshing beer, savoring the taste, and picked up the menu because my stomach was sending a clear message: feed me! I considered the four pages of delicacies—what should I choose? I knew that my mother, a professionally trained cook with a reputation among family and friends for turning out amazing traditional dishes, would enjoy sampling the items on this menu. It was a hard decision, especially since I always tend to default to one of my favorites, sausage. Here, I had a choice of more than a dozen different sausage combinations. Or should it be sauerbraten, a delicious portion of beef marinated for at least a day in a vinegar-and-onion mixture, then cooked to perfection and served sliced with a side of red cabbage infused with apples and clove and a soft-ball-sized bread dumpling. My mouth began to water just at the thought of it, and my nose detected its aroma floating around the room as others feasted on that delicacy.

I enjoyed a few more sips of beer to wash down the fresh-baked bread and cold sweet-cream butter that the server had brought the table. I gazed around the room, no longer awestruck by the surroundings but unexpectedly realizing what I was doing. All that training I with Smith and others suddenly came into focus as I began to scan the room. Had I really been that conditioned? A moment of fright shot through me, pausing with my stein in midair at the revelation that I was now seeing the other dinners in a different light. Had I become jaded? It couldn't be this easy to condition someone to immediate suspicion, could it? Smith had complimented me after only a month of training on how quickly I was catching on. My relaxed vacation state disappeared as I again looked around the restaurant. Were any of Jones's men following me, like the old man in the bar with Smith? At that moment, I understood that my view of the world would never be the same again.

As my mind wrestled with the moment's paranoia, a band started playing German drinking songs at the other end of the room. Taking a big swig of beer, I talked myself down, relaxed, and enjoyed the music and the surroundings.

I settled on sauerbraten with spätzle, which I thought were what my mother would have ordered. It wasn't long before the waitress placed a large oval platter with several layers of sliced brown marinated beef in front of me. Each slice was about a quarter-inch thick and covered with a beautiful brown gravy, dense yet translucent. At one end of the oval plate sat a mound of yellow spätzle topped by some of the same brown gravy. The firmness and the color indicated that these small dumplings had been made fresh recently, and on their own they would make a delicious meal. My nose gathered the marinated beef's fragrance, mixed with the wafts of fresh beef gravy, as it should be. As side dishes she brought a small bowl of red cabbage and a refill of the bread basket and butter. I used the side of my fork to cut into a slice of meat; it split in half. No knife is needed if the entrée is prepared correctly. Turning the fork over, as is the custom in Europe, I speared the cut piece of meat, scooped up some gravy, and used my knife to push some spätzle onto the meat and took it into my mouth.

My mother's version was good, but this was great. I alternated the meat with dumplings and the red cabbage, which also was fantastic. A second beer, also tall, helped to wash the meal down.

When the server came to clear away the empty plate, without a trace of gravy left, thanks to the fresh bread, she asked if I wanted dessert. Having seen a tray of scrumptious-looking pastry being carried about, I was tempted but said no, wanting to continue to savor the wonderful combination of flavors of the sauerbraten. Between the meal, beers, and travel, my body was ready to head back to my down-filled bed by the time the check came. On the way out, I stopped at the front to look at the post-card rack. I found a postcard that featured the restaurant along with a col-lage of menu items, including the sauerbraten. I decided to buy one and mail it the next morning to let Mutti know I had arrived safely and was having a good time. Politely, I put on the back, "Good, but not as good as yours!" I knew that would help to allay some fears she might have had about my trip.

The "Assignment"

At 7:45 the next morning I was in the lobby, waiting for Tom to arrive. A different man, with stiff bearing, walked in a few minutes later, approached me without any hesitation, and said, "Tom was unable to be here this morning; Mr. Jones is waiting for you. Please come with me." He turned and walked toward the door. Seeing through the window the same car that had brought me the night before, I followed him.

We got into the sedan and, without further conversation, pulled out into traffic. Half an hour later we pulled into a parking garage below an office building. Walking ahead of me, the driver showed me to an elevator, got in, and pushed the button. We got out on the fourth floor and walked through several doors before reaching one that he opened after punching in a code on a pad on the wall. Hearing the buzzer from the open door, Jones popped out of an office and welcomed me with a big smile and his hand out. As we walked down the hall, Jones turned and asked, "Before we get in there, let me ask you one more time, are you still willing to help us with this?"

"Yes," said I, without any equivocation in my voice. I had made up my mind that I was in this for the long haul, whatever the outcome.

"OK, then, let's get started," said Jones as we entered a meeting room with a screen at one end and half a dozen chairs arranged around a large table.

The moment we sat down, a door opened and a man came in, carrying several files, and seated himself across the table.

"This is Mike," Jones said. "He and I will be working with you while you are on this mission." That was the first time I heard the word *mission*, which neither Smith nor any other trainer had uttered previously. My heart raced as I thought, *Did I really sign up for a "mission"?* I thought back to the TV show *Mission Impossible. No*, I told myself, *this is only a vacation and a chance to help the government—none of that spy shit for me—Manfred, don't get carried away!*

"I know we have been vague with you about what we are asking you to do and whom we represent, but you are not stupid, and by now you've probably figured it out," said Jones. "We are *not*," he emphasized, "part of the CIA or some other government spy agency. We work with military investigations."

OK, I thought, *but that still does not explain the self-defense and weapons training I had received, and what is military intelligence anyway?* I thought of military intelligence as being the people in the field who help spot the enemy. Beyond that, I had no clue about their purpose.

Mike explained, "Over the last couple of years, state-of-the-art weapons and information about new US weapons used in Europe have been stolen from our bases in Germany. We believe service members are being set up to steal secrets and weapons of all kinds. The drug problem in the US military based in Germany has become severe. With the war winding down in Vietnam, soldiers who still have time to serve have been moved to German bases. Many soldiers became addicted to drugs in Vietnam. They are now stealing from the military to support their drug habit. From what we have been able to learn, there appears to be a criminal gang operating from behind the Iron Curtain, selling information and weapons to the highest bidder worldwide, including the Soviets.

"From service members who confessed to participating in previous thefts, we learned that a young woman either seduced them or enticed them with money; in other words, set them up. Working out of Budapest, this woman has been very successful in recruiting GIs on trips to Germany. We know who she is, but we do not know when she will come back across the border again. We need your help to bring her back across the border so we can arrest her."

"Me?" I blurted out, astonished. "How am I supposed to do that?"

Both men smiled at my outburst. Jones said, "We do not know which base or weapons she plans to hit next, so we cannot trap her here. We want to turn the tables on her by having you lure her into the West, where we can arrest her."

My mind spun, and adrenaline coursed through my body. I poured Coke in a glass with ice. Drinking it gave me a moment to reflect on what I had just been told. I sat there for a minute, taking it all in, and finally responded in an earnest tone, "OK, so what do you want me to do?"

Jones spoke first. "We selected you because you can represent yourself legitimately as both a citizen of your native country and the United States at the same time. To complete the cover, we will give you an identity that will allow you to carry out what needs to be done. You will become a freelance writer and photographer for *Playboy*, looking for a story about good-looking women behind the Iron Curtain. This is how you will, we hope, meet up with her. From previous encounters, we know she is exceptionally good looking, in her late twenties, and fascinated with all things American—especially American pop culture. You and the cover we have built for you will be the honey to draw her out into our trap."

"And just how do you expect me to that?" I interrupted.

"We want you to entice her to come to Vienna with you for a photo shoot. It's a city she knows, so going there should not alarm her. You will explain to her that your trip to Budapest is simply a scouting mission. Any pictures you take must still be approved by higher-up editorial staff. You can tell her that the magazine wants to have professional facilities available for the final shoot. For that reason, you and she will need to be in Vienna.

"As you know, the Hungarian regime does not look favorably on such Western decadence like *Playboy*. We believe her ego and need for fame are big enough for her to take the bait. Moreover, since she has traveled outside of Hungary previously, she should not consider such a trip remarkable."

We met for the rest of the day. Jones and Mike gave me further instructions and information about her, where they thought I could meet up with her, how to make contact, and other details I would need to carry out the assignment. They also provided me with a leather camera bag and camera, instructing me to take pictures along the way, specifically while at home.

Mike said, "We want you to continue your vacation, go to your hometown, meet with family and friends, do everything to reestablish yourself in the community. Then you will go on a sightseeing trip to Vienna, where we will meet you again and brief you further."

Jones intoned, "By now, you should understand the risk involved. Over the last few months we have tried to train you to be safe, but you will be on your own once you cross the border. We will not support you or acknowledge any involvement with us. As far as the United States government knows, you are a student on vacation. You're on your own!" He looked me straight in the eye and asked, "For the last time, are you a go with this?"

"Let's do it," I said with firmness in my voice that surprised even me.

Tante Frieda and the Picture

The following morning, I sat at a café table in the Frankfurt train station; in front of me was a plate with a freshly baked roll, a large pat of sweet butter, a couple of slices of cured ham, and a small dish of apricot jam. Good cured ham is a favorite of mine, a delight I missed back in the States. I sat back, watching the scenery, and savored every morsel of breakfast. The aroma of freshly brewed coffee, sweetened and lightened with cream, wafted from my small cup. Even though I generally don't drink coffee, I knew I had to fit in as much as possible, so I took small sips. (I love coffee, its taste and smell, but not how it affects my body—making me jittery at first and then fatigued.) Past the delicious fragrance of the coffee and cured ham was the tang emanating from the newer diesel locomotives and the coal-fed odor of the steam locomotives.

The strong coal smell may have been unpleasant to some, but for me, it was nostalgic. My grandfather, after all, had been an engineer on one of the monster steam locomotives sitting a few tracks over from me. A picture of my grandfather and his locomotive still hung in my parents' home. I thought about the train trips through the Alps my parents had taken with me while I was young. I especially loved the tunnels. I would go into the corridor of the train and stick my head out the window, taking in the coal fumes that raced alongside, not realizing they were poisonous fumes. It felt like I was taking in all the power given off by the locomotive.

Looking down at my watch, I saw that my train was scheduled to pull into the station within fifteen minutes. I wanted to be at trackside to experience once more the feeling of the heat and steam given off by the locomotive as it slowly passed everyone on the platform. I left enough money to cover the bill and a tip under the coffee cup, picked up my suitcase, and headed to the tunnel leading up to the platform. Just as I reached the platform, a large engine came by, its huge wheels turning slowly. Steam released from the brakes blocked out the sound of metal-to-metal grinding as the wheels came to a stop. It was magical. It put me into another world and another time.

Once the inbound passengers had gotten off, the conductor sounded his whistle, loud enough to overcome the trains' noise, to alert those waiting on the platform that they could now board. The conductor wore an immaculate dark blue uniform with gold and red piping, a high cap, and a black visor. He greeted each passenger as he or she stepped up into the car, helping women board with a gracefully extended hand or arm. Once onboard, each of us walked down narrow hallways to our respective seat or cabin. Before long, the locomotive's steam whistle blew and the train began its slow movement out of the station, picking up speed as it cruised through the city and into the countryside.

Comfortably seated in my cabin, I felt joy fill every part of my being. Rushing by the window were lush green valleys, the roadways carved out of the sides of the mountain, a raging river, or a tunnel. My heart raced, knowing that I would soon be home and see friends and family I had missed greatly.

Dusk was settling in the countryside when the train began to slow and I heard the familiar release of steam. The train slowed as it entered the station on the first stop on my "vacation." Although there had been many lovely towns, small and large, along the way, this stop was important for me, and an end of the line.

Grabbing my suitcase, I moved to the door with four other people and waited for the train to come to a full stop. I could see that the train station was poorly lit and small, with only one building. Stepping off the train, I saw my aunt standing off to one side, beneath a lamppost. She wore a long coat and a scarf tied around her head to protect her from the fine cool mist that usually came off the mountains in the evening, even though the calendar said it was summer.

"Manfred?" she cautiously asked as I approached her.

"Yes, it's me. Guten Abend, Tante Frieda," I replied in German, using the German name for aunt. She rushed to me and gave me a big hug, one much stronger than I anticipated from a woman in her late seventies.

"How much you have grown," she gushed with joy in her voice, "You look handsome; you're a grown man." Had it been light enough, she would have seen me blush.

The last time we saw each other was also on a train platform, but one much larger, when my parents and I were leaving for America. I could still picture my aunt, her husband, my grandmother, and the other friends who had come to see us off.

As Aunt Frieda and I walked down the sidewalk toward town, I admired the solitude and peacefulness surrounding us. Scattered lights could be seen behind shutters or through windows of homes along the way. The air was fresh and clean, and no sound disturbed the tranquility of the moment other than our steps on the pavement. After walking for a few minutes through darkened streets, we arrived at her home. She lived on the second floor of a home she owned while renting out the lower level. At her age, it might have been better for her to live on the first level; nonetheless, she had always lived upstairs and saw no reason to change.

She had prepared a traditional spread of cheeses, cold cuts, slices of bread, and vegetables, assuming I had not eaten dinner on the train. After she showed me where I would sleep and gave me a chance to clean up, we sat down to enjoy the meal. I drank a hearty local beer with it, while my aunt had a cup of coffee, having eaten her dinner earlier in the evening. She looked much older than I remembered, frail, and her face lined with old age. Speaking now in my native dialect, it didn't take long for me to feel at home. Politely I answered all questions she threw at me about my family while enjoying the bounty in front of me. I loved being in her company again.

It felt like old times. After a second beer, I saw that she was getting tired and excused myself, claiming to be tired from the long train ride myself. I retreated to my small room, but I was anything but tired. The excitement of actually being here, something I honestly had not expected to experience ever again, made me feel very much alive. I unpacked my clothes and lay back on the bed, taking in the moment while wondering what lay ahead for me in the next couple of weeks.

When I got up in the morning, my aunt had coffee and rolls ready, which she had picked up fresh from the baker down the street. It felt familiar sitting in this cozy room, with a plate of butter and jams, and the wonderful aroma of fresh hard rolls in front of me. I was home again. It reminded me of summer weeks I had spent with her when I was young.

Considering her age and frail health, I knew this might be the last time I could have a conversation with her about her life. I had previously been too young to care; now, I knew better than not to take the opportunity. I had heard scattered pieces from my parents about the interesting life she had as a nanny to one of Austria's former royal families. This was my occasion to find out more. Throughout the morning, she took great delight in sharing her life experiences with me.

She, in turn, had questions about America. How were my parents doing? What was my life like? She wanted to know all about my fiancée, Judy. Our breakfast conversation lasted for a long time.

She explained that at age thirteen, she was hired as a nanny for the Esterhazy family, an important part of the Austro-Hungarian royalty. She stayed with the family though her entire career, taking care of Countess

Aunt Frieda in 1914 before going to work for the Esterhazy family, part of Austrian royalty.

Agnes Esterhazy, who later became a well-known European actress and showed me an autographed picture. She told me about life with the royal family, how kind they were, and how much she enjoyed living with them, especially the Countess and other children she cared for. I found it strange that my grandparents had sent her off at such an early age, though she explained that such apprenticeships were not uncommon in those days. She joined the family within days of turning fourteen, the legal age of apprenticeship. I listened attentively, enjoying every second of her story.

After lunch and a nap, we walked to the local cemetery to place flowers on the grave of my uncle, who had died a year earlier. His father, Peter Rossegger, had been the Austrian equivalent of America's Mark Twain, having written a series of books about the Austrian people's lives.

After afternoon *Kaffee und Kuchen*, while I packed my bags, she asked me if I wanted anything to remember her by. I looked around an apartment containing old furniture, vases, and ceramic figurines from another age, and nothing interested me or seemed practical to bring home with me to America. Sensing my lack of interest, my aunt pointed to a picture hanging on the wall.

"Would you like to have that picture?" she asked. The blue, green, and red painting showed two people warmly embracing. It looked very modern and out of place among her things, not the kind of art you would expect from someone her age.

"Yes," I responded, hesitant, not knowing what else to choose but knowing I had to accept something.

"Let me tell you about that picture," she said in a low, almost wistful tone. She sat down on the sofa and proceeded to tell me about her trip to the 1937 Paris World Exposition, during her last days of working for the Esterhazy family. They considered the trip a reward for her long and dedicated service to the family. The theme of the exposition was "Art and Science," all in the impending shadow of Nazism in Germany. Hoping art would prevail over science and war, Pablo Picasso had created a large wall painting entitled *Guernica* for the exposition, remembering the German air force attack on the Basque town of that name. He wanted to show that war was not an answer. Artists, scientists, and architects were encouraged to submit their versions of a new, peaceful world.

As part of Countess Esterhazy's entourage, my aunt met Picasso and several of his fellow artists. One fell madly in love with her. I was amused to see my aunt blush, turning into a shy schoolgirl as she told the story of how this painter followed her home and for three years, on and off, tried to convince her to marry him. Eventually, she forced him to abandon his pursuit when she became engaged to my uncle. For years after that, the artist stayed in touch with her, writing letters and sending postcards. Finally, in grief—at least, that is what she believed—he painted the picture she wanted to now give me. He wanted her to have it as a remembrance of their relationship. I stared at the picture, recalling the family lore that my aunt was alleged to have had two children out of wedlock. Now, hearing this story, I wondered if there perhaps was some truth to that story, since she had no other children of her own. Gratefully, and somewhat awed, I accepted the picture, which now has a prominent place in our home (as well as the cover of this book).

Examining the picture closely, I could not make out the signature. Seeing my puzzlement, my aunt said, "Beking was the name of the painter; he was world famous, you know, and good friend of Picasso." Between the German pronunciation and the Austrian dialect, unfortunately, I could not figure out the artist's name. Nevertheless, since he was showing works at the World Exhibition and traveled in Picasso's circle of friends, he must have been prominent. I was speechless; this was much more of a story than I had ever anticipated. I accepted the picture, packed it in some newspaper, gathered my belongings, and departed for the train station. To this day, I still do not know who the artist was.

In front of the small stationhouse, while others moved past us to board the train, we said goodbye. "Auf Wiedersehen"—see you again—we said to each other, although both of us knew that it was highly likely that this was the last time we would hold each other close. Avoiding the sadness, I pulled away, picked up my suitcase, and moved toward the train, sending a last look, a smile, and a brief wave back to her.

I boarded the train, found my seat, and pulled down the window so she could see me. She stood there with the afternoon sun lighting up her face while slowly waving at me. I could not tell from a distance, but I was certain there were tears in her eyes, as in mine; we both understood that we would never lay eyes on each other again. I tightly clutched the bag containing the picture as if I were holding on to her. As the train pulled out of the station and my aunt disappeared in the distance, tears filled my eyes.

The train followed the main route that my grandfather had worked as a train engineer, and he joined my aunt in my thoughts as I stared out the window, letting the landscape drift by. My second-class car had comfortable padded seats facing each other over a table that could be folded up under the window. Across from me sat an older couple—retired farmers, I assumed, from the look of their weather-beaten hands. The trip would take about two hours and carried us through mountains, tunnels, and small towns, with one or two stops along the way. How strange to feel the excitement of being back home again alongside the sadness of likely saying goodbye forever. Worse, I had to see my loved ones while deceiving them about the real reason for the visit.

Staring out, I felt conflicted. I had to face what lay ahead. Was it the sadness of the reality, or the happiness of spending time with friends and family? I had to make up my mind if I were to concentrate on the task at hand. Feelings would only get in the way.

As the train came out of a tunnel and rounded a curve, my hometown appeared before me. The setting sun glowed on the red slate roofs of the old buildings of the central city and threw large shadows onto the backside of the Schlossberg, the iconic round "castle mountain" in the center of the city. It had been a fortress for centuries but now was a tourist and recreation destination. Its former dungeons had been turned into luxury boxes for an outdoor theater. I was surprised at how the city had been transformed in the thirteen years since I'd left. New buildings towered over the landscape, including signs of a growing suburb.

The train slowed as it entered the Graz Hauptbahnhof, the main train station, which held a dozen or more passenger trains and at least an equal number of freights. The powerful-looking black steam engines of old stood next to shiny, sleek diesel engines painted in Austria's red and white. In their midst were the boxy green electric locomotives. The country had plenty of electric energy, so many of the intracountry routes used electric trains. The station was a bustling place with crowds of people moving to and from trains. I got off, descended a set of stairs, walked a short distance through a tunnel walkway, and ascended another flight of stairs to catch the intercity electric commuter train.

Fifteen minutes later, I stepped off on the outskirts of the city. As the train pulled away, I stopped to take in a three-hundred-and-sixty-degree sweep of my surroundings.

Behind me, in the west, I saw the mountains on which my parents and I went hiking and picnicking on our Sunday outings. Looking up, I could make out roads and a few of the small inns and pubs where we had eaten. Taking a deep breath, I smelled the air coming off the mountains, fresh with a slight hint of pine from the lush green forests. Turning in the other direction, I saw how things had changed. The old, narrow, two-lane road with grassy shoulders that I had known growing up—the road leading to my home—was now a wide city street with sidewalks on both sides and a bike path.

When I left Austria in 1957, the country was just entering a new era of growth and economic prosperity. This evening, I could see the progress it had brought. Looking over my left shoulder, I saw the large white four-story apartment buildings where my cousins Werner, Ingrid, and Ernst and parents lived. Werner's dad was my father's only surviving brother; his other brother, Franz, had died in a tragic bus accident many years ago.

Feeling like a stranger, rather than someone returning home, I picked up my suitcase and started walking. Every now and then I stopped, put the suitcase down, and looked around, amazed at the changes that had taken place. I walked past the closed grocery store where my mother had worked and from which she used to sneak me sandwiches. Past the candy store where I'd spent my few hard-earned or found *Groschen*, pennies, on gum or sweets. Next came the butcher shop that was owned by the father of one of my friends. Visiting him was always an adventure; they slaughtered animals in a building behind the store to make delicious smoked meats and sausages, along with regular cuts of meat. His dad always got joy out of impressing me with a new kind of sausage he had just produced. Since my family could not afford meats routinely, I gladly accepted any offerings that came my way.

Brown fence surrounding our house.

My slow, reminiscence-laden walk ended twenty minutes later when I stood next to the weathered wooden fence surrounding the house where I had spent the first eleven years of my life. By now, the sun was sinking behind the mountains, leaving only a red glow to show me the way. I softly touched the weathered brown wood, running my fingers along the fence like a needle touching an LP that could bring back all my memories. I recalled the delicious gooseberries and red currants that had grown on the other side of the fence, from which my grandmother made fantastic jams. Or the times when my friends and I had peeing contests to see who could shoot higher. At last, I stepped up to the door, took a deep breath, and pushed the small black button to the right of the frame. Through the open window I heard the bell ringing inside the house.

"Hallo, who is there?" a weak yet assured-sounding voice called out in in a deep Austrian dialect.

"Oma, it's me, Manfred!"

"Manfred," the voice responded with great delight, "I'll be right there."

Soon, I heard the shuffling of feet on cement and the door being unlocked from the other side. My grandmother swung the door aside, and we fell into each other's arms in a long and tight embrace. Tears streaming down her face, she kept repeating, "I can't believe it, you are really here. I can't believe it!" Tears streamed down my face, too—tears of pure joy, unlike the last time we had seen each other. I gathered my bag and followed her inside. The smell of something good cooking on the stove hit me as I walked into the kitchen. It was so tiny. I had spent much of my youth in what had seemed to be a spacious room. It was small and crowded by standards I had become accustomed to in American kitchens. Sitting on the corner bench, playing games with my grandfather, I used to look such a long way across the room to see Oma bustling about. Now I felt closed in. It made me realize how much I had grown. Being in this room, though my eyes were seeing it as a man, I felt like a little boy again.

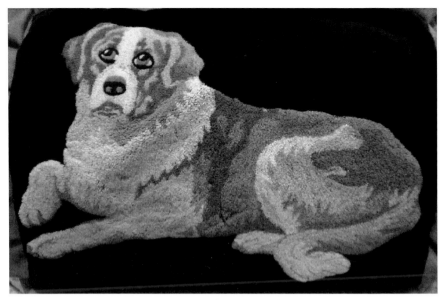

My pretend pet as a child.

She showed me into the adjoining room, her living room, where I would be sleeping on an old, ornate Ottoman sofa bed. It still had the two crochet pillows, made in 1921, of a Saint Bernard and the other of a cat. While young, I'd never had any pets; instead, I used to curl up with one or the other pillow and pretend the crocheted animals were my pet. Both heirlooms now holding a place of honor in our home. The room felt like a walk back into history. In the corner still stood the dark green *Kachelofen*, a ceramic glazed-tile stove that had not been used for years. On the right stood the heavy credenza made of dark brown burnished and polished wood, decorated with marquetry and glass panels on either side. The center section was backed by a mirror. Wine glasses, statues, and similar knick-knacks sat on various shelves. The Persian carpet under my feet was soft. It had been walked on by many feet, and on it my grandfather had taken his last breath. I plopped my suitcase down on the sofa, turned, and gave her another big hug as eleven years of my childhood here flooded through me. Typical of her, she admonished me not to get all sentimental because she had dinner on the stove, and it was going to burn if we didn't eat soon.

Dinner consisted of a white meat goulash, spätzle, and some mashed vegetables. I wasn't sure what I was eating and didn't ask. It was well known in the family that my grandmother had little regard for food safety, a point my mother had reminded me of before leaving on this trip. Having seen her rub green stuff off a roast before putting it in a frying pan, I had some fear about eating here. I refilled my wine glass several times in the hope of killing any bad bacteria hidden in the meal. We chatted late into the evening, both of us happy to be again in each other's company.

I spent the next week reacquainting myself with the community, visiting friends and family members, and sightseeing. I wanted to be sure that my knowledge of the city was current. Jones had advised me to take pictures of myself with family members and leave some film in the camera, in addition to carrying pictures with me.

Cousin Erika

I took one photo of my cousin Erika while we had lunch at the most recognizable historic landmark in town, a restaurant on top of the Schlossberg. Aware of the true nature of my trip, I made sure to enjoy every minute spent with friends and family. I had no clue what to expect in the next phase of this "vacation," so I absorbed every minute of fun and pleasure I could find, even going to a casino with my cousin Ingrid. She loved the pomp and glitz, especially while showing off her good-looking American cousin.

When family or friends asked why my fiancée had not accompanied me, I explained that I wanted to make up for lost time with family, and besides, with our marriage coming up, she could not take time off from work. Everyone understood that.

The Assignment Begins

After a week at my grandmother's, I packed a small suitcase she gave me. Its style added authenticity to my Austrian persona. I boarded one of the sleek red-and-white express trains—one of the first European efforts at a high-speed electric commuter train—and arrived in Vienna midmorning. I checked into the hotel Jones had arranged, dropped my bags in the room, and took a taxi to Jones's office. Plans had been for us to spend this day and the next on reviewing the mission. As we began the briefing, Jones first stressed that I would use my Austrian passport while traveling. As far as anyone was concerned, I was a young man from Graz, on vacation, wanting to follow my ancestors' trail and do some sightseeing. This would also be my response to border guards and customs agents who inquired into the nature of my trip. As evidence I could give my grandmother's address and offer friends and family as references. If necessary, I could support my case by showing pictures of myself with friends in various locations around Graz. Only a detailed inquiry would be able to prove otherwise. I hoped this slight ruse would keep me safe and out of a Hungarian prison.

Once in Budapest, though, I would, at the appropriate times, turn into a young freelance photographer from Chicago, working for *Playboy* magazine. Although I had always been a camera buff, I hoped the additional training I'd received from a portrait photographer would make me look legitimate. Jones instructed me to be sure to act "American," freely spending money at the appropriate cafés. To make the story real, Jones's staff had bought me a new set of clothing to match my photographer persona: hip jeans, classy and colorful shirts, and boots. It was a far cry from my own uptight college style.

The rest of the briefing was spent on how to get in touch with my target. They had watched her for some time and gave me detailed instructions on where she shopped and what she liked to do. I was to make myself visible to her and take it from there. On the last day in Vienna, I received instructions on how to get in touch with Jones in case of an emergency. He was to be my "cousin," whom I would call for help. Before leaving, Jones asked me to open the camera bag. He took it, removed the camera equipment, and squeezed the sides to lift out the bag's felt liner. He then inserted a small automatic pistol and two extra clips at the bottom of the bag.

"Use only if necessary—and you'll know when."

Stunned, I recognized it as the same type of gun I had used during training. The seriousness of what I was about to embark upon made my hair stand up on the back of my neck, and for a second, I wondered if it was not too late to pull out. I wanted to shout, "I didn't bargain for this!" That thought disappeared as quickly as it came into my head. As we finished the meeting, Jones reminded me that I was on my own once he walked out the door, and the US government had never heard of me!

Early the next morning I was on a train to Budapest, sitting in coach class with families and other tourists. I had deliberately selected a train that made stops at many small communities along the way. My weekend suitcase was in the overhead luggage net, but I kept the camera bag next to me on the seat. We traveled through Burgenland, the Austrian equivalent of the Midwest plains. There were no tall mountains, only hills that held some of the county's best wine-growing regions.

Train station near Hungarian border and possible ancestral home.

The train stopped at Bad Tatzmannsdorf, which I believe could have been my ancestral home. It is famous for its warm springs and health spas, enjoyed by many notable European artists, musicians, and even royalty. If asked, I would point to the town's name as one reason for my travels— searching for my family's background.

An hour or so into the trip, the train stopped at the Hungarian border. My heart pounded as guards with pistols at their sides and rifles slung across their backs came through to check everyone's passport. My car was loaded with families with noisy young children, causing the guards to rush through the carriage. When they reached me, I took the initiative by greeting them in my native language, hoping to establish my identity. They took the passport, looked at me and at my picture, and gave it back, and then moved on to the next person. To them, I was just another regular person on the train. As the train pulled away from the border post, I set my head against the window, hoping to cool my throbbing brain, relieved at having passed the first test and perhaps the riskiest part of the journey. Only then did I realize I had been hugging the camera case tightly under my right shoulder the whole time. *This is for real!* I thought.

In Budapest the train pulled into a large train station very much like the one in my hometown, crowded with old black locomotives, shiny new diesel locomotives, and some electric commuters. People came and went from trains, no one paying much attention to a hip-looking young man getting off the train. Once across the border, I had taken the opportunity to change in the bathroom from my traditional Austrian clothing into my "American" look and move to a different part of the train.

I stepped out of the train station and hailed a taxi, making sure I asked in English for the small hotel that had been arranged for me through a well-known travel agency. I checked in, knowing that each newly arriving guest is reported to the police. I had no idea if I would be watched. However, Smith and Jones had suggested that it was very possible because I was posing as an American.

Having learned my lesson in Frankfurt, I took my time to unpack and settle in. The hotel was old and small, yet modern for a former communist-ruled country. It had a large radio in the room and a phone with no numbers. I had no doubt that someone could be listening in on any calls I might make. Still, I relaxed on the large down-filled duvet and pillows on the bed. The beige walls were clean but showed some wear. The window was tall and narrow, with thick curtains to keep out the light. A small vase with three fresh flowers stood on a small dressing table next to the window along with a white ceramic washbasin and a white pitcher of water. Towels and a washcloth hung from a metal bar on the right side of the table.

I ate at the hotel restaurant that evening to better acclimate myself, listen to other people, and watch their behavior. After all, this was still a communist country, although signs of Western encroachment could be seen everywhere. I had witnessed from afar the trauma the city had endured in 1956 during the Hungarian uprising against Russian communist rule. Many people had fled the country, escaping across minefields and barbed wire-fences. I remembered how my school had held food and clothing drives for refugees from the conflict. Student groups took trips to help distribute relief aid at the border. If they got too close to the border, communist guards fired at them.

When the waiter came, I asked if he spoke English, authenticating my American identity. Jones and I had agreed that I would use my Austrian persona only to enter the country as a tourist. Once in, I would be an American photographer. We did not know whether our person of interest had any contacts with the police. Thus, it safer to maintain the same cover as on my visa.

No, he didn't, the waiter said in halting English. Nevertheless, we could communicate enough to allow me to order a traditional dish of goulash with a fresh-baked roll, salad, and a stout Hungarian beer. The goulash was dark red and spicy, as it should be, with large, delicious chunks of flavorful beef floating in it. My mother's goulash, a favorite of friends and family, was thicker and not as spicy, but nevertheless just as good. I called it the Austrian version of Hungarian goulash.

The next day, feeling more comfortable, I took a bus to one of the many market squares in town. Under the previous strict communist rule, capitalism was frowned upon. Following the 1956 uprising, the regime, in an attempt to show its liberalism, allowed and even encouraged small private restaurants, cafés, and bars. Indeed, street vendors made up a large part of the private economy and social life.

I strolled around, making sure I looked like a tourist: taking pictures, pausing, looking into shops, window shopping and stopping at street vendors to buy drinks and food. I picked up a *Hoppacska* sandwich, a cross between a hamburger and a Philly steak sandwich, which was huge, filling, and very tasty. The following day I obtained recommendations from the staff at the hotel for sightseeing venues. I made sure they knew I wanted to take pictures, should the police ask about me while I was out. The hotel owner was happy to provide me with several cultural locations; however, he also warned me of places to avoid. As I walked about the city, I practiced the skills I'd learned to see if I was being followed, remembering Smith's mantra: "Be comfortable, but alert."

On the third day, Saturday, after wandering around for a bit, I made my first foray to a market square where I hoped to see the person of interest. On a shady side street I found a bakery and café housed in a building whose cornerstone showed the date of 1632. I claimed a sidewalk table where I could sit against the building, facing out. On my left was the bakery's window, giving me a view into the restaurant and of the people walking by. On Saturdays, most stores and shops closed for the weekend at 3:00 p.m., when people step out for leisure. Groups of adults and couples took seats at the tables inside and outside the bakery. Waiters in black slacks and white shirts efficiently moved among the guests, taking orders and delivering trays of strong-smelling coffee, heaps of ice cream topped with whipped cream, and pastries of all kinds. I used the classic tourist approach of pointing at menu items or sample trays brought out by waiter and smiling to get my need across. Slowly sipping my coffee, eating a pastry and ice cream, I looked very much like any other customer. Here, where coffee was king, I did not want to draw unwanted attention by ordering my preferred tea. Thus, I idled away a couple of hours watching café patrons and passersby, every now and then looking at a magazine I had picked up along the way.

I knew my chances of bumping into my intended target were slim, but this is the job that I had been given and I intended to make the best out of it. Truthfully, I did not think there was much of a chance of running into her. I had an appointed number of days during which I would attempt to make contact, and if not, I would get back on the train and go home. My mission would have been a success regardless, and I would get what had been promised, a good job in Grand Rapids and a 4F on my draft record to keep me out of Vietnam.

The Trap

The next day dawned warm and sunny, and I found another café, one suggested by Jones, close to the one I had visited the day before. In most European countries, Sunday is a family day. Families spend time together, eat out, play recreational games, and visit family and friends. Hungary was no different. Seating was limited on a busy Sunday afternoon. After carefully scanning the crowd, I found a table outside where I could watch people going by yet be sheltered in the shadow of the overhanging trees planted along the sidewalk. The air had that wonderful sunny afternoon feel and smell to it. Blended in were the aromas of fresh coffee, baked goods, and smoke. Although I do not like cigarette smoke, it seemed oddly appropriate this afternoon. Everyone was dressed in their Sunday best. Men wore suits and ties. Women wore beautiful summer dresses, and some even wore small pillbox hats with decorative netting. After all, this was a communist country with conservative and Catholic virtues.

I started with a glass of popular Hungarian white wine and a slice of Dobos torte, a Hungarian wafer cake layered with chocolate buttercream and topped with caramel and a side dish of freshly sweetened whipped cream. For a moment my mind wandered away from why I was here, fixated instead on the pleasure I was about to experience.

As the first forkful of sweet delight entered into my mouth, the laughter of a small child caught my attention. I glanced over my right shoulder at a young boy, about four years old, his lower face covered with chocolate ice cream. His mother, sitting across from him, was frantically reaching across the table to clean him up while he squirmed and laughed, avoiding her white linen napkin at all costs. She finally succeeded and sat back down. Amused, I smiled at the boy. He giggled at me, took a big spoonful of chocolate in his mouth, and let half of it run back out again. His mother turned to see who was causing her the undue struggle with her son and caught me smiling and making faces at him. When my embarrassment turned into a smile, her expression changed from frustration to puzzlement, probably wondering if the stranger thought she was abusing her child. When she turned and the sun hit her face, I realized it was her, the object of my trip. My heart began to race as I realized this was the moment I was here for. *Stay calm, don't screw it up*, was the thought going through my head.

I tried to recall the pictures I had been shown by Jones. Although they were not as clear as they could have been, nevertheless, the brown eyes, the long brown hair, and the slender figure left no doubt that it was her. I could not believe it! As she got up from her seat and moved closer to the boy, I noticed that she wore a tight white blouse and an even tighter brown skirt. *Damn*, I cursed Jones silently, *they did not tell me that I would be dealing with a mother and her son!* They had made her out as a ruthless thief and danger to our military, not a single mother with a cute little boy. Had they told me, I wondered, would I still have agreed to do this? All I knew was that this was going to complicate things, and yet this was my opportunity!

I tried to gain the boy's attention by blatantly waving at him and smiling, moving my hand over my eyes, and playing peek-a-boo with him. He put his hand up to his eyes and started his own game of peek-a-boo with me. His mother sat down again, turned, and saw me still peek-aboo-ing him. I attempted to look guilty and made hand gestures common to travelers in foreign countries while saying, slowly, "I am sorry." I exaggerated every word, not loud enough to be heard by anyone sitting nearby but clear enough that she could understand.

"No problem. Thank you for helping," came the response in a good, albeit accented English, and she turned away with a slight smile.

"Oh, you speak English," I asked, in my most astonished voice. She turned back and said, "Yes, not so good. I learned it in school."

"It sounds good to me," I said—thinking, *It is exceptionally good!*

I shifted my chair to make direct eye contact with her. "How did you know I spoke English?" I asked.

"You look like a tourist," she replied with a smile. Then she froze and said, "I'm sorry, I hope I did not offend you, but you are dressed like you are not from here." I concentrated on continuing my eye contact with her son, who was smiling at me, and asked if I could say hi to him. She paused to think about it, agreed, and then asked a passing waiter something in Hungarian. I wasn't sure what she said but decided to keep my attention on her son, recognizing that was the means of keeping up the conversation with her.

I moved closer, and she introduced herself as Lillian or Lil and her little boy as Josef. We started with small talk; I asked about Josef, how old he was, whether he went to school or had any brothers or sisters. The conversation seemed to progress, so I offered to buy her another coffee and an ice cream for Josef. Just then, the waiter returned with a fresh white placemat and three colored pencils and a small glass of raspberry juice for Josef. Lillian accepted the offer of coffee but objected to any more ice cream for him, stating that he had had enough for one day. I took that as a sign that she was willing to continue our conversation and ordered myself a coffee topped with fresh whipped cream. My adrenaline was pumping at this point, and I really didn't need the coffee, but I needed to stall for time while I judged how the conversation was going. We talked a bit about Josef, and like any mother, she was happy to tell me all about him while he drew pictures on the placemat, every now and again cocking his head at me as though he was listening.

Eventually, she asked why I was in Budapest. I told her that I was a photographer but didn't go into details. She seemed appropriately interested but probably knew enough not to ask any more questions in a public café. She told me that she was a businesswoman—nothing further, and I didn't ask. Then she asked if I was visiting on my own or with family. No, I responded, I was all alone, hinting that there was no one special, only me wanting to see the city's sights. I said that I had heard many good things about the city, how old it was and what an important role it played in European history. That seemed to impress her.

"What kind of pictures do you want to take?" she asked. She sounded somewhat suspicious.

I explained that I worked for an American magazine that was interested in the changing Hungarian culture, specifically, how the country was becoming increasingly modern, youth life, and the movement closer to Western values. Lil asked which magazine, but I diverted her by asking if she knew where I might find a guide who could show me around the city. Unfortunately, Lil said, since she lived here, she'd never had a reason to hire a guide, so she could not help me. Instead, she picked up her purse from the floor next to her chair, dug in it, and found a pencil and piece of paper on which Josef had drawn a picture. She wrote down some numbers and said that if I called her tomorrow afternoon, she might be able to find someone who could show me around. I put on my best dismayed look and protested that I did not expect her to go out of her way for me; I just wanted a reference—all while hoping like hell that she would not accept my protests. If she did, I had no plan B to stay connected to her.

As the afternoon began to fade, we agreed that I would call her the next day. She stood up, shouldered her bag, cleaned off Josef's mouth one more time with the white cloth napkin, and picked him up off the chair. As I watched her walking away on the sidewalk, Josef turned and waved goodbye to me.

Stunned at my success, I sat there for a few more minutes, watching the setting sun's shadows crawl across the red tile roofs of the old city. I rehashed everything we had said, wondering if anything could have given me away. I concluded that no, everything had gone as well as or better than expected, and that in itself worried me. I ordered a glass of wine to help me calm down from the caffeine high.

When I called Lil shortly after lunch on Monday, she answered the phone on the second ring—thank goodness! Had it been anyone else, I wasn't sure how I would have responded except to hang up. She sounded cheery and gave a warm, "I'm glad to hear from you!" We chatted briefly, and then, to my utter surprise, she offered to show me around herself because she had not been able to come up with a reputable guide. "I do not work tomorrow. It will be a nice day; it will be fun to show you my city."

Wanting to set the hook, I asked, "Will you bring Josef along?"

"No, he does not have enough patience. I will let my mother babysit him." She giggled slightly after the word *babysit*, as if she was proud to get that American word out correctly. She then suggested we meet at the café where we first met.

The next day, after a whirlwind afternoon tour of some of the major city sights, we relaxed at another café with a glass of good Hungarian white wine each and some appetizers. After the second glass of wine, Lil explained that she was in the import/export business and had traveled to Germany and other European countries. She shared that on those trips, she had enjoyed picking up a variety of Western magazines.

I sensed the curiosity and interest rising as she tried to draw out the name of my "employer." Cautiously, I divulged bits and pieces of my work, not giving away too much all at once. When I finally admitted to working for *Playboy*, she blushed slightly, calling it a "naughty" magazine. I didn't know if that revelation had ruined our plans. Had Jones misjudged her?

Lil recovered and now seemed amused by the idea. I quickly interjected that I was not looking for nude models, simply the new beautiful Hungarian woman.

With a sly smile, she said, "I understand!"

As nicely as things were progressing, I did not forget why I was here. While sightseeing, I had kept a close watch, as taught, to see if we were followed or observed, knowing Lil worked with others who might be watching us or protecting her. I took her picture in front of historical buildings and statues, reinforcing what I had been telling her—that she should be a model. Lil demurred, claiming not to be beautiful enough for a magazine, yet I could tell she was enjoying every minute of posing and the adulation. *She is eating it up*, I told myself, careful not to become overconfident, knowing how easily she could charm men.

After this great start, two days passed without any contact further from Lil. I was slightly concerned but knew I could not rush her; the next move was going to be telling, and it was up to her. Meanwhile, I continued building my cover, even taking pictures of other young women on the street. Not wanting to risk it, I finally called her. To my surprise, Lil agreed to have dinner with me the next evening. Pleading ignorance about the local restaurant scene, I asked her to select a place. Oh yes, she'd be glad to help, and she knew of "a cozy little place."

The restaurant was in a charming little underground alcove that had served first as prison cells and then, during World War II, as a bunker. Curved exposed bricks made up the ceiling, and tables were set into recesses, providing privacy. The clean but worn tile floor showed its age. I wondered what the tiles would say if they could talk; what had they seen over the years? The atmosphere was romantic; nice white linen tablecloths, candles, and a gypsy playing the violin in a corner. Several glasses of excellent Hungarian white wine and a fabulous meal provided an air of allure to the evening. By the time dessert arrived, along with a smooth brandy in a heated snifter, Lil was holding my hand across the table and looking warmly into my eyes.

After paying the waiter, as is the custom in Europe, we walked out arm in arm into the warm summer night, toward a taxi stand. Stopping before the taxi stand, Lil turned and looked deeply into my eyes. Then she asked if I wanted to come to her apartment. Maybe I could take some pictures of her? A sly smile on her face hinted of possibilities to come. I accepted the invitation and spent the next few nights with her, going to park and shopping with her and her son during the day, taking pictures of her and not just the beautiful city.

The Final Curtain

Eight days later, I stood on a Vienna train station platform, waiting for the express from Budapest to arrive. At midmorning, the station was busy. No one paid much attention to others on the platform as people bustled on or off their trains. The station was an old structure with a rich history. Over the floors had walked famous musicians, writers, philosophers, physicians, kings, and queens. I did not stop to fully appreciate my surroundings. Instead, I was scanning to see who was around.

Oh my God, I thought, *have these people brainwashed me so that forever I will be vigilant?* Was I, so to speak, forgetting to smell the roses? I shook the thought aside and took a whiff of the mix of diesel and coal smoke in the air. Trains crossing Europe or Asia were now modern diesel-powered machines, and I missed the coal engines' sulfurous smell from my childhood.

My train pulled into the station, and without thinking, I sighed deeply.

Nerves, I thought. *It has come down to this, the final act of the drama.* Six months ago I could not have anticipated the tension, fear, lies, and joys packed into the last couple of weeks of my life.

Whooshing steam and the screech of large steel wheels pierced my thoughts as the train stopped in front of me. Formerly part of the Orient Express line, it now carried high-paying passengers between Vienna and Budapest. In homage to the past, a powerful steam locomotive pulled ornately decorated cars with curtained windows recalling the regal past when train travel was a luxury. I looked for car number six, from which Lil would alight.

I walked to my right on the platform to be closer to where I judged she would get off the train. The train came to a stop with a final whoosh of the brakes. The doors opened, and the conductor got out to place two metal stairs at the bottom of the door. Once the conductor had stepped aside, I saw Lil walking up to the door, a sporty piece of luggage in her hand. She was dressed in a beautiful long camel-hair coat, her hair up and conservatively hidden under a pillbox hat with a small ribbon of black lace around it. My heart pounded in my chest as if I were on my first date, knowing with certainty that this would be my last meeting with her. Guilt overwhelmed me briefly. For a split second, the thought of warning her off entered my mind as I remembered Josef. That thought evaporated like water on a hot summer highway as I realized that this was the moment for which I had worked and taken all these risks. Shoving all emotions aside, I put a smile on my face for Lil to see. *Get on with it!* I told myself.

Stepping down to the platform, Lil saw me and rushed over to embrace me, kissed my cheek, and gave me a quick furtive kiss on the lips.

"Oh, it is so good to see you again!" she said, looking intensely into my eyes, and then planted a passionate kiss on my lips.

"Where is Josef?" I asked, drawing us apart slightly.

"Oh, I could not bring him; I want this to be just for us," she said with glee in her eyes. "Mother is taking care of him."

"Great," I said, quietly heaving a sigh of relief. I worried about what would happen to Josef after today. I had not anticipated having a child involved in the job. Knowing his grandmother was caring for him somehow made this unpleasant situation more tolerable.

"Let's get out of here," I said. I had steeled myself, knowing what would happen next. Lil's passionate kiss and the thought of Josef had penetrated the wall that I had built up to deal with this moment. I was eager to finish this play and let the curtain come down on the final act.

She took my left arm in both of hers and leaned her head lightly on my shoulder while I picked up her bag and carried it in my right hand. We had reached the middle of the cavernous depot, with people milling about, when suddenly, from behind us, a voice said in English, "Lillian Krmczak, may we have a word with you?" Jones and another man appeared and took her arm from mine while two other men in suits approached from the front and four uniformed police officers closed in on either flank. She looked at me in shock. Protesting that the men should release her and calling out for me to help her, she was led away.

I walked toward a side staircase leading down to more platforms and handed off her suitcase to two approaching men, who handed me my own suitcase. I walked down the stairs, trying not to think about what just transpired, knowing what would happen next. Can you feel good about having done a bad deed, even if it is virtuous? Walking as fast as I could without running, I got away from there as quickly as possible.

Two hours later, I was sitting in my grandmother's kitchen. In front of me was a plate of ham, smoked cold cuts, cheeses, and fresh bread, along with a salad of fresh lettuce and tomatoes from her garden, covered with the pumpkinseed oil dressing famous in that part of Austria. The second bottle of local pilsner was sitting in front of me. The first had cleared the bad taste of the day's events from my mouth. This one was to wash down the wonderful meal.

"So, how was your vacation? Did you have fun?" Oma asked.

"You wouldn't believe it if I told you. Yes, I saw a lot of interesting things," I replied, putting on a smile for her, yet doubting myself. "Let me tell you about them tomorrow!"

Smith and Jones kept their word. My spring internship became a full-time job. The president of the firm had been secretary to General Dwight D. Eisenhower during World War II, and the executive vice president had worked for the Office of Strategic Services, predecessor to the CIA. Understanding that I had done some work for the government, without any questions asked, both were happy to cooperate.

I received a good salary, an unlimited expense account, and a plush office with large mahogany furniture to start my career. My peers, meanwhile, were looking for jobs during a downturn in the economy. As my first project, I wrote a training manual, *Your Guide to Successful Retirement*, the first publication of its kind. We used it as a marketing tool to attract lucrative pension and insurance business. As an "author," I then provided training to many Michigan firms and presentations to corporations in New York and other cities.

Some months later, while waiting in a client's lobby, I picked up a magazine. Inside I saw an article entitled "Hungarian Women Convicted of Leading Espionage and Theft Ring." I put the magazine down and stared off into the distance with a clear conscience.

Remember, Manfred, it never really happened!

Judy and I were married on September 19, 1970, in Benton Harbor, with family and friends cheering us on. We eventually moved to Lansing so I could work for the State of Michigan. Judy took a job as the executive secretary to the president of Michigan National Bank, then the state's largest bank. Our daughter Tracy was born in Lansing on January 28, 1974.

PART II

Maria's Story

In the stories that follow of our years apart, I have worked hard to capture Maria's experience as she shared them with me. My words cannot be as true or exact as her experience, but she has graciously allowed me to include her point of view and kept me on a realistic path. Maria has added, "Any errors in the narrative are exclusively related to my loving husband's wanting to make sense of my life."

CHAPTER 6

MARIA'S EARLY YEARS

"[Women]..gathered in groups in their best swimsuits and straw hats, competing for each other's spouses, a pointless endeavor, really, since the men scarcely glanced at them; much more interested in talking politics - the only topic in Chile..."

Isabel Allende in Paula, *describing Chilean family weekend outings at the beach.*

Maria's family was part of a proud and long line of political activists. Her activism, which I witnessed firsthand in college and have subsequently witnessed, goes back to her grandfather, whom she admired and loved. Born in 1878, he, over the next sixty years, was a leading figure in Chile's political movements, particularly the

Maria's grandparents

socialist and communist parties. In 1912 he helped to found the Socialist Workers Party. In 1922 he was one of the founders of the Communist Party of Chile, only to be expelled from it in 1930. In the intervening years he took on a number of positions in local government. Despite his political leanings, in 1925 he was elected a senator for two provinces. Not agreeing with the then president, he was exiled to Easter Island. He escaped, and after hiding out for six months in Santiago, he again ran for Congress and was successfully elected to a four-year term from 1933 to 1937. After his term he was appointed Chilean Ambassador to Mexico, a position he served in from 1939 to 1942. Later he would also serve as Minister of Public Works and Communication, and Minister of Economy and Commerce, ending his public career as Ambassador to Panama in 1953. He died in 1967.

Maria inherited her grandfather's strong belief in social activism, his compassion for others less fortunate, and his love of art. In 1910 her grandfather was president of the Social Workers Congress, a profession Maria has made her career. After high school he entered an art program and was even offered an opportunity to study in Naples, Italy. Maria, too, loves art, having produced and shown some of her works in Minneapolis. Her grandfather's legacy clearly lives within her.

With this background in social and political activism, it is no wonder that dinner conversations with her parents and brother frequently involved lively discussion about politics and world events rather than the discussions about favorite sports or teams common at US dinner tables. According to Maria, these were serious debates where humor was not expected nor allowed. These discussion shaped Maria's life and outlook on the world. She learned early to challenge others and think about world events. She would carry on that tradition with her own children, Amanda and Bob, taking them to museums, art exhibits, cultural, and political events.

Maria's father, Mario Rafael Marino Proby, was a trained geologist, and her mother, Fresia de las Mercedes Hidalgo Rojas, graduated from a prominent Chilean university and received a PhD from the Universidad Nacional de Mexico.

Maria's father worked for the national oil company, seeking new areas to explore for oil. He traveled often for work, while Maria's mother taught school.

Fortunately, like most professional families in her country, they had a housekeeper who cared for Maria and her younger brother.

Maria grew up admiring her maternal grandmother, Maria Engracia Rojas Gonzalez, whom she simply called Abuela. She had had a rough life, having been forced into marriage after a man several decades older than she impregnated her; Maria's mother was the product of that relationship. Abuela was warm, kind, and pleasant, even when Maria tried to aggravate her. She was not a big woman, and yet she kept everyone, from the maids to Maria's mother, in line with her voice and stern looks. Later in life, Maria would wonder if the knowledge of Abuela's background had pushed her mother to seek acceptance in social circles she deemed as "quality" people. Had she also then tried to push Maria in the "right" direction?

Maria's mother was frequently unhappy when her husband was gone, leaving her responsible for raising the children. She could not share or show emotions well and struggled with parenting. Maria explained to me that her mother was prone to outbursts of rage, often aimed at Maria.

Mario was the favored child and was mostly spared their mother's anger due to an illness from which he suffered as a young boy. Maria told me she never knew what would displease her mother. To compensate, Maria tried hard to do whatever her mother asked, hoping to avoid punishment. Later in life, Maria relented, knowing there was no way to please her mother.

Although Maria and her mother struggled, Maria and her father had a bond that endured and matured. When her father was home, he spent a lot of time with Maria. He was a handsome man, not too tall, but slender. He dedicated as much time to his daughter as she wanted, much to the dismay of her mother. They would sit together, and he would read to her. As she sat on his lap, he would tell her about his latest dig and show her samples of rocks and other artifacts from his trips. The places he described were far away and interesting, and Maria wanted to see them all—especially the rugged areas of Chile. At times, she would play with or pull his bushy eyebrows and mustache and then run from the mock fight that ensued. She was not an athletic girl, so she would never get far from him. Maria treasured every minute her father spent with her.

He had a real avarice for books, magazines, and professional journals, which he shared with Maria. He took the time to explain details she was too young to understand herself. He also enjoyed music, and Maria would listen with him to the newest long-playing record he had bought—Elvis, Sarah Vaughan, Tennessee Ernie Ford, and other American country and western artists. Listening to each was an imaginary journey they could take together without ever leaving home. It also gave Maria her first taste of the English language and US culture.

When the family took car trips, her father would invent mystery games for his children to solve. He was always challenging Maria and Mario to think and be involved. Her father would pose a question, like, "A child holding a box goes up to a house and rings the doorbell. The owner comes to the door, looks into the box, says thank you, and sends the child to the next house. The child stops at four other houses, all with the same result. What was in the box?" Maria and Mario had to guess the correct answer by asking their father yes-or-no questions only.

When Maria was seven years old, the governor of the province where they lived, an old man who happened to be their neighbor, invited Maria to see his office. The man knew her parents, so Maria had no fear. Over a period of a year, the man kept inviting her back. He would kiss her and touch her, and he asked her to touch him. Maria did not know what was happening, but it made her very uncomfortable. One day, she mentioned to her mother that the neighbor had kissed her. Maria's mother told her that the man was like her grandfather. Maria did not know what to do. Intimidated by the man's insistence, she continued "visiting" him even though the situation was uncomfortable and sometimes painful. It was not until a year later, after listening to some older girls, that Maria understood for the first time that she had been sexually abused.

Education in Chile

In Chile, education was not the well-prescribed routine of US public schools. Rather, it was a hierarchical system of private schools in which class, family, and finances, along with academic performance, were the predominant factors in furthering one's education. Even at an early age, Maria was bright and precocious. Above all, her mother cared about making sure Maria got into the "right" school and started behaving like the proper young woman that she was about to become.

By the time Maria was ready for high school she began attending a boarding school run by the Catholic church. Having listened to adventures of her grandfather, father and even mother, given the opportunity, Maria decided to signed up for a study- abroad program, leading her to Grandville, Michigan.

Becoming a High School Exchange Student

Maria arrived here to start the senior year of high school. Grandville was a small but growing suburb west of Grand Rapids, only a few miles south of the college where we would meet three years later. In Grandville she lived with a Christian Reform family, thrusting Maria into a new culture, language, and religious persuasion. In the spring of that school year she had a chance to attend the prom. Ironically, and as fate would have it, her date was Terry Prangley, younger brother of my good friend Richard, whom I would later work with for many years.

Highschool picture

Fate crossed Maria's path again a few years later when she and her first husband rented a second-floor apartment in downtown Grand Rapids. Richard, in his first year out of the institution, had, along with another former resident, rented the first-floor apartment of the same home. They casually interacted on holidays, having joint parties in the basement rec room. Maria had forgotten about that until one evening when, after she and I had been married for some time, we went to dinner with friends in Grand Rapids. Driving down a hill toward a restaurant, I pointed out to Maria the home where Richard first lived. Maria exclaimed, "That's where Jeff and I lived! No kidding, Richard was the one of the 'boys' that we used to hang out with on holidays." Even so, she did not connect her prom date with Richard, never realizing it had been his younger brother. Maria and I again were astonished how fate had again intervened in our lives. Maria had met Richard with me after we had already been married, but neither made the connection of having lived in the same house almost three decades earlier. Now, Richard loves to regale me with stories about the time he spent with Maria and her husband.

Based on her time in Grandville, Maria learned about the new college that had just started up, Grand Valley State University. Returning to Chile after her year as an exchange student, Maria convinced her parents that this would be a place for her to get her college education. Although her parents knew little about the college, they knew Maria would have her exchange parents nearby, should she need any assistance.

I believe that in allowing Maria to return to Michigan to attend college, her parents knew she would get a good education and be removed from some of the political and social turbulence that was starting to affect Chile.

CHAPTER 7

FIGHTING FOR THE CIVIL RIGHTS OF OTHERS

Maria stood next to the man who was about to be pronounced her husband.

"Do you, Jeff, take Maria as your wedded spouse?" the officiant intoned in the most solemn voice. "Yes," Jeff replied with a broad smile on his face and a quick wink over his shoulder to his parents standing nearby.

What am I doing here? Maria thought. *I'm the only brown person in this entire room and family. How did I end up here?*

She and Jeff were in the home of his family, along with a large group of wedding guests most of whom she barely knew, but all significant leaders in the labor movement. This was a gathering of labor royalty. Maria was all alone; neither her family nor friends were there to support her. Her parents had not been able to afford the trip—or perhaps they did not want to see her wed? Maria was not sure. All she knew that within the next few minutes, she would be married to the son of a high-ranking member of Michigan's labor movement.

Maria wasn't sure that she loved him the way that she always had thought she would love a man who was going to be her husband. They had met at college, where he had invited her to attend a campaign meeting for the man running to become the first Black mayor of the city of Detroit. Jeff was brash and outgoing—refreshing, compared to some of the other men she knew, including her work-study boss, Manfred.

Jeff was the only one who seemed stable; he could provide for her, yet he also had that revolutionary zeal that excited her. Jeff had served in the Peace Corps in Africa, had beautiful blue eyes, was charming, and politically active; all things that attracted Maria to him. She cared for him deeply and committed herself to make the marriage work. She would be a dutiful wife.

Maria's own family had deep roots in social activism in Chile, the foundation for her own protests against the Vietnam war. Maria had come of age while the US government was actively engaged in overthrowing the Chilean government. She had protested and seen police brutality up close. So, marrying into this family seemed a logical extension of her own political roots.

Mississippi Voter Drive

"Ladies and gentlemen, in preparation for landing in Memphis, the captain has asked that you extinguish all smoking devices, put your tray table in the locked position, and your seatback upright."

Maria awoke, groggy, her head on Jeff's shoulder. They'd both had a couple of drinks before boarding the flight to help them relax and both had fallen asleep. Maria opened her eyes and looked around the cabin. She wondered why anyone was concerned about the evils of cigarette smoking; the secondhand smoke inside the plane was enough to give anyone lung cancer! Two hours in the air and the inside of the cabin looked like a foggy night in London town.

"Are you ready for this?" Jeff asked, rousing her to a full state of consciousness. "Hell no," is what she wanted to say, but instead she said, "I'm ready if you are," gave him a smile, and squeezed his arm.

What have I gotten myself into? Maria thought. *Less than a year ago, I was still a college student, and tonight I'm on my way to register Black folks to vote in Clarksdale, Mississippi! How did all this happen?*

Maria had no clue where Clarksdale was. This was her fifth year of living in the United States. She had spent most of that time, except for short excursions including a trip to join a war protest in Washington, DC, in white, middle-class, conservative Christian western Michigan. Now she was on a plane to work for a month or more in poverty-stricken rural Mississippi. There was a good chance that she and the others might be attacked or even killed, as had happened to other "Northerners"—as the mostly white volunteers were called by those opposed to giving African Americans the right to vote. It was risky to help with voter registration and desegregation drives almost anywhere in the South.

Before Maria had a chance to dwell longer on her predicament, she felt a bump as the wheels touched down, and the plane rolled on the tarmac until it came to a stop. Maria and Jeff grabbed their meager belongings out of the overhead bin and headed for the door. As soon as the plane door opened, oppressive heat surged into the smoke-filled cabin. They stood in the aisle, waiting for the crew to get their bearings and attach the stairs so the passengers could deplane. Walking across the tarmac to the terminal in the evening light, they felt crushing heat come up off the cement, and their clothing began to feel moist. Once they entered the terminal, appreciating the air conditioning, Jeff and Maria waited for the rest of their team. Jeff was the leader of this group of young people who had volunteered to assist in the voter drive. Each group looked tired yet simultaneously exhilarated as they walked into the refreshing terminal air. This was an era of change. History was in the making, and these six young idealists from Michigan were excited to be part of that history.

"Hey, Jeff!" a booming voice rang out. Aaron Henry, a large Black man with slightly graying temples approached, followed by two women and two younger Black men. Mr. Henry rushed over and hugged Jeff and Maria as if they were his own long-lost children, oblivious to the heat and sweat each extruded. The welcomes continued with introductions, and each person in the party hugging and greeting the others. Most people in the terminal took little note of the events. Only a few stared suspiciously at the group of Black folks meeting a group of young white people. Times were racially tense throughout the country, and Memphis was no different, especially ever since the assassination of Dr. Martin Luther King Jr. three years earlier. For a while, it had been hoped that tragic event would make people realize how damaging racial hatred can be. Sadly, the shock of his death had soon been forgotten, and the long hot summer of integration and voter registration had raised up many of the old evils.

"Come on, folks, we've got the vans parked outside. I don't want to give anyone an excuse to plant a ticket on us or take us off to jail for being illegally parked," said Mr. Henry, smiling. He was a prominent and long-time civil rights leader in Mississippi. Although raised by sharecropper parents, he had attended school and became a pharmacist. In 1959 Mr. Henry became the president of the NAACP of Mississippi. He was a frequent target of racial violence, and in one notable incident, he was chained to the back of a garbage truck and paraded through town. None of these actions deterred him. Tonight, he had six new young and eager "up north" kids who would help him register as many of his fellow citizens as they could.

Mr. Henry led them out to two waiting white vans, and they all crowded in. They rolled out as the setting summer sun lit the sky in deep red and orange. Soon Memphis and the airport faded away behind them, replaced by fields and grasslands that had once been the site of plantations where enslaved people labored. The setting sun gave the lush green fields a golden beauty that contrasted with the area's poverty.

Clarksdale lies about seventy miles southwest of Memphis down Highway 64. It was founded in the early 1800s and survived only due to the labor of enslaved Africans, who formed tillable land out of swamps and grassland. In 1850 the county census showed 38,711 slaves, 13,153 whites, and one "Free Man of Color." After the Civil War, and with the advent of better transportation and the dawning of the Industrial Revolution, towns and counties in the Deep South changed drastically, having lost their primary source of economic strength, sharecropping and farming. From 1910 to 1920, Mississippi's African American population decreased by 74,303. Clarksdale, like many other rural southern towns, struggled to maintain itself. The Civil Rights Movement was seen by members of this predominantly white society as the final nail in the long fight against changes to the rural lifestyle. Today, Clarksdale is still a small town, now dependent on tourism rather than plantation income. It is the home of the Blues Hall of Fame and the Blues Foundation, which attract visitors to the former homes of entertainment notables such as musicians Sam Cooke, Ike Turner, and Muddy Waters, and writer Tennessee Williams, who, it is said, modeled much of his writing on his youth in Clarksdale.

Jeff, as the group's leader, sat up front with Mr. Henry. Maria and two others, along with their two local hosts, sat in the next two rows. Mr. Henry began to explain how happy he was that they had "come down" and that the "Black folk" of Clarksdale were waiting for them. Little did Maria realize that he meant that literally. While Maria had hoped to settle in with their host family that evening, Mr. Henry instead took them to a Baptist church where about three hundred people had gathered. Embarrassed, the group from up north made its way up the aisle among the kind of looks normally given to a blushing bride walking arm in arm with her father. To make it worse, the northerners were seated in the front row. Mr. Henry stepped up to the pulpit and raised his hands to hush the crowd.

Until that moment, the sounds from the crowd had been intense: a mix of laughter, loud discussions, and children's giggling voices. Maria guessed that the crowd was wondering what these six white kids could do to help them. She recalled the speech that night.

"Brothers and sisters," Mr. Henry began in a pastoral voice, "let us pray!" He led the congregation in a prayer that thanked God "for bring-ing these young people to this God-ordained mission in Clarksdale, Mississippi." He went on to ask God for his divine intervention over the next month, "To keep everyone here and in the community safe, as they venture forth to register all of the Negroes in Washington County." There were a lot of "Amen" and "Yes, Lord" exclamations. The joy and genuineness of the responses made a deep impression on Maria.

The oppressive heat and humidity and well-worn brown wooden benches reminded Maria of the time when she was sixteen. Her dad had come home and announced that he had booked a family cruise to Panama, including a trip through the Panama Canal. The cruise was a lot of fun, and she and her brother enjoyed the freedom to go wherever they wanted on the ship. In Panama itself, however, the heat and humidity made the trip less bearable. *No wonder so many people died of malaria during its construction*, Maria had thought. The heat left you in a puddle of sweat. Yet tonight, as Maria looked at the crowd seated behind them, she saw that the ladies were not sweating like she was, and only a few men wiped their heads with colorful handkerchiefs. Maria saw joy on the faces of most of the community members. The few serious faces, she would later learn, were probably the informants for the sheriff or another white organization, or those who feared change and the trouble it might bring. It was well known that most people wanted change, although many felt comfortable with the status quo or afraid to rock the boat and bring down the wrath of the white power that still solidly controlled most of Mississippi.

Maria turned back to Mr. Henry, who was still talking in the pulpit. While he no longer sounded like a pastor, his voice still had a booming voice of authority.

"You know," Maria recalled him saying, his voice rising to a serious and authoritative tone, "some in this county do not approve of what we're doing here. In other parts of Mississippi, young people from the north have been killed or disappeared. That ain't gonna happen here! Am I right?"

A resounding chorus of "Amen!" and "No way!" rang out throughout the congregation.

Maria suddenly realized that she could not sense a scintilla of tiredness, heat, or exhaustion. She was pumped, ready to go to work, right now!

She wanted to jump up and scream "Hallelujah" or something—just what, she did not know. But the adrenaline coursing through her veins made her want to get up and get going!

Looking at Jeff's face, she saw his fierce look of admiration for Mr. Henry, so she thought it best to just shut up. The atmosphere reminded Maria of the palpable excitement in the demonstrations she had participated in during the uprisings against the Chilean government. Mr. Henry finished with a few more words of motivation and then told everyone to go home, be safe, and "get to work!"

As soon as they stood up, Maria and the volunteers were rushed by well-wishers who crowded in to thank them and shake their hands. The northerners felt very embarrassed by all the attention. It had been their perception that they would come down here and quietly go to work, not become instant celebrities, drawing unwanted attention to themselves. The reception had been just the opposite.

After everyone had departed the church, Mr. Henry and his staff rounded the volunteers up and took them to their hosts for the next month. Mrs. Thompson, a matronly looking older Black woman, had agreed to put Maria and Jeff up for the duration. Her home was located on the outskirts of what was then called the "Colored" section of town. She welcomed them warmly to her neat and cozy home, addressing them as "Miss Maria" and "Mister Jeff." Mrs. Thompson showed them to a small room in the back of the house. It had previously been occupied by a couple of her children. Now it would be their bedroom and home away from home. During their entire stay, they would repeatedly ask her to call them just by their first names, and yet she never dropped the formality. It was always "Miss" or "Mister," even though she knew they were married—not that it would really have mattered to her. After a while, Maria gave up, knowing old traditions die hard.

The next couple of days began a routine that would last for most of their stay. Go to the church, which had become the center of activity; get lists of names and directions; and head out into the city or countryside to find the names' owners and register them. Even though word had been spread about their activities, most people were still initially leery when these unknown white kids knocked on their doors. Some Black families, clearly feeling intimidated, were not sure why they should register. Others were unsure what registration would do for them since it was not directly a vote. Memories of enslavement, Jim Crow laws, and threats had left folks in these parts fearful. Even so, a significant number of locals opened their doors to them.

Jeff passed off his duties as group leader to someone else after only a few days and left the group to attend to affairs the next county over, where some of the state leadership had its offices and national civil rights leaders would be visiting. Jeff made it his business to be where the action was. After a couple of weeks' absence, Jeff called Maria and told her he had to return to Michigan but would come back for her before the month was out. He said that she and Stacy, a young Jewish woman from a Detroit suburb, would partner up on their registration drives instead. Maria felt abandoned. They had been married less than six months, and Jeff was already leaving her in an unknown area with strangers. It did not feel good.

Maria's features did not immediately give away her ethnicity, but once she spoke, anyone could tell she was not "white." Maria considered herself a woman of color. In these parts of Mississippi, there were only two kinds of people, Black or white.

Unexpectedly, Maria had her first encounter with overt racism in Clarksdale in a form she did not expect. Mr. Chen, a Chinese American man, ran what would today be called a convenience store at the edge of the African American section of town. He catered to both Black and white neighborhoods, although mostly Black customers. Maria found out early that it was the cheapest place in town to buy cigarettes. One day, when Maria stopped into the store to buy cigarettes, Mr. Chen berated her in broken English, "Why are you here, stirring up trouble? Go away! Quit helping the Negros." Had it not been so serious, Maria would have thought the whole episode ludicrous. Here was a nonwhite resident, acting just as racist as the people who were preventing the majority of the county's residents from voting. She wanted to laugh in his face and tell him what an idiot he was, but she knew better. She had to consider her safety and that of the others. She took her cigarettes and left, under her breath, mumbling a curse in Spanish.

"Don't say anything!"

Safety was a big concern. Something could happen to any of them at any time. Mr. Henry had warned them never to go anywhere alone—while on the job, they should always stay in pairs. Mr. Henry pounded caution into them every day. He did not want anything to happen on his watch.

One afternoon, Maria and Stacy drove out into the county to register some folks who lived on a very remote farm. The family had welcomed them and asked them to stay for dinner. Mindful of Southern hospitality, they did not turn down the offer, but as they left afterward, concern entered their minds as they noticed that the sun had begun to set.

It had been a busy and hot day; both were tired. A few miles down the lonely dirt road toward Clarksdale, the car sputtered and stopped. They realized that after driving all day to reach as many families as possible, they had forgotten to pay attention to the gas gauge. They cursed their neglect, and then fear rose in their minds and souls. Here they were, two young, white-looking northern women, known sympathizers with the African American community, conducting business that threatened the fabric of the existing society, alone on a dark country road. They had no telephone, and no one knew their whereabouts. Each remembered the news reports of about young men who had been killed in similar situations by whites opposed to integration and voter registration. What would happen to two young women? One Jewish, the other Hispanic.

Although the road was in the middle of proverbial nowhere, it was not completely untraveled, serving as a connecter between two other county roads. As they sat in the darkness, contemplating what to do, the headlights of a car appeared coming toward them. Maria yelped, "Quick, let's get out and flag them down!" Her hand reached for the door handle.

"Are you nuts?" Stacy screamed. "Look at you: do you look like a white girl?"

"Oh, shit," Maria exploded, the seriousness of the situation hitting her.

"Whatever happens, you sit low and do not say a word, understand?" Stacy barked at Maria. Suddenly scared, Maria just nodded.

The car slowly pulled up on the other side of the road and stopped, keeping its lights on and the motor running. Maria saw a man reach into the backseat of the car and then open the door. In the dim light from his car's headlights, Maria could see that he was an older man, lean and strong. He was carrying a shotgun over his shoulder and wearing a broad-brimmed cowboy hat. As he approached, Stacey again hissed at Maria, "Do not say a word!"

When he got to the car, the man leaned down and asked Stacy, "Howdy, young lady, what seems to be the problem?"

With the heat and no air conditioning in the car, all the windows were down. Stacy smiled and said, in a voice dripping charm, "Why you know us girls, we were so busy talking that we did not notice how low we were on gas, and we completely ran out. Can you help us?"

About then, both Maria and Stacy noticed the sheriff's badge pinned on the man's shirt. *Oh shit*, Maria thought, *this is not going to turn out good.* Law enforcement had been complicit in some of the violence carried out in the area against both Black residents and visiting northerners.

Just then, a voice came from the sheriff's car. It sounded like a young girl's voice.

"Daddy, what's wrong?"

The man replied, "It's OK, honey, these girls just ran out of gas."

The girl's reply was muffled. The sheriff bent down to look in the window, smiled, and asked, "Where are you two from?"

Maria started to say something, but Stacy interjected quickly, "We're visiting a friend, Mrs. Hill. She suggested we see some of her family today; that's why we're out here." Probably, the sheriff knew full well what two young people visiting Mrs. Hill were doing here, but he did not make any mention of it.

"You two are in luck. I keep a spare can of gas in my car; let me get it and put it in your tank. It should provide you enough to get home tonight. Tomorrow you can fill it up and bring it back to me." He walked over to his car, placed the shotgun on the ground, opened his trunk and pulled out a round red metal gas can, came over, and emptied it into their gas tank.

"Now, remember, drop it off any time tomorrow—no hurry." With that, he leaned into the car and placed it on the backseat floorboard. As his head went back out through the window, he glanced at Maria and asked, "You OK?"

Before Maria could answer, Stacy jumped in again with "Sorry, my friend was just very scared. We did not know who was pulling up. Thank goodness it was you, Sheriff."

"Glad to help out. Now you girls get on home; you don't want some n*****s to find you all alone on this road." With that epitaph spoken, he crossed the road, got in his car, put it in gear, and pulled off.

"M*********er," Maria yelled out, all the anxiety and anger gathered over the last few minutes exploding out of her. The frustration of being down here by herself, the stupidity of this country's racism, got the best of her. She vented all the feelings she had held at bay on their way back to Clarksdale. The wind rushing through the open windows carried away all her venom.

A week later, it was time to leave and Jeff had not returned as promised. The many friends they had made warmly said goodbye. The volunteers got into the two vans that had brought them what now seemed to Maria an eternity ago. As she and Stacy took their seats, a man rushed up with a big bag and said, in a very cheery voice, "Wait, I got a souvenir for you to take back up north." With that, he placed the bag, containing a huge fresh watermelon, still warm from the field and weighing well over twenty pounds, in Maria's lap. Not without a few chuckles and comments along the way, the watermelon made it all the way back to Detroit, where Maria shared it with Jeff and his parents.

A few months passed, and the campaign season heated up again. By November, Jeff had signed up for the Democratic campaign full time. The following spring, he came home one night and announced that they were heading back down to Clarksdale. He had accepted a job running a campaign in Mississippi. The previous year's voting drive had been successful, and they now had African American candidates who needed help. His father insisted that they purchase a new car, and in it they headed south in early May.

Two months later, Maria realized that most of her married life so far had been spent away from her husband. Jeff was away again in various parts of Mississippi, working on the two things he relished the most: campaigning and—she soon learned—other women. Meanwhile, Maria was left to herself in Clarksdale, living with a young Black couple who had not wanted to host a stranger in their home but could not refuse Mr. Henry's request. In early summer, Maria decided she had enough of helping people in a country still foreign to her. She packed up and went home to Chile to visit her parents. Her visit would turn into a six-month stay that changed her life forever.

CHAPTER 8

GOING HOME TO TURMOIL

The Chile that Maria returned to was a country in turmoil. Right-wing billionaires and economists tried to control the national economy for their own profits. In 1970, its citizens chose a more socialist path and democratically elected a left-wing president, Salvador Allende. But Allende and his populist reforms weren't popular with one group: US corporations including ITT, Pepsi, and Anaconda Copper, which leaned heavily on a friend in the White House, Richard Nixon, and his chief foreign policy architect Henry Kissinger, to do something. What they did over the next three years—starting with the CIA-backed assassination of a Chilean general in 1970—was one of the bloodiest and most morally unconscionable chapters in the history of US foreign relations. It culminated with history's original "September 11" attack—a violent American-aided coup September 11, 1973, that led to Allende's death, the empowerment of military dictator Augusto Pinochet, and a reign of terror in which at least three thousand political opponents, and perhaps many more, were murdered or "disappeared." Soccer stadiums became concentration camps for thousands, and many were brutally tortured.

The events of 1972 and 1973 were not sudden incidents. They had an extended history dating back to the 1960s, when large American firms started to take resources and wealth out of Chile. The US State Department's Office of the Historian describes it in the formal archives of the United States:

> Relations between the United States and Chile deteriorated in the 1960s due to U.S. concerns regarding the

Chilean Left and the rise of Chilean nationalization of certain industries, especially copper. The Alliance for Progress, signed in 1961 by President John F. Kennedy, was designed to prevent the spread of socialism throughout the hemisphere. . . . The prospect of the nationalization [being taken over by the government of Chile] of two of the leading Chilean copper companies, Anaconda and Kennicott—both owned by corporations based in the United States—along with the growth of socialist sentiment throughout the hemisphere led the United States to send aid and assistance overtly and covertly to the Chilean Government, as well as to political parties such as the Christian Democratic Party (PDC).

The U.S. Government used covert funds in Chile during this election period, not for any one's candidate's use but to prevent Allende's election.

Allende wanted to reform health care, agriculture, and education and was invested in further nationalizing businesses. He increased the percentage of farms and businesses that were nationalized. Wages increased throughout the administration, and for the first few months, inflation was held at bay. On the surface, the reforms appeared to be successful. It became clear, however, that the successes were not balancing out the problems. . . . These issues led to a series of demonstrations and strikes from 1971 to 1973.

Such was the chaos that Maria's beloved country found itself before I met her. As we grew closer, Maria shared with me that she and friends had participated in protests in Chile, never being specific about incidents. Still, I learned that she knew what tear gas smells like, what happens when peaceful protestors encounter police with clubs and truncheons, and worse, what can happen to demonstrators captured and led off by the police or military. In such an uncontrolled environment one can only speculate about the horrors that happened to protestors, whether male or female, while held captive in a lawless society.

In 2020, as the Covid-19 pandemic and its variants which ravaged the world, the killing of George Floyd in Minneapolis and the riots that it sparked throughout the country weighed especially heavily on Maria. I knew that seeing footage of government and military forces putting down peaceful protests, spraying tear gas, using live and rubber ammunition, and beating and running down protestors made her tense and anxious. As we watched such violence unfolding close to home, I realized from her comments that she was re-experiencing moments from her life in Chile in the early 1970s. Some pain never goes away.

CHAPTER 9

HANNAHVILLE: AN AWAKENING

Eventually Maria went back to Michigan to divorce her husband, recognizing their marriage had deteriorated. In 1976, seeking a fresh start, Maria got a job working with youth at the Hannahville Indian Reservation near Escanaba, Michigan. The reservation was distant from any urban environment that could trigger flashbacks or remembrances best forgotten. Here, Maria saw that she could make a difference.

The Hannahville Indian Community is a federally recognized Potawatomi tribe residing in Michigan's Upper Peninsula, approximately 15 miles (24 km) west of Escanaba on an 8.5755square-mile reservation. The 2000 census reported a resident population of 395 persons within its territory, most of whom were of Native American heritage. As of June 3, 2013, the tribe had an enrolled membership of 891 people. According to the 1990 Census of Population and Housing for Michigan, the per capita income for the Hannahville community in 1989 was $4,625, whereas the per capita income for the state of Michigan was $14,154.

The people of Hannahville are descendants of Potawatomi people who refused to leave Michigan in 1834 during the great Indian removal. They moved away from Michigan for a period, living with the Menominee in northern Wisconsin and the Ojibwe and Ottawa peoples in Canada. The Potawatomi, together with the Ojibwe and Odawa, are part of the Council of the Three Fires. In 1853 some Potawatomi returned to Michigan, and one group settled along the mouth of the Big Cedar River at Lake Michigan.

Hannahville changed Maria again. At this time, casinos had not yet become the economic driver it is for many tribes today. Living on the reservation and working with young people there opened her eyes to the immense poverty, crime, and social ills present on reservations and their roots in historic and ongoing discrimination against Native peoples in the United States. Tribe members educated her about the proud history and heritage of American Indians and the discrimination, genocide, and horrors Native people had endured historically under white colonization. She saw how hard tribal leaders worked to improve the lives of their people and the importance of traditions and culture. She soon felt part of the community and enjoyed her life there.

Although she had never worked with youth before, Maria enjoyed her new job. She wrote a grant to obtain minibikes to get the young people involved in healthy activities. Today, Maria is still proud of what she did for the youth in her program.

Maria also met and fell in love with Tom, a member of the tribe. Their relationship flourished, and they began to talk about marriage. Unfortunately, that was not to be. One night, Tom was killed in a car accident on US-2, the main two-lane highway crossing the southern part of the Upper Peninsula. His death devastated and traumatized Maria. After all she had been through in the last few years, she had finally found an anchor in her life and looked forward to building a future with him. Now that dream had shattered.

Return to Chile

Tom's death devasted Maria, so she decided to return to Chile. This time, she chose not to get involved in politics. She got a job working for the United Nations and sought out a therapist to help her cope with the tragic events of her life. Maria found it somewhat ironic, as she explained in one of her early emails to me, that the therapist was an Austrian immigrant.

After almost a year in Chile, Maria returned to Grand Rapids and got a job as an outreach worker for the Hispanic Center. After seeing the ills on two continents, she wanted to help people. She knew that if she wanted to make an impact, she had to go back to school. After finishing undergrad at Grand Valley State University (GVSU), Maria enrolled at the University of Michigan and completed her master's in social work in 1980, thus completing a cycle started by her grandfather. Over the next decade Maria would use her skills and training to help and support others, for which work she was recognized and honored.

In 1992 Maria would be recognized as a distinguished alumnus by GVSU for her work and dedication to helping people. Her accomplishments were summarized at the award ceremony as:

> *After starting her career in youth services in 1975 at the Hannahville Potawatomi Indian Reservation, Maria Marino, '80, earned her bachelor of philosophy at Grand Valley State University. Upon graduation, Marino worked as both a job skills instructor and Executive Director for the Hispanic Center of West Michigan.*
>
> *She has also worked as a social worker for the Family Outreach Center and Manistee's Community Health Clinic and Public Schools.*
>
> *Marino is also credited with founding Maria Marino and Associates, a private mental health practice which provides therapeutic services to children and their families in St. Paul, Minnesota. Within this practice, Marino has started projects including the Ramsey County Head Start, American Indian Family Services, and CLUES (Chicanos Latinos Unidos en Servicio).*

Maria would also receive the Women of the Year Recognition for Community Service from the YWCA and the National Conservation and Community Service Award.

Love and Family

In 1980, after finishing her degree, Maria met the man who would become her second husband and the father of their children, Amanda and Bob. Tim was from West Michigan. He had learned Spanish in school, so their mutual appreciation of the language attracted them to each other. Early into the relationship, Tim suggested that he could sell a house he owned and they could use the money to travel through South America. At first Maria thought he was kidding. Once she realized he was serious, however, she agreed to the plan. Before leaving, they got married in Grand Rapids. Maria knew she could not bring a man into her parents' home and share a bed with him without being married.

Maria at Machu Pichu

After Maria's parents became acquainted with their new son-in-law, Maria and Tim traveled to Punta Arenas, the southernmost populated area of Chile. It is literally at the bottom of the world—a starting point for anyone traveling to Antarctica for research or tourism. Over the next year they traveled the entire length of the coast of South America, fulfilling a dream Maria had had as a child. They visited Indigenous villages, world-famous sites such as Machu Picchu, and the Atacama Desert. They hiked and traveled by bus, train, and local forms of transportation supplied by farmers.

When they reached Guatemala, the country was going through another civil war supported by the CIA. It was risky to be around tourist attractions, especially for Americans, who were blamed for much of the unrest. Nightly they heard gunshots and explosions. Even in the daytime, they had to be careful where to go. Exploiting her Chilean nationality, Maria arranged for visits to Mayan temples when few others were present because of the ongoing violence. She and Tim were shown hidden areas of the temples that normal tourists would not have seen. Maria also caught up with a close friend from Santiago who was reporting on the civil war. He warned them that danger was too close, so they flew home to the United States earlier than planned rather than continuing their journey to completion through Mexico.

Maria still thinks about this adventure frequently, and over the years she has shared many stories from it with friends and me. It has been fun to see her recollecting those exploits with joy and excitement. And, as we watch travel shows about South America on TV, Maria delightfully points out places she has been and fills me in on details the programs omit.

Maria and Tim settled in Grand Rapids, Michigan. MSW degree in hand, Maria was asked to take over the city's troubled Hispanic Center. As CEO, Maria built the center into a thriving agency that still serves many people today. Maria and Tim settled in Grand Rapids, Michigan. As CEO, Maria built the center into a thriving agency that still serves many people today. Her efforts were described in a featured article in the Grand Rapids Press on May 8, 1991:

> "Hispanic center's director leaving May 17 to work on doctoral degree."
>
> *It's been three and a half years since Maria Marino-Idsinga took over as the director of the financially troubled Hispanic Center of Western Michigan and began guiding its comeback. Now she's ready to give it the ultimate test: Can the agency continue to grow without her? "I hope so, or I haven't done my job," said Marino-Idsinga, 42." I think I'm leaving an agency that's doing very well, an agency with a certain amount of credibility."..."Marino-Idsinga's outspoken, aggressive style of leadership will be missed," said Wende Aligihre, vice chairwoman of the board of directors.*
>
> *"Under her direction, the Hispanic Center has done a 180 degree turn around," she said. "She has an excellent handle*

on what is going on in the Hispanic community and she's been able to convince others of the needs of the Hispanic community and come up with wonderful programs to meet those needs."…The agency, formed in 1978, ran into shaky financial ground in 1986. With a $23,000 deficit and waning confidence from its main funding sources – the center's board brought in the Catholic Human Development Office to manage the agency for two years. Marino-Idsinga, hired as director in November 1987, took over full management responsibilities in May 1989. Program additions to the center include:

- *Clinica Santa Maria, a clinic run by St. Mary's Hospital and staffed with bilingual professionals.*

- *The restoration of the summer youth employment program*

- *An outreach worker who provides services in area resident's homes.*

- *A Spanish language and culture class for Grand Rapids police.*

With a background in social work, rather than administration, Marino-Idsinga had to learn how to manage budgets and personnel in order to translate her vision for the future into services that touch people's lives today. In tackling those tasks, she said she ended up learning as much about herself as she did about administration. "Being a minority working in the mainstream system, you always feel you have to prove who you are over and over and over and that your ability is questioned simply because you're of color," she said. "I don't have to do that anymore. I don't have to have that armor up.

It's amazing to me how much this job has given me a sense
of being, a sense of self, a sense of Hispanic self," she said.

While tackling this difficult effort, Maria also put her husband through law school and raised Amanda, born in 1986, and Bob, born in 1988. Regrettably, juggling a career, two young children, and a husband in law school took a toll on their marriage. Overwhelmed with studies and raising a family, Maria dropped out of the doctorate program. After divorcing her husband, Maria took a job as a therapist, moving to Manistee, in the northwest corner of the state, along Lake Michigan.

Fate intervened again to keep us apart. My job included working with several local community mental health agencies in lower Michigan—including the agency in Manistee where Maria worked. Yet, each time I was there, Maria was out of the office and we never connected.

CHAPTER 10

MEETING THE FAMILY

In December 2005, immediately after Christmas, I met Maria's parents on my first trip with her, Amanda, and Bob. I was looking forward to seeing Chile, a magnificent country whose natural beauty is largely unappreciated by the rest of the world. From the driest desert in the north to the bitter cold of Punta Arenas near the southernmost tip of Chile, close to the Strait of Magellan, leading to Antarctica, Chile is one of nature's wonders.

Like most new suitors, I was both excited and fearful to be meeting her parents for the first time. Although Maria and I had known each other for years, I had only met her children for the first time in May 2005, and we were still in the process of getting to know each other. At the time, Amanda was eighteen and Bob seventeen. They were very independent souls, so I had to earn their trust. Taking this trip was a risk, but what better way for me to get to know the family? Coincidentally, Maria's brother Mario and his family came to Santiago from Minneapolis to spend time with his wife's family—a family reunion of sorts.

Her parents' house was located in an upper-middle-class neighborhood. It was modest by American standards but very nice. It sat behind an iron fence and brick wall, both lush with greenery. A small backyard contained lemon trees and other fragrant shrubs, and a pine tree standing six feet high or more. When we arrived, it was decorated with Christmas ornaments—a shock to me in the context of Santiago's warm and sunny climate. I had never seen a Christmas without some snow or cold temperatures, but in Santiago at that time of the year, temperatures hover in the mid-eighties every day, with blue sky and the Andes in the background. The lovely garden and green grass were surrounded by eight-foot-high and three-foot-thick shrubbery on all sides. Cats, which made the yard their home either temporarily or permanently, lounged in the shade of the bushes. They were companions for Maria's dad, and he lovingly spoiled them.

Inside, the house was decorated with ornate artworks collected over time by Maria's grandfather, through her father's travels, or during her mother's time in Mexico. Behind a large dinner table was an ornate hutch with two large Chinese vases on either side and other precious items, and an ivory puzzle ball. A large chandelier over the table provided additional ambiance. Mealtimes meant not only good food but also good conversations lasting long after the meal was done, with Maria acting as my translator. Sitting at the dinner table, I could sense how stimulating discussions had been carried out here while Maria was growing up.

Both of her parents were elderly and affected by various medical problems, her mother more so than her father. In my opinion, age and illness made her mother, whom Maria described as never very outgoing, withdrawn. Nevertheless, she approved of my marriage to Maria. Although also ill, her father was very much engaged and, with Maria's help, a wonderful conversationalist. Their acceptance was very reassuring, and I immediately felt at home.

Fooled by Mother Nature

Maria, Amanda, Bob, and I drove a couple of hours north of Santiago to a small town that houses a famous beach. That day the temperature hovered in the mid-nineties. It was the last week of December—midsummer for that part of the world—and not a cloud was in the sky. The beach was beautiful, and the ocean was deep blue, with azure waves topped by pure white crests inviting us to cool off. I could not resist the large rolling waves, and I rushed to be the first to jump into the water. As soon as the water hit my body, I felt an icy wet sting on my very hot body. Leaping back onto the beach, I saw Maria laughing uproariously.

"What's the matter?" she asked, barely able to get the words out above the hilarity of seeing her macho husband whimpering from the cold water. The beauty of the beach and the blue of the ocean had lulled me into forgetting that the ocean currents there come up from Antarctica. Despite the air temperature, they rarely match the ocean temperatures further north. Frozen to the bone, I took a long while to warm up on the pristine beach. Still, watching the waves roll in, I cherished each minute of enjoying the wonderful water in front of me.

A couple of days later, Maria took Bob and me on a tour of Santiago while Amanda was being introduced by her cousin Pancha to childhood friends. As we came into town, I was astonished by the sight of Cerro San Cristóbal, a small mountain in the northern part of Santiago. It reminded me of being home in Graz. Cerro San Cristóbal is about 2,800 feet high and rises about 1,000 feet above the rest of Santiago. It is a major tourist attraction, just like the Schlossberg in Graz.

Maria took us to the top of San Cristóbal via and old funicular railway. The view was spectacular! We could see the entire city below us. Santiago has a population of around 5.6 million inhabitants, while Graz has approximately three hundred thousand people. At the restaurant Maria and I showed Bob how to conduct a wine tasting. He enjoyed the process, and by the time we finished we had almost two dozen wine glasses in front of us. Later, driving through the city, Maria gave historical context to many areas, including the government plaza, where the infamous 1973 coup took place. It was a wonderful excursion.

The Families' Guardian Angel

As her parents aged, it had become more difficult for them to carry out routine daily housekeeping functions. Fortunately, Maria's parents had found a guardian angel and caretaker years earlier in a young woman named Pilar. Having a maid was not unusual in Chilean culture, especially among successful professional families. In Chile, a maid's job was not looked down on but rather was an accepted profession for many women. Early in the job, Pilar became pregnant. Rather than dismissing her, as might have been the usual thing to do, Maria's parents offered to take Pilar and her newborn daughter in. They provided her a small apartment in the back of the house, where eventually, Pilar and her daughter's father would live. They even hosted the wedding of Pilar and her husband at their home.

By the time I arrived, Pilar's daughter was in high school and preparing for college entrance exams. While carrying out her domestic duties, Pilar, an intelligent and determined woman, had also attended school to become a nursing assistant. This was a tremendous blessing for Maria's parents as they continued to be overtaken by age and illness. Maria is convinced that, had it not been for Pilar, her parents' illness would have taken them from this earth years earlier.

Some Losses Are Difficult to Understand

A couple of years later, Maria received a call from Pilar that her father was hospitalized. The doctors suggested he would not live more than a few days, and she recommended that we come immediately. Maria, her children, and I flew to Santiago as soon as we could make arrangements. By the time we got there, her father had been moved from the hospital back home in the expectation that the end was near. Pilar refused to give in, insisting that she could bring him around. She did, and he lived another wonderful five years under her loving care. Her mother, unfortunately, passed away a couple of months after the incident. And, sadly, Maria was not able to be there for her father's passing but was reassured by the knowledge that he was in very good hands with Pilar. Maria flew to Santiago for the funeral once it was arranged.

After the funeral, Maria had a chance to grieve with Pilar, who by now had become a close friend and confidant. Maria knew that she would need to return to Santiago another time to settle the estate. The home had many precious and memorable items that were of particular value to Maria, but after the funeral, she could only take a few precious items to keep safe.

Arriving at customs in Atlanta, Maria was asked if she had anything to declare. Maria being an honest person, said yes, and showed the agent a brown wooden box containing an ivory puzzle ball the size of a softball and its stand.

The puzzle ball was ornately carved and had twelve nested, rotating balls, each intricately carved with animals and oriental designs. After examining the object, the customs agent declared the item to be illegal under a protected species act and confiscated it.

Knowing its history and meaning to the family, Maria was devasted. She argued that the item had been in her family since at least 1940, when her grandfather had brought it from Mexico. As far as Maria knew, it was among several gifts given to him by the Mexican government. The customs agent would not listen, took the box, and asked her to move on. There was no appeal.

Picking her up at the Minneapolis airport, I could see Maria was distressed. At home, she told me the entire story. The next day I contacted the Dallas District Office of the Fish and Wildlife Services (FWS), to whom, Maria had been told, the puzzle ball would be sent. FWS was responsible for the recovery of any ivory items confiscated by Customs Service. The agent with whom I spoke was friendly enough but explained that strict laws exist to prevent ivory's import in order to protect African elephants. In his mind, it was a closed case.

He did say that I could go through an appeals process where a magistrate would review the case. Of course, I was not about to have the government take away a precious family heirloom. Family heirlooms have special meaning to immigrants, something nonimmigrants do not fully understand. I decided to appeal the decision.

A few weeks later, I received a letter stating the appeal had been denied. At issue was the fact that Maria could not prove that the puzzle ball had been in her family, or that it was over one hundred years old, one of the limited exceptions to the federal law. Nevertheless, I called the magistrate. Although sympathetic, he did not think much could be done since the Obama administration was cracking down on ivory imports. NBC's *Today* show, with the support of the Obama administration, filmed a pyre of confiscated ivory being burned in Times Square, New York. The magistrate did allow that if we could prove that it was over one hundred years old, he would be willing to reconsider his decision.

Maria knew it had been in the family since her grandfather brought it from Mexico but did not know how old the item itself was. We both guessed that it was Ming Dynasty era, based on pictures in books on Chinese art. Meanwhile, I was determined to fight the system. Maria was overcome at the loss, blaming herself for being honest and declaring the item. She wanted to hear no more and let me do all the appeals. I looked up experts from the *Antiques Roadshow* TV program and found one Asian art expert willing, for a fee, to drive from Houston to Dallas, examine the puzzle ball at the FWS office, and provide an expert declaration. He did so and then submitted a certificate of authentication to the magistrate, declaring that it was probably made in the nineteenth century. This made it over one hundred years old, but obviously, he could not provide a specific date when it was made. A close friend of the family, an attorney in Santiago, vouched in writing that she has seen the puzzle ball on the dining room hutch for many years. Despite that testimony, the FWS would not budge. The entire process took almost a year, only to conclude with a dead end.

A few months later, out of curiosity, I called the FWS agent again and asked what had happened to the ball, fearful that it had been destroyed—a call I could not share with Maria, knowing how sensitive a topic this was for her. The agent discovered that it had been transferred to an FWS holding site in New Mexico that handles precious items, especially eagle feathers for Native tribes. A kind agent at that center found it, having not known what was in the case. Trying to reassure me, the officer said as far as she knew, it would remain there until someone asked for it. She volunteered that they sometimes loaned out items for display to museums. Knowing it had not been destroyed, I risk sharing that fact with Maria. It gave both of us some consolation.

Two years ago, while having a beer with my son Steve, I told him this story. He suggested that I contact the Minneapolis Institute of Art, which has an extensive collection of Asian artworks, to see if they would be interested in displaying it. He thought it would be a surprise to and reassurance for Maria if they could procure it, and she could see it safe.

Skeptical, I put off contacting the museum until May 2020, when I explained the circumstances to the head of the Department of Asian Art and showed him a picture of the puzzle ball. After some time, he informed me that the law prevented even the intermuseum loan of ivory items. He considered the puzzle ball, based on my pictures, very interesting and intriguing, but he regretted being unable to help out.

There are many losses we face as we go through life. How severe they are depends on where we live, who we are, and the circumstances, and who we lose. The puzzle ball had been a touchstone connecting Maria to her grandfather and family history. It had a cherished place in the family home, and she had hoped to display it in our home providing continuity of a precious heirloom. Some people may not think that losing an ornamental item is a big deal, but within an immigrant family, heirlooms can bind a family together.

PART III

Two Special Decades: Career, Loss, And Reunion

CHAPTER 11

TWO DECADES THAT SHAPED MY LIFE

In the fall of 1970 my life and responsibilities as an adult began in earnest. College days were done, and my "vacation" to Europe had earned me a well-paying job in a consulting firm in Grand Rapids. Marriage to Judy was heaven. Many of my college friends, married and into nascent careers, also lived in the city, allowing us to carry on an active social life. A year later, in August 1971, spurred by high inflation rates, President Nixon imposed wage and price controls in an effort to gain control of price levels in the US economy. My consulting income was derived from commissions, so when he implemented *Executive Order 11615*, freezing wages and commissions, my income dried up. Fortunately, Judy had a good job, which allowed me time to find a new job.

Having written a training manual for employees promoting preretirement, a first for private industry, I had gained a reputation in the state and national aging sector. A month after losing my first job, I was offered a position at the Michigan Commission on Aging, starting my almost four-decade career in state government. Believing myself a capitalist, I scorned working for government, sure that I would only be in the job until Nixon left office. My loathing for him was such that it motivated me to become a US citizen, just so I could vote against him in the 1972 election.

A few months after I moved to Lansing and started the new job as project director for the Retired Senior Volunteer Program (RSVP). At the same time, the executive director of the office was fired for improper conduct and the Legislature created an entirely new agency, the Office of Services for the Aging (OSA). I was asked to be one of four people to start the office and revise the state's aging programs. I also met a man who would become my boss and career mentor, C. Patrick Babcock. Pat was my first boss at OSA, then in the governor's office, and also the Department of Mental Health. In his long career in state government, he also headed up the Department of Labor and the biggest department, Social Services. He ended his career as a senior vice president for the Kellogg Foundation, where he worked on many national projects. Apart from his outstanding professional credentials, Pat was also one of the kindest and humble human beings. He nurtured not only me but also other professionals, and he became a good friend and supporter of my friend Richard. He made the idea of a traveling mental health exhibit a possibility by having the department provide the initial seed funding.

Becoming an Advocate for Seniors

At OSA my first job was implementing the new Older Americans Act Comprehensive Services Amendments establishing Area Agencies on Aging. The amendments added a new Title V, which authorized grants to local community agencies for multi-purpose senior centers. This meant the state had to be divided into ten "areas" to implement the act. This process proved the axiom that no good deed goes unpunished. While the program would help seniors throughout the state, its implementation brought out political and other rivalries; some even personal. Ironically, the two most difficult areas were (perhaps not surprisingly) the metropolitan Detroit area, which just recently had selected its first Black mayor, and the sparse, but heavily aged, Upper Peninsula.

I loved the political infighting and intrigues and was very good at negotiating agreements to achieve our goal. I threw myself into the job, thereby neglecting my marriage. Judy was patient and kind; I was obsessed with creating something new. Our marriage ended amicably in divorce in 1976 with Judy and Tracy moving back to Holland where Judy's mother lived and would be Tracy's loving caretaker while Judy worked as executive secretary to the president of a home products manufacturer.

Career or Family?

My successful effort at setting up the ten Area Agencies gained me attention withing the higher levels of state government. I was asked to become special projects director for then Gov. William G. Milliken, the kindest, fairest, and most ethical politician I ever met. On behalf of the governor, I reviewed major projects that the five human service department initiated. I also became the front man for the governor in the process of moving persons from mental institutions and hospitals into community residential settings. NIMBY, or Not In My Back Yard, became the rallying cry for citizens who did not want "these" people in their community or neighborhood. Standing in front of groups of angry citizens I had tomatoes thrown at me, car tires slashed, and life threatened. The governor would not back down. He saw what positive things could happen when people with disability were given a chance. Gov. Milliken was responsible for the eventual release of my friend Richard from the Coldwater Regional Center for Developmental Disabilities, where he had been unjustly housed for seventeen years. Richard and the governor ended up being friends.

Reunion with Another Roommate

On one of my trips to Detroit to check on the senior services I had dinner with Karen, who after her divorce had moved from Minneapolis back to live with her parents in a Detroit suburb. Karen, former roommate of Maria and Judy, became my second wife a year later. My career blossomed and just prior to the general election in 1980 a new director was hired for the Department of Mental Health. His hiring was a signal toward community living and away from large institutions. He was a world-famous psychiatrist best known for being the first to recognize what is called

Stockholm syndrome and his work on the science of hostage negotiations. Unfortunately, although he had impressive academic credentials, his understanding of the political sphere was limited. In order to avoid a major embarrassment, two months before the election, the governor ask me to become an assistant to the mental health director, with the purpose of helping him avoid political pitfalls. I asked the governor not to send me there based on what I perceived was the worst run human service department. Its culture was institution based, not at all willing to change. Surprisingly, the governor relented and ask that I at least stay until the election was over in two months. "*Sure,*" I agreed! I can put up with almost anything for two months. Reality though was something else. Twenty-seven years later, in February 2007, I finally retired from the same department.

My first supervisor at the department was another man who had made a name for himself throughout his career in law enforcement. He became one of my professional heroes, one whose philosophy and attitude I have tried to emulate throughout the rest of my career. He taught me that no matter how complex the circumstances, there are always alternatives to given solutions—a lesson I applied in many meetings and negotiations. Wesley A. Pomeroy was described in his *New York Times* obituary:

> *As a peace-loving peace officer who maintained order with such friendly persuasion at the 1964 Republican National Convention in San Francisco that he was recruited by the Justice Department and who later became a counterculture hero as the benign and highly effective security chief at the 1969 Woodstock music festival [bringing in the Hell's Angels motorcycle gang to keep the peace]. . . . If Mr. Pomeroy had had his way, the revolutionaries of the 1960's would not have had much to rebel against. That was because Mr. Pomeroy, a member of the American Civil Liberties Union and an advocate of the decriminalization of marijuana, was a law enforcement officer who viewed protesters as citizens, not criminals, and whose approach to crowd control was to*

coddle, even if it meant sharing police communications sys-
tems with a rally's organizers and teaching angry counter
protesters how to set up picket lines.

Wes was a kind and caring man who taught me a lot about law enforcement and had me participate in many law enforcement events.

"A Lesson I Didn't Learn"

When I started my career in mental health, Michigan had twenty-three state institutions housing over 26,000 persons with developmental or mental disability. My first month on the job I was responsible for helping to oversee the closing of four hospitals and managing the layoff of 3,200 employees. While this was going on, a new bureau was formed to set up a comprehensive county based mental health system. At the time, there were fifty-four independent county run community mental health agencies. These agencies were consolidated under a regional system that infused them with additional state and federal dollars to supplement the small county revenue. For example, one of the smallest counties in the Upper Peninsula went from a budget of slightly more than half a million dollars to over five million dollars.

Not having learned my lesson the first time around, I threw myself into work. By 1985, the transition to community-based services was moving into full swing. I was working fifty plus hours. I would come home in time for dinner and to see the kids off to bed. I'd then sit down and crack open my briefcase full of work. Two or three strong drinks later, and numbed from booze, I fell into bed. Somewhere after doing this every day for over a year, I realized I could not keep it up. My body does not deal well with excessive stress. For the sake of my family and my health, I demoted myself, taking the job of one of my staff who retired. The job was mental health area manager for the Upper Peninsula, located in Marquette.

I started the job in Marquette on a stormy day in February in the midst of a severe snowstorm. In August, Karen and the kids joined me. We rented a house, this time large enough to accommodate the entire family. The following summer we found a house to buy. It was a perfect fit for a young family. Located just south of the city, amongst woods, at the end of a cul-de-sac, with a large lawn in front and back. The children loved being able to ride bikes and play without concern for traffic. With Marie and Anna still not in school, Karen and I agreed that she should stay home to care for them. Once each was in school, Karen planned to get her teaching degree. The time the children were growing up was a wonderful time. We enjoyed the many outdoor activities available and made friends through a church Karen joined. After graduating from Northern Michigan University, Karen never found a teaching job to her suiting, working instead in the church preschool. I credit Karen's staying home for the amazing adults Marie, Anna, and Steve have become.

Helping Richard Achieve his Dream

By the start of 1990 service changes for persons with mental disabilities envisioned a decade earlier were beginning to take shape. Agencies in my area were providing new and enhanced services. I was driving at least twice a month to Lansing for staff meetings and my work with Richard. His vision coming out of the institution was to educate children and the general public about mental disabilities to, as he would say, "Prevent what happened to me, happen to others."

Richard was outspoken about his advocacy. He gained the attention of CBS's *Sunday Morning Show*, which featured him going back into the institution where he spent seventeen years of his life. We formed a non-profit of which I was president, made up of the state's major disability groups, to develop a traveling exhibit to educate children. Richard's efforts were acknowledged by the national Association for Retarded Citizens (ARC) honoring him with a new award, presented to him in Nashville by Mickey Rooney, the actor. The award was named after Bill Sackter, whose life was represented in two *Bill* movies, with Mickey Rooney playing the lead. Richard was also invited to the White House by President Reagan to witness the signing of a disability related law. John Schneider, a columnist for the Lansing State Journal, who had helped Richard early on and also become his friend, wrote a book about Richard entitled *Waiting for Home: The Richard Prangley Story*. The title was homage to Richard's biggest dream, to have his own home where he could have a workshop, garden, and paint walls any color he liked. Not being able to read or write, I accompanied Richard on these travels, working with designers and contractors on the exhibit and negotiating with the publisher once John had finished the book. Eventually, once enough books had been sold, and he had earned money from speaking engagements, I co-signed a mortgage for him to get his own home—where he still lives. While these efforts helped Richard, it meant even more time away from my family and added stress to our relationship.

One Job is Never Enough

Meanwhile, I still had to carry out my full-time job in the Upper Peninsula. There, with my counterpart from the Department of Social Services, we started the Upper Peninsula Children's Coalition in response to children from the Upper Peninsula with emotional or mental challenges having to be moved to Wisconsin or lower Michigan for services, hundreds of miles away from their family. I became chairman of that group, which at its zenith, had over a hundred-member child service agencies from throughout the region. We gained national recognition for our cooperative efforts, to the point where former First Lady Hillary Clinton, in 1997, came to talk to our group for over two hours. Unfortunately, at the state level the political winds were changing and the progressive thinking of the '80s was replaced with the election of a Republican governor. The newly appointed department director had close ties to former President George H. Bush, and decades later, to the Trump administration. The advocacy for disabled persons I had been part of for more than a decade was seen as a threat to their fiscal conservatism. At the close of the 1990s, opposed to my advocacy efforts, I was threatened with being fired. Unable to do so, because of my reputation as an advocate, he chose to close the Marquette office, forcing me to come to work in Lansing. Little did he know that this move also started me on one of the most personally rewarding careers as state traumatic brain injury director—a job I held within the department until retirement in 2007.

During this decade, my children were all in school and doing well. Steve, the oldest, graduated from high school in 1997 while I was serving on the school board. A moment I will never forget occurred when I was proudly able to hand him his diploma on the stage, in front of family and friends. Karen did not want to move downstate, resulting in my having to commute six and a half hours each way on weekends between Lansing and Marquette.

The times living in Marquette provided many highs, lows, and sadness. Commuting was stressful and it took its toll on our marriage. Marie, Anna, and Steve missed not having me there. Once in Lansing, I commuted two hours each way during the week from Benton Harbor to Lansing. The Benton Harbor house was available after my mother's passing in 1997 where she had lived alone since Papa's death in 1993 (Their passing will be described later). The stress of those commutes forced me to rent an apartment in Lansing, requiring a second job at night in a convenience store and later a distribution warehouse so I could pay for it. Steve joined me later and for eighteen months we were roommates.

CHAPTER 12

NEVER HAD A CHANCE TO SAY GOODBYE

We were a close family. As the only child, my parents had always been there for me. I had no brothers or sisters to guide or help me. Mutti and Papa raised me, taught me, and protected me.

As I grew and became my own man, with a family and job, I was not always consciously aware of them my parents—I was too occupied with my own life. Still, they were always there, only a phone call or a trip away. On holidays and special occasions, I could share with them love, good times, good food, and gifts. I could share special moments as their grandchildren were born and grew up, and their school events and sports. Important occasions in their lives were celebrated with Oma and Opa. Then, one day, you realize your parents are gone—tragically, as in my dad's case, or slowly, as in mom's case. Suddenly, that security, that bedrock of your life, is no longer there. You never really realized it was there, and yet it was, and it sustained you. And then you don't have them to turn to any longer, to share your joy, happiness, or problems as you had done forever. A black hole opens up in your heart, and your life has to be recalibrated.

My recalibrations occurred four years apart, and under very different circumstances. Although Mutti's death was inevitable, the pain was no less. Still, it does not compare with the pain of losing Papa, because I never had a chance to say goodbye. Only a smile and a wave, and the memory of a hug are what I have as a parting memory.

He Would Be Proud

March 3, 1993, Grand Rapids, Michigan. All day I had been waiting for this moment, anxiously looking down the hallway to see if I could see them coming. Mutti and Papa had driven from Benton Harbor to see Richard and me at the Amway Plaza Hotel, where the Michigan Association for Exceptional Children's annual conference was taking place. My parents knew Richard's story well. He had been mislabeled and inappropriately placed into an institution for the developmentally disabled for seventeen years. They knew how hard we had been working to tell his story, specifically to educate others about people with mental or intellectual disabilities and to fight the stigma of mental disabilities.

Mutti & Papa using disability kiosk.

Richard had been a visitor to their house on many occasions, and they loved him—especially my dad, who did not know much about disabilities but was very impressed with what Richard had accomplished since being on his own. Mutti was impressed that Richard was incapable of being bitter, always having an upbeat spirit. And Papa felt compassion for his struggle, which I think he identified with as an immigrant, trying to find your way in a new world while not always understanding what was going on around you.

After a wonderful dinner together, Richard and I had gone ahead to prepare our project, the Mental Health Educational Exhibit. Throughout the day, attendees had come to try out our kiosk, a tool that educated students about mental disabilities. We encouraged teachers to try it out in the hope of bringing the kiosk to their school districts. Using a touch screen, the user could bring up information about any mental disability and see videos of people with disabilities explaining what their lives were like. This was before the internet or YouTube, not to mention smartphones. PCs were just being introduced to classrooms, and laptops and tablets were not yet available. It had been my job, over the course of two years, to develop the concept of the kiosk, help write the script, hire the professionals we needed, and raise the funds for its creation. The videos were created using actors with disabilities. Users could play a game that dispelled myths about disabilities and "Learn that it's OK to be different," which was the underlying theme of the exhibit. This conference was our big launch for the project.

The computer technology was state of the art for 1993. We used an Apple Macintosh computer to run a program that was loaded on a twelve-inch gold-plated disc. This Mac was the most sophisticated device of its kind available. Educators favored Apple computers, in part because the company made them available cheaply to schools. Few people knew about touch screens, and the educators who came by were amazed by the technology. The computer sat in a bright red box the size of an ATM, with only the touch screen visible. A few feet behind the kiosk were four large cloth panels serving as a backdrop. Each showed pictures of people with disabilities and their stories, including Richard's. Bright maroon signage with gold headers against the camel-colored cloth covering provided an attractive and welcoming display.

Richard and I were sitting in front of the kiosk when I glanced to my left, down a hallway between exhibitors' booths, when I caught sight of Mutti and Papa. My dad looked from side to side, intrigued by the various exhibits, while Mutti searched for us. As they approached, Richard and I got up from our metal folding chairs to meet them. I gave Mutti a big hug while Richard stuck his hand out and shook my dad's hand vigorously, saying, "Hi, Dad!" He turned to me to add, "You know because he's your dad, he's my dad too!" We all laughed and bade both of them to sit down in front of the terminal.

Richard started out, proudly explaining, "Here, let me show you what it's all about," while touching the screen with his finger. Up came a tic-tac-toe square, and a voice said, "What would you like to do? Touch any of the boxes to continue." Richard beamed with excitement, and my dad inched closer to the screen. Richard explained that all Papa had to do was touch one of the boxes, and a story would come up.

Mutti urged Papa to try it. He touched one of the boxes on the screen and was amazed when the screen changed. A video came up, showing a young man on an empty stage pointing at them and saying, "Now that word, *disability*, let's talk about that. We are all different. No one is alike . . ." My parents listened and watched in fascination. After the first story was done, Papa eagerly pushed the next box. Silent throughout, he pushed the next on-screen buttons as prompted, while Mutti let out gasps or a slight "Oh no" as the stories showed discrimination and stigmatization of people with disabilities. After about forty minutes, the program ended, and my dad sat back and said, "That is amazing, really interesting. How does this work?"

The engineer in him came out, wanting to know the technology behind what he had just seen. Mom turned to look at Richard and, with moist eyes, said, "I'm so proud of you." She took his hand in hers, probably understanding, for the first time, what Richard had gone through.

I took Papa around the back of the kiosk and opened it up to show him the Macintosh computer. I took out the disk, the size of an LP record, and explained that everything he had just seen and heard was contained on it. He looked at it with wonder, shaking his head with amazement. I explained that the story and pictures are translated into bits and bytes burned unto the disk and then read by the computer. Being a lover of technology, he was captivated by what he saw. I could see it in his eyes. He appreciated what this new technology could do.

He was not a man to show his emotions, I think, because he was afraid to look weak, but here was something that really impressed him, and he showed it. I recall, on holiday visits to our home in Marquette, he would not go to the Christmas Eve service with our family, knowing he would probably become emotionally overwhelmed by the pageantry. Perhaps he worried about it raising thoughts of his own Christmases growing up, afraid to shed some tears. Mutti asked me to accept this, even though it hurt not to have him participate with his grandchildren and family in the service.

We went around the front of the kiosk, and I could see he was very pleased. He gave me a big hug and told me that I had done a great job. That compliment meant a lot to me; my heart swelled with pride. It had always been hard to please him, but this night I knew I had. I felt good! Mutti looked on with a smile, recognizing the connection that Papa and I had made.

Richard asked them, "Well, what do you think? Will it help kids?" Both answered, "Oh yes," and reached out their hands to congratulate him. Then Dad broke off the gladhanding, saying they had to leave to get back home, at least an hour's drive. I reluctantly agreed; I'd rather have spent more time in the glow of this good feeling. We hugged once more, and I kissed both on the cheek as we parted. I watched them walk down the same hallway they had come. Each glanced back once, giving us a slight wave before turning left at the corner to walk out to the parking lot. I turned away from Richard so he wouldn't see the moisture in my eyes; my heart, though, swelled with pride.

The Longest Night

Fourteen days later, March 17, 1993. It was about 10:20 p.m. as I walked into our house in Marquette. It had been a long day. I had worked in my office until about three thirty and then driven to the Dickinson–Iron County Community Mental Health Agency's board of directors meeting, about an hour and a half away. The meeting had run longer than expected. It being March in the Upper Peninsula, a snowstorm had started while I was in the meeting. In Iron Mountain, in the northwest central part of the Upper Peninsula, the weather was not yet too bad; nevertheless, I had to drive carefully on the snow-covered roads, watching for the ever-present deer attempting to cross the road. The weather forecast had warned of a nor'easter coming in from the peninsula's eastern side. Nor'easters are particularly dangerous snowstorms because they pick up a lot of moisture coming over Lake Superior and then dump it once the system hits land.

I walked into the quiet house, knowing that the kids were asleep on a school night. When I stepped in from the garage, our family room was dark. *Strange*, I thought. Karen would usually be watching TV there, waiting for me to get home. Hanging my coat on the hooks next to the door, I walked up through the kitchen into the hallway, past Steve's bedroom and into our bedroom. Karen was sitting with Anna, our second oldest, on our bed, both looking ashen. Karen had her arm around Anna, whose head was on Karen's shoulder. Anna has always been a sensitive child, and I could see she was upset.

"What happened?" I asked, thinking that something bad had happened to Anna. I took off my suit coat and started to loosen my tie.

"I've got some bad news," said Karen. "Sit down."

"No, go ahead, what is it?" I replied in my usual self-assured and know-it-all tone.

"We got a call about forty minutes ago that your dad has been hospitalized with what they think is a heart attack. Your mom is in the hospital with him, but they do not know yet how bad it is. A nurse from the ICU called and left her name. You need to call her back to find out more. Ask for her when you call." She reached across Anna to hand me a slip of paper. This was in the days before cell phones, so there had been no way of getting hold of me until I had arrived home.

Stunned, I took the piece of paper and walked back down the hallway to the living room where we kept a phone on Karen's work desk. My heart was racing like crazy as I dialed the number, thinking, *What happened, how bad is it, is he OK?*

"ICU," came a voice when the phone was picked up. I identified myself and asked for the nurse, whose name, ironically, was also Karen. She came on the line, and I identified myself, by now barely able to get the words out, my heart beating out of my chest, breathing hard.

"I'm sorry, Mr. Tatzmann," the nurse said somberly and very professionally, "but it appears your father may have had a serious heart attack. Your mother is here with him. From what she tells us, it sounds like he collapsed in their dining room around eight o'clock tonight. He was in pain but refused to have your mother call an ambulance. After an hour or so with no change and unable to move, your mother called the ambulance anyway. They rushed him here and have been working trying to stabilize him. He is in very serious condition. Where are you? You might consider coming here as soon as you can."

I only heard the words "He is in a very serious condition" and "come as soon as you can," nothing after that.

"Mr. Tatzmann, if you do come here, please ask for me, and call us back at any time for updates. Either one of the other ICU nurses or I will be able to give you an update. Your mother is very upset, but we will take good care of her."

"Thank you, "I stammered, "I'm on my way."

I walked back into the bedroom, and the look on my face must have given away the seriousness of the news because Anna started crying. She was close to all of her grandparents—more so Karen's, but she loved both sets immensely. Karen was trying to hold it together to support me. I briefly described the situation for them as I reached for the top shelf of our bedroom closet where I kept my traveling suitcase. My job required a lot of travel, including once-a-month trip to Lansing to meet with my bosses. I kept a partially packed, black soft-sided carry-on handy. I opened dresser drawers and pulled out underwear and socks. Karen, realizing what I was doing, said she would put some hot water on for tea.

I got a couple of shirts and some slacks out of the closet and then hesitatingly looked at my formal black suit, covered by a plastic suit carrier, and a white shirt next to it. Not wanting to think of the possible necessity, yet understanding reality, I threw the suit on the bed next to the carry-on and placed the white shirt on its travel hanger, laying a black tie on top of it. I pulled out my formal black dress shoes and stuffed them into the carry-on, along with a set of black socks.

Karen put her head in the door and asked how many tea bags I wanted in my cup. "Three," I replied. Both of us knew what was in store for me. This was one of the times when I wished I were a coffee drinker, but I knew that I needed a clear head for what was to come. Karen prepared the tea and came back into the bedroom. Karen told Anna to get under the covers; she could sleep in bed with her tonight. I think that was for both their benefits.

I zipped up the carry-on, went to the bathroom, kissed both goodbye, and grabbed my bag and suit. Turning at the door, I asked Karen to let my mom or anyone else who called know that I was on my way. I said that I would call her first thing in the morning with any update, knowing that the kids would need to get up early for school anyway. The car was still warm inside as I pulled out of the driveway, but the tracks I had made coming home were already covered by a layer of snow and no longer visible. It was going to be a long night.

Only two roads run the entirety of the Upper Peninsula from east to west. M-28 is the northern route. Coming out of Marquette, it runs along the shore of Lake Superior for long stretches until after Munising, when it moves inland through the middle of the peninsula. It's subject to severe lake-effect snowstorms, when the wind causes whiteouts that make it impossible to see the hand in front of your face. The state police sometimes close it when drifting snow creates high berms across the road. The other major east–west road is US-2, the highway that hugs the shore on the top of Lake Michigan. Truckers coming from lower Michigan and traveling to Wisconsin and Minnesota used this road frequently. It is better traveled than M-28, where, on some late nights, I have driven for an hour and not seen another vehicle.

Seeing the snow pile up, and knowing a nor'easter was on its way, I decided to head south out of town. The ship the *Edmund Fitzgerald* sank during such a storm. Not wanting to get stuck somewhere in the middle of the Upper Peninsula in a blinding snowstorm, I took my chances on the storm being less severe on the southern route.

Coming out of our subdivision, I turned left onto M-41. By now, it was a bit after eleven o'clock, so there was no traffic. I pushed the gas pedal as far as I thought safe, not too worried about the snow. Rather, I focused on looking for deer, which were especially bad around Trenary, about halfway to Rapid River, where I needed to turn east on US-2. The last thing I wanted was an accident that meant my mother would have to attend two funerals. Still, I was pushing well beyond sixty miles per hour on the fifty-four miles to Rapid River. By the time I got there, I realized that I had neglected to check how much gas I had, having already driven many miles today. The gauge showed only a quarter tank left. Knowing there were few gas stations open between Rapid River and St. Ignace, I stopped at a little white house with two pumps in front of it.

I got out and inserted the nozzle into the tank. Not wanting to freeze in the cold wind, I stepped inside and found three guys sitting on stools, each wearing a thick woolen parka. One guy was behind a counter—the owner or manager, I assumed. They greeted me suspiciously, probably wondering what anyone was doing out on a night like this. Likewise, I wondered what these three guys were doing up so late, sitting in this place.

I simply said, "Hi," and grabbed some munchies off a metal rack near the door—mostly sugary stuff, to keep me awake. The guy behind the counter buttoned up his parka and went outside to read the meter on the pump so I could pay. While he was outside, I asked the other two guys if they had heard what the road conditions were going east. "No," both replied, but based on the weather conditions, they did not think it was too good; both quickly added, though, it was probably better than "up north," meaning M-28.

"Where are you going?" one guy asks.

"My dad is dying in a hospital downstate, and I want to get there," I replied.

"Oh shit, I'm really sorry for you," the one closest to me said.

The other guy came back in and rang up my munchies and the gas. I paid and went back out, wiping off snowflakes that had gathered on the car while I was inside. Taking in a couple of deep breaths of fresh air, I took off my coat and threw it in the back seat, then got into the car and turned into the darkness of US-2. With the snow coming down hard, the darkness was total. The only view out the windshield was large snowflakes streaming toward me; everything else was black.

Prior experience had taught me that it was dangerous to stare straight into the snow coming down. One can become easily hypnotized and drift off the road. I kept my eyes moving from right to left and back to avoid being entranced and to spot any deer that might want to cross the road. I knew the odds of a deer jumping out at this time of night were slim, since they had enough sense to hunker down somewhere during a snowstorm. Nevertheless, the vigil kept me awake. I was driving on adrenaline and knew it.

I saw no other vehicles on the road. Whenever the snow let up a bit, I pushed the car to eighty and beyond. I barely slowed down as I flew past the state police post in Manistique, knowing that at this time of the night, the town was asleep and the cops probably were not out. I saw four out of their five squad cars parked in the lot next to the building and felt safe that I would not be stopped tonight, fully aware of how long it takes to get to Benton Harbor. I was doing everything I could to make good time.

Almost two hours later, the storm let up a bit. In the distance, I saw the lights of Big Mac, formally known as the Mackinac Bridge, the seven-mile span connecting the Upper and Lower Peninsulas. As I got closer, I saw Clyde's Drive-In diner on the left. Normally, whether with family or alone, I would stop to get one of their famous hamburgers, greasy and loaded with mustard and sweet onions. Clyde's is a Michigan tradition. Closed tonight, it served as a way marker, giving me slight hope that I was making a good time. Once I crossed the Mackinac Bridge I would be on I-75, where I could make even better time. The state highway department did a good job of keeping the road clear, and I knew the road well from traveling to Lansing for meetings at least once a month. The sixty-mile stretch south of the bridge to Gaylord, especially around Vanderbilt, was known as snow alley. I hoped that tonight's winds and snow, coming out of the north, would not yet have affected this part of the road.

I crossed the bridge close to 2:00 a.m. With no other southbound traffic, I zipped down the highway, hitting a hundred a couple of times when I felt it safe to do so. There was no traffic on my side of the highway. I saw only one Detroit *Free Press* truck heading north, apparently delivering newspapers to the Upper Peninsula. In under forty minutes I reached Gaylord, a popular stopping point for tourists and vacationers on their way to the Upper Peninsula. I needed to stop for a bathroom break, but more importantly, now three hours later, I needed to call to find out my dad's status. I pulled off the highway at the first exit and walked into the closest motel, a Comfort Inn. I'm sure I must have been a sight walking up to the desk, exhausted and in a state of deep anxiety.

I asked the desk clerk for a room, and she said they had plenty available. I explained my situation and asked if they had a half-day rate since I was only planning to stay for two or three hours to rest up and use the phone. No, she said, they do not have a half-day rate and was unsympathetic to my plight. Reluctantly and upset, I paid in advance, took the keys, and went to my room. I went to the bathroom, washed my face, and then sat at the edge of the bed and withdrew from my shirt pocket the piece of paper with the ICU phone number and name of RN. I dialed the number, and a nurse answered. I identified myself and asked for Nurse Karen. After a minute's wait, Karen came on the phone. Before I could say anything, she said, "Mr. Tatzmann, I'm sorry to tell you your father passed away a half-hour ago."

She explained that my mother had a chance to say goodbye to him and that some family members were with her now. Through tears, I asked what caused the death, and she said it was a heart attack. By the time he came into the hospital, she said, too much damage had been done to his heart, and they could no longer save him. "I'm truly sorry for your loss," she said, sounding very comforting. I could barely get a "Thank you" out and hung up the phone. I had to get to Benton Harbor as soon as possible, now to comfort Mutti.

Exhausted, I laid my head back on the pillow and wept. After sleeping for only an hour and a half I woke, probably from the adrenaline kicking in. I washed, got gas and a Starbucks coffee in a glass bottle, and headed out again. I needed the jitteriness of the coffee to keep me going. Every now and then, I rolled down the window to get a blast of cold air to refresh me.

Driving as fast as I thought prudent, "half an hour" was all I could think of! Should I have stopped somewhere and had them place a phone next to him so I could say goodbye? Where, though? Nothing was open along that stretch of road. It hurt so much, not having been able to say goodbye and tell him how much I loved him.

There was no snow blowing in this part of the state, but my vision blurred with the tears that kept coming back into my eyes no matter how often I wiped the back of my hand across them. My thoughts raced to the question of how important that last hug was and my last look at him as he walked out of the conference hall in Grand Rapids. Knowing that it was my last image of him, forever.

Near 6:30 a.m. I briefly stopped at a Shell station in Cadillac, knowing Karen would be getting the kids up for school; with a choking voice, I told her the news. She asked if I was OK after driving all night. I didn't say much because I couldn't. I just tore myself away from the phone. Adrenaline cursing through my body.

With tears still in my eyes, I arrived in Benton Harbor about eight thirty in the morning. Mutti opened the door, and for a few seconds, we just stared at each other; then we threw our arms around each other, holding on tight. Surprisingly, Mutti did not cry, but she was very happy that I was there. I sensed a great deal of relief.

I picked up my bag and walked through the kitchen to the dining room. The large dining table that always stood in the middle of the brown area rug was at an angle, apparently where the EMS guys had moved it to help my dad. There were no stains or spots where they might have spilled some IV to indicate where he might have lain. I stared at the space on the carpet where I knew he had fought his last fight.

It occurred to me that the last two generations of men in my family had met this fate, dying of a heart attack in March of their seventy-second year. In 2018 I would be diagnosed with a genetic blood-clotting condition that causes pulmonary embolism. Chances are good that my dad, grandfather, and I believe, great-grandfather all died of a pulmonary embolism incorrectly diagnosed as a heart attack.

Looking into the living room, I saw a sheet, comforter, and pillow on the green recliner where Mutti must have gotten a few hours of sleep. As exhausted as she must have been, she had not been able to sleep the previous night in the bed she had shared with Papa for forty-eight years. Turning away from me toward the kitchen, she said she would make us both a quick breakfast. Then we would need to go to the hospital to get his body released to the funeral home. I took my bags and suit into my former bedroom, now a guest room, and got cleaned up for a long day ahead.

After a brief breakfast of *Brötchen*, fresh rolls with butter and jelly, we got in the car and drove to the hospital. On the way there, she told me what had happened, and I could hear the pain and guilt she felt about not calling the ambulance sooner. Why had she listened to him? Why was he so stubborn and proud? I told her we both knew how stubborn he was about health care, something that ran deep in the family; and continues still. Nevertheless, the guilt never left her, even until her dying days.

Karen and the kids came down a day later. Many people attended his funeral on March 20, 1993, his seventy-second birthday. Dad had worked for LECO for over thirty years and made many friends. Those who knew him from the German club he helped to found also came to say good-bye. He and Mutti had been instrumental, along with four other couples, in starting the Benton Harbor chapter of the Deutsch-Amerikanischer Nationalkongress (German American National Congress), or DANK, for which he served as treasurer for many years.

Although he worked in totally different field at LECO, his early days as a mechanic never left him. Weather permitting, he could be found in the garage working on a car or an old used tractor, prone to breakdowns. He loved mowing the almost three acres of lawn on which our house sat, especially when any of the grandchildren visited. He'd give them rides on his lap or in a trailer behind the tractor. Even though he didn't get many chances to see them, Opa loved his grandchildren and always asked about them. He was not prone to shows of emotion—except when it came to his grandchildren. He let his inner child come out on those occasions, and he would play with them and be silly and carefree, breaking down his Austrian stoicism.

He did not have an easy life. The war was hard on him; then, he took his family and start a new life in America, not knowing the language and having little money. Yet, he always had a job, and although never rich, he made sure his family was never without necessities. His great joy in life was spending time with friends and family.

Papa transformed an old, dilapidated farmhouse into our home, a gathering place where card games, board games, and love prevailed. Mutti's dinners were always a reason to celebrate, no excuse needed to have friends and family over.

Looking back, I wish Papa and I could have been closer. We loved each other immensely and yet were never really close. Our individual stubbornness and egos got in the way. In many ways, I deliberately opposed him. Why? Just to prove I could be my own man. In games we competed fiercely, never giving each other an edge. It's stupid to say, but we were never friends. I'm sure it hurt him that I never took up one of his passions—chess. He was very intelligent and could play three games at a time, which he usually did during lunch breaks at work. My own stubbornness didn't allow me to learn, even though it would have pleased him immensely.

My life's biggest regret is not having had a chance to say goodbye to him—to let him know how much I loved him!

CHAPTER 13

A VISION IN THE CLOUDS?

The midafternoon September sun beat down on me as I jogged down the country road an hour after having watched Mutti being wheeled out of the house in a body bag. Exhausted—although not from running only a mile and a half—I stopped at an intersection, set my hands on my knees, and took a deep breath. The ordeal of the last two weeks had ended today.

A warm breeze floated over me. Something told me to look up into the blue sky at the large white puffy clouds. I saw my mother, father, grandmother, and other deceased family members very plainly, all looking down on me from behind one cloud. Looking like she was in her late twenties or early thirties, my mother smiled reassuringly. She was there for only a split second, but I could see she was happy and well, much better than she had been for the last three years. Was the vision real, or was I hallucinating? My heart still tells me it was real.

After a courageous three-year battle with cancer, Mutti had been in hospice care at home for the last two weeks. Her opponent started as breast cancer, and eventually became lung cancer and, finally, a liver cancer that killed her. Thankfully, through the final two weeks of this ordeal, I had not been alone. My aunts Elschen and Helga, and my uncle Fritz, among other family members, came out to comfort her and help me care for her. Helga, the youngest of her three sisters, stayed with me at my parents' house, where I had lived until I went to college. I had always looked up to Helga and considered her more like an older sister. I only called her "aunt" when I wanted to tease her. She lived with her husband and two daughters in New

Jersey, where she was the bookkeeper for his plastics business. Elschen was the second oldest of the four sisters in the family. She lived nearby in St. Joseph, by herself, after my Uncle Gunther died. Her son Detlef and his family lived a short drive away from her. Fritz, the only remaining son in the Lenk family, had flown down from Edmonton, Canada, to be with my mom. He was pastor of a German Church of God and provided spiritual comfort to all of us during this difficult time. Before moving to Edmonton, he had been pastor for a German congregation in Stevensville, Michigan, attended by family members on my mother's side.

During the last two weeks, when Mutti knew the end was near, having her sisters and brother nearby had provided her a great deal of comfort—more so, probably, than the pain medication she was on. Fritz prayed with her and read to her from his German Bible, and together the siblings sang songs they had grown up with in Germany. Many had been taught to them by their father, a man of great faith and spirituality.

Helga would repeat her selfless caregiving twenty-three years later, in 2020, when Aunt Elsbeth was in her last days due to heart failure. It also allowed her to be close to the other sister, Frieda, who lived a few miles away and suffered from a form of dementia and weakening physically. Frieda and her husband, Helmut, had retired to Florida a few years earlier.

Fortunately, Frieda's granddaughter Anita was there to care for her over her last three years. Elsbeth and Frieda would die within two months of each other in 2020, and Fritz followed them two months later. Sadly, due to the Coronavirus pandemic, I could not attend any of their funerals.

Throughout Mutti's last days, I had spent a lot of time with her, holding her hand, stroking her head, and telling her about her grandchildren. Sometimes we reminisced about events and things we did as a family. In her last week, we were not certain how aware she was of our care and love. Was her body giving out, or was the morphine she was on making her so sleepy that she was not aware of those around her? In the last two days, Mutti's breathing became labored. I kept wiping her parched lips with a moist cloth and dripping water from crushed ice into her mouth, hoping it would provide some relief. We all knew that the end was not far off.

Remembering the experience with my dad, each night I leaned my cheek against hers for a minute or two and kissed her goodnight before I went off to sleep—never knowing if that was the last kiss I could give her.

Helga and Elschen took turns sleeping in the bed next to Mutti's hospital bed. On Saturday morning we could see her breathing was very labored, and at 2:35 p.m. she took her last breath. I kissed her goodbye one last time, and we all gathered around to hold her hands while Fritz provided a final prayer.

A Farewell Journey

Mutti was aware of the possibilities of her cancer diagnosis. She described her journey in a journal she started two years, six months, and twenty-seven days before the end:

> After almost nine years of being cancer-free and feeling wonderful and frequently with much energy, I found out during an exam with Dr. Carter, on April 15, 1994, that my lungs had some fluid in them. They suspect it was the result of a cold during the winter months, which I could not shake. Dr. Carter ordered a draining of the left lung, which was not a very pleasant experience at all. Still, it had to be done since my breathing was difficult, and it was hard to catch my breath. For a few days afterward, I felt better, but then the same thing occurred on my right side. I had a lot of phlegm and pain on my right side every time I breathed. Dr. Carter speculated that it had to be something else and suggested a bone scan be done. The results showed that cancer had returned and spread. Further tests and X-rays confirmed the diagnosis.

A cancer specialist, Dr. Betty Koshy, was brought in, and she decided to approach the situation aggressively by immediately starting chemo. Manfred and I had a big meeting and consultation with her. She took her time to explain everything to us. She gave us both the good and bad news and explained what would happen with the chemo.

After Mutti's initial breast cancer diagnosis in 1985, she'd had a radical mastectomy, which we hoped would end the cancer scare. She and my dad spent the next eight years enjoying their retirement, visiting friends, and seeing their grandchildren in Marquette. That joy came to a crushing end for her on the evening of March 17, 1993, with Papa's death. Papa's death was hard on Mutti. They had been the love of each other's lives. Like most married couples, they had their differences but loved each other dearly. Throughout the marriage, Mutti had difficulties dealing with the Tatzmann family trait of stubbornness and control, causing many migraine headaches for her.

After Papa died, she was left alone in a large house—the same one they had purchased in 1963, only six years after immigrating—with a big lawn. Owning an old house always gave Papa something to putz around with, fix, or replace. But things that had given him great joy caused Mutti dread. How was she going to take care of everything?

They had minimal savings because their jobs had never paid well. Papa's company was too cheap to give its employees a pension; after he retired, they lived off Social Security. She worried: would she have enough money to take care of repairs? Luckily, the house was paid off, having cost only $4,600 when they bought it. The price was reasonable because it had been moved from a nearby location so I-94 could be built and was dilapidated when they bought it. For example, the former owner had used the basement as a garage. When we moved in, the basement had almost three feet of water in it. The three of us did most of the work to fix it up and make it our home. Mutti loved this house, and yet she was afraid because its location was not in the best area of town. For the first time in her life, she was all alone.

At this time, I was living in Marquette. Steve, Anna, and Marie were young. Work was difficult and kept me busy. At one point, Karen suggested that Mutti could move up to be close to us. Marquette had a good medical center where she could receive care. We looked at some condominiums where she might live, but she wanted to stay in the home she loved, near her sisters and her very large circle of friends. Instead, I used my monthly work meetings in Lansing as a chance to stop in, see her, and make necessary repairs, and, during the growing season, to mow the lawn. While she was glad to see me and cooked all my favorite foods, I could see the unhappiness and fear in her face each time. As often as I asked about her moving, she was steadfast in wanting to stay in the house. Still, I worried about her a lot. She felt a constant fear of becoming the victim of a burglary, or worse. Eventually, I think, it was stress that caused the cancer cells, dormant for over nine years, to return and attack her system again.

Once the cancer return had been discovered, her doctor decided that she wanted to treat this new cancer aggressively. Mutti decided to describe her journey through cancer treatment in her diary:

> *May 15,1994—I had my first chemo treatment. It didn't seem like it would be too bad at first. But then the following three to four days, it hit. I felt like nothing, tired, exhausted, nervous, and felt like sleeping all day. On top of that, I had a sore throat, couldn't swallow anything, and when hunger hit and I tried to eat something, the stomach didn't like it. Luckily, Dr. Koshy had prescribed some medication, which I had to take every four to six hours before eating anything, or as needed with a lot of water. She told me I should drink a lot of fluids, juice, water, or any other kind of liquid. It was especially important!! I was glad that the house's air conditioner worked so well since the clean air helped me breathe.*

May 31, 1994—I had an MRI of all my organs but haven't received the results yet. I don't feel too good, have no ambition, and am tired, but I'll bake a cake anyway because Manfred is coming.

This was so characteristic of her: no matter how tired and miserable she felt, only rarely did she let on. She gathered strength from giving joy to others. Cooking for friends and family, but especially for me, was one of her great joys. Over the next two years, as her body deteriorated, she could no longer go out to visit friends. Instead, she summoned all her energy and have them over for *Kaffee und Kuchen,* the traditional German afternoon coffee and cake. Although it was difficult for me knowing she was living in the house all by herself, I took some slight comfort and solace in knowing she had a great circle of friends and extended family members nearby to help her out.

June 3, 1994—Two weeks later, and my hair is coming out by the handful! I don't even want to comb my hair anymore since every time I do, more comes out. Tomorrow Reneé and Christa will come by [Christa is the wife of my deceased uncle Manfred; their daughter Reneé is a beautician]. Reneé will cut off the rest of my hair and fit me for a nice wig! On Monday, I have to go to the blood test again, and afterward, Gudrun [a friend] and I will drive by the Cancer Society to pick out two wigs. They don't cost anything, but I'll give them a donation.

Since Saturday, all my hair has fallen out, I'm a "baldy" again! I wore my wig for the first time, and it looks exceptionally good. Although around the house, I simply wear a turban. It isn't as warm as the wig and not as heavy. The temperature outside is unbearable, 85 to 90 degrees, and I don't even want to go out. I'm supposed to stay out of the sun anyway.

At the end of June, I'll start the chemo again. Right after that, I didn't feel too good again, and my Fourth of July weekend wasn't particularly good at all. I spent most of it in bed. Sometimes it feels as if I had a severe flu, but it doesn't do any good to feel sorry for yourself. It's something you have to work through if you want to get better.

Before, Manfred came down for each of my chemo sessions. It felt good not to be alone and have him here. He won't be here for the next one since the entire family will be coming for the weekend and then leaving on vacation from here. Herman, their sweet dog, will stay with me, so I'll have a little company and distraction.

August 31, 1994—Today, I'm to receive the sixth and final chemo treatment. Afterward, they want to treat me with medication. We'll see how that works out. Manfred is coming down again and will be with me at the chemo. The last and final chemo is behind me.

I'm looking forward to just being on medication. One tablet in the morning with breakfast and one tablet in the evening with dinner. The medication is expensive, but if it helps, it's well worth the money.

I had a thorough physical checkup and the doctor says I'm making good progress. My initial cancer count was 2,890, and now I'm down to 200. How they count that is beyond me, all I know is that the smaller the number, the better, and the chemo seems to have helped!!

February 1995—During this month, I had all kinds of blood tests and saw Dr. Koshy. She is pleased with me, and my blood pressure is also way down. I have to admit that I'm feeling quite good. Some days I get a pain here and there, but Dr. Koshy says I also have arthritis. During my chemo, I

found out I have lost twentysix pounds since I had no appe-
tite. I've gained five pounds back, but I still want to watch
it. Although I think it won't hurt to gain some more weight
back, just in case something else happens, I'll have some-
thing to fall back on and won't look too emaciated. I'll wait
and see what the test might bring.

May 1995—My tests on May 10 all went well. Dr. Koshy
was very satisfied. My cancer count is down to 120. My
blood tests and lab test all proved to be OK. The chest X-ray
looked good. They could not find any fluid on my lungs. My
blood pressure was down to 87/138. If I intend to go on a
trip, she will want to see me again in August.

August 2, 1995—All the tests came back OK, and she cleared
me to travel if I want to since I'll be on medication anyway.
She recommended I take someone along to help out, espe-
cially in carrying all the luggage.

We were all elated that Mutti had made it through all these treatments over the last year. It seemed to have worked. Mutti was very optimis-
tic that she had, with prayers and great medical care, beaten cancer again.
She knew the chemo had taken a toll on her body, and it was still not as
strong as before. Nevertheless, she felt good. Good enough that she wanted
to go see her family and friends in Europe.

I will never know what was in her heart, or deep down what she was
thinking. I'm sure that even though she never said it, she remained uneasy
that cancer could return at any time. So, while she was feeling good, Mutti
wanted to see her loved ones in Europe one more time. She had not been
there for a few years; the last time was with my dad. She wrote in her diary:

So, I decided one more time to travel to Europe from August
14 to September 4 and asked Manfred and Stephen to come
along. It didn't take much to convince them!! We are flying
with Lufthansa.

It was a special time for Manfred and me since he and I had not been back to Europe together since we left there in 1957. He had not been back for more than twenty-five years himself. It was especially exciting and gratifying that we could show Stephen our "Heimat." It was exciting for Stephen because he could try out the German he had been taking for two years in high school. He tried it wherever he could and made quite a lot of progress. He was very proud when people understood him, and he could speak with them. He was impressed with Germany and Austria and enjoyed seeing everything.

I was torn by the idea of this trip. I felt guilty about not being able to help Mutti, with me being stuck in the Upper Peninsula. Despite that, I knew in my heart that it would probably be her last visit to see family and friends. I was worried about Mutti paying for the trip since I knew her funds were limited. Additionally, I worried that the trip would take a great toll on her body, still recovering from the chemo. As Mutti put it in her diary, the trip was a "very special time" for all of us. Steve was sixteen, old enough to understand why the trip was important, and he wanted to help out. With a young family, I did not have the money for such a vacation, and Karen, unfortunately, had a problem with Steve going along, even though she knew it was Mutti's wish. (To make up for it, I would take Karen, Anna, and Marie on vacation to Cancun, Mexico, the next year.)

Saying Goodbye a Last Time

In Frankfurt, we rented a car and drove to Greifenstein, a small, old village in the Bavarian hills about an hour north of Frankfurt, where Mutti's' cousin operated a church camp and had a beautiful home. The plan was for all the cousins to meet there for a reunion.

At that time, we had no cell or smartphones, so when we arrived in Greifenstein we stopped at a pay phone to call her cousin for directions to his home. Steve and I got out of the car to stretch our legs while Mutti was on the phone. Looking around, Steve and I were hypnotized by the sweet aroma of baked goods. Like two cartoon characters, we followed our noses and drifted across the cobblestone street soaked by an early morning rain toward a bakery. I was overjoyed to be able to show Steve a real German bakery. We entered, and our nostrils exploded with the fragrance produced by shelves of freshly baked loaves of bread and trays of fresh hard rolls of all kinds. In bins sat brown, golden, smooth, round, and braided rolls, inviting us. Behind a large glass counter we found oodles of pastries. Staring at the sweet delights like two men who had been stranded on an island without food, we noticed that crawling around and over the scrumptious pastries were some kind of insects. I could see the shocked look on Steve's face. Both of us had been ready to dig into something, anything, sweet. Seeing insects crawling all over the pastry, our appetite faded. I looked instead at the loaves of bread, which were not covered with bugs.

A woman dressed all in white appeared from a doorway behind the counter. A hairnet covered her black hair. She had on a large apron dusted with flour, sugar, dabs of jelly, and food coloring.

"Guten Tag," she greeted me cheerfully. "Can I help you?" she asked in German.

I explained that we had just arrived from America, and I had been telling my son that I was looking forward to getting some real German pastries. Pausing, I looked at the pastries covered with insects. Feeling like a dumb tourist, I asked, "Are they safe to eat?"

She opened the back of the counter, pushing a glass door to the side, and lowered herself to look into the pastry section to see what I meant. I pointed to the crawling things. She reached in to grasp one of the sweets, and the nearby bugs flew away.

Laughing, she popped back up from behind the counter. "You mean you don't have this in America?" I let her know that a store would be shut down if it had bugs on or near the food.

She laughed, while another woman who had also come from the back looked at us questioningly and said, "Those are not bugs; they're *Wespen*"—German for "wasps." No larger than a half-inch from head to tail, they were remarkably busy. "The *Wespen* are good. They eat any bad bugs or even bacteria that may be there and keep everything clean. I know it looks strange, but they are our helpers."

I had never heard of such a thing, but it made sense to me. Knowing how strict the German government was about food purity, I felt satisfied. Steve and I got at least a dozen different kinds of sweets and proudly marched across the street, stuffing our mouths with goodies. Mutti saw us coming and broke out laughing, saying, "I knew it would not be too long before you'd find something like this! What did you bring me?" She told us that her cousin would meet us there and then we would follow him to his house in our car.

During the next couple of days, while Mutti was catching up with all her cousins, who had come in from different parts of Germany, Steve and I went exploring.

The city was named after Greifenstein Castle, which was built in 1169 but fell out of use by the mid-1600s. Although most of the buildings on the castle grounds had deteriorated, the local historical society preserved parts of it as a tourist attraction. Steve had never seen a castle up close and was intrigued. We spent the next few days exploring every part of it. The lookout tower was still in place, which gave Steve and me a wonderful opportunity to view the area from the top.

After a couple of days in Greifenstein, we traveled the famous German Autobahn through Bavaria to Austria. We stopped only once to overnight at a small village near the Bavarian–Austrian border, careful not to overtax Mutti's strength. The next afternoon we arrived in Graz.

Graz is the second-largest city in Austria, with close to three hundred thousand inhabitants. Few Americans have heard about it unless they are fans of the actor and former California governor Arnold Schwarzenegger, who came from a suburb of Graz (and with whom I rode a bus to school), or if they are associated with one of the international car companies. There is a good reason why Graz is called the Detroit of Austria. Most large car manufacturers have a plant there. It's located in a broad valley in the most southern part of Austria, an hour from the Slovenian border. The river Mur runs through the middle of the city.

I was astonished at how much everything had changed in my hometown. The two-lane roads used for commerce while growing up were now urban highways. Seeing a mall, including the Austrian equivalent of a Home Depot, shocked me into realizing how long I had been gone. How much our *Heimat* had transformed itself into a modern country.

Our first stop was a visit to my cousin Ingrid, or Inge, as we have always called her. She had inherited the house in which I grew up after my grandmother died, and she and her son, Oliver, two years younger than Steve, lived there. It was fun meeting Oliver, whom I had known only from pictures. Oliver's dad had left before Oliver was born. Inge raised her son alone, and their closeness showed.

It was an eerie feeling being in the house again. The last time I had been there was twenty-five years earlier, sitting with my grandmother in the summer of 1970. Now, it looked quite different. Inge had modernized it and changed things around. The corner bench under the kitchen window, where I had sat for hours and hours with my grandfather, was gone, replaced by cupboards. The small one-faucet sink that my grandmother used for everything had been redone to a modern counter and sink. Mutti was delighted to see the changes Inge had made to the home we knew so well. Oma had never wanted to make any changes.

The drafty bathroom, where we had once used newspaper instead of toilet paper, was gone, replaced by a modern bathroom with hot and cold running water and real toilet paper. I wistfully looked up the stairs to what used to be our apartment but could not go up because Inge had rented it out. Looking at the dark brown wood of the stairs going up took me back in time. I recalled the feet of family and many friends passing over them. They reminded me of a silly game I used to play when I was little, jumping from one set of stairs to the next, seeing how far I could jump and still land safely.

The basement, which had been a mess the last time I saw it, had also been cleaned up. It was almost sad, seeing everything orderly, not the clutter I had been used to. Nevertheless, on a back bench I found the old grape press that Opa had used to make his own wine. When I was about five or six, I would help as he picked the red grapes that grew in our yard and dumped them, supplemented by grapes grown by neighbors, into the slatted-wood press. The grapes, although called red, had a beautiful dark blue skin on them.

The wine press was about two feet tall and round, holding about one bucketful of grapes. Opa would turn the screw at the top, driving down a board that crushed the grapes. Deep red juice would come out of a spigot at the bottom of the press. Much as maple buckets are hung from maple trees to catch the sap to make syrup, the grape juice would run into a bucket hanging from the press. I would sit across from the spigot and every now and then dip my finger into the bucket. Opa would then transfer the grape juice to large glass containers to ferment over time, becoming wine. Glass tubes coming out of big corks at the top of the containers would show whether the juice was fermented. It was fun keeping a watch on the process over time.

After one pressing was done, only seeds and dark compressed skins were left at the bottom. They had to be fished out by hand, which was my job. By the end of the process, my hands were as purple as grape skin from dipping my hand into the mush. I snacked on some, but most of mush was spread in the garden. As soon as we dumped it out, birds would flock down and eagerly attack the grape seeds. The next day we would see the results all over the yard: purple bird poop everywhere.

Due to the weather conditions, we could not always grow enough grapes, so Opa made enough bottles to last him for more than a year. Occasionally, when Opa was having a small glass of wine, he would let me take a sip. I loved the deep rich flavors, sometimes a bit sour, at other times strong and flavorful. The taste has stuck with me to this day.

Showing Off My City

We did not stay at Inge's house. One of Mutti's best friends, Herta, was on vacation, so she let us stay in her apartment in the city's old section. It was a second-floor walkup in a large old building with many apartments. Steve and I loved the area. Mutti was delighted to be in an environment she knew so well, like the tapestry and furniture. She loved how the apartment was decorated, reminding her of what she might have had, had we stayed. It had a small kitchen, an eating area, and a moderate-sized living/dining room in a true European style. Steve and I shared the couch, which turned into a bed.

Behind the building we could see Graz's iconic Schlossberg. In front of the building, a tram went by every few minutes. The trams provided a clean, safe, and easy ride to anywhere in the city without worrying about parking a car. It was the same transit system for which my dad had worked, on which I used to go joyriding when young. For me, it was an ideal place—a place I would love to live again.

A small but fully supplied grocery store was a hundred yards left down the street from us. Directly across the street was a bakery, next to a café with garden seating. Two doors right from the entrance to our building was a butcher shop, and a few steps further down was an apothecary, or pharmacy as they are called in the United States. What more could a person ask for? A park and walking paths were less than a block away, while a wide and clean sidewalk ran along the street.

Most every day was warm, but not hot, with a blue sky. Steve and I enjoyed leaning out the window and watching the world go by. We observed people walking or getting on and off the trams, along with a few cars going by. The street was busy but never crowded. I still relish having shared these moments with Steve.

On a typical day I would drive Mutti to the home of whatever friend she was visiting, greet them and visit for a while, and then take off with Steve to see the sights. One day, I took Steve and Oliver to the Schöckl, the highest mountain in the area at a little over 3,000 feet tall. It did not compare with the Alps, hours north, and which easily are 10,000 feet and higher. We went up by cable car and viewed Graz and the countryside for miles around.

One day, when Mutti needed a rest day, Steve and I walked to the iconic Schlossberg, which rises to about 1,200 feet in the middle of the city and dates back a thousand years. The castle was never conquered, despite many wars fought around it. At the top, visible for miles around, is the clock tower or *Uhrturm*. Visitors frequently have a hard time figuring out the time of day when looking at its six-foot-high clock hands. That comes from a simple deception that started during Turkish invasions centuries ago. To confuse enemies, inhabitants of the castle reversed the hands: the short hand points to the minutes and the long hand to the hour. It has been kept that way ever since. Even today, it tends to confuse people. Steve was impressed with what he saw and the story behind it. A few years later, he had the clock tower tattooed on one of his calves to honor our heritage and his Opa. He also had a fighting tiger tattooed on the other calf to honor his other grandfather, a former Marine, who fought during World War II in some of the worst battles in the South Pacific. I am immensely proud of how he honors his heritage.

In the 1500s a cable system was used to haul goods to the top of the Schlossberg. Eventually, that system became a funicular car system that is still used today to ferry visitors up. The Schlossberg is the city's largest tourist attraction, with restaurants and a theater at the top. The theater's expensive box seats were originally prison cells carved into the bedrock of the mountain. During World War II, the city dug tunnels into the Schlossberg as a bunker to protect the citizens from Allied bombing of this industrial center. Now the tunnels are shopping arcades.

After two weeks, saying goodbye to our friends was heart wrenching. No one dared say it, but everyone accepted that it would probably be the last time they would see Mutti. The drive from Graz through the mountains into Bavaria was very solemn. Steve understood the moment's sadness and spoke little, just watching the beautiful scenery go by for hours.

The Final Goodbye

Our last stop was Frankfurt, Germany. Some very good friends of my parents, Albert and Inge Hiller, who had lived in Benton Harbor for many years, had moved back to Germany several years earlier to open a hotel and restaurant. I am godfather to their two children. By the time we visited in 1995, they had sold their business and were enjoying retirement.

One of Steve's best friends from high school was an exchange student in a city nearby. Steve had arranged to catch up with him, so we dropped him off with his friend's host family. The boys had a night out, enjoying German *Gemütlichkeit*, in this case, a lot of German beer.

Meanwhile, Mutti had a wonderful time reminiscing with her friends Ingrid and Albert about their times in Michigan. I could see the trip was becoming more and more physically exhausting for her. Yet, the joy she got out of seeing her longtime friends gave her strength and happiness. Though we didn't know it at the time, this momentum would carry her through the upcoming time of pain and struggle.

We spent the last two days in Frankfurt with my childhood friend Werner and his wife, Gudrun. Werner's parents, Mutti and Papa, had been the best of friends the entire time we lived in Graz; consequently, Werner and I grew up like brothers. They lived with her father in a beautiful three-story split-level home. Their garden, large by European standards, was filled with flowers and ornate shrubbery. Werner and Gudrun had two sons, both grown and living away from home. Gudrun's father was in his eighties, yet vibrant and fun to talk with. We had some great meals on their beautiful patio. Mutti shared many stories about the two families and us boys growing up, delighting Gudrun, who had never heard these tales of her husband's childhood before. Our two days there reconnected Mutti with a past that was immensely meaningful and happy for her. We drank a toast to those who could not be there—to Papa, and to Werner's parents, Robert and Herta—and relived the memories and joy of those days gone by. We all understood what an amazing life they had shared. For Mutti, it was the cherry on top of the cake as far as this trip was concerned. She hoped otherwise but knew cancer could come back at any time. So, she embraced this time as a possible closing chapter of her life.

A Valiant but Losing Fight

Mutti wrote in her diary:

Fall 1995—It will soon be fall and the evenings are getting longer. Many things are coming up soon. At the end of October, I have to have a blood test, X-rays, and bone scans again. I'm hoping everything turns out OK, but you never stop worrying! Elschen is hoping I will travel to Tennessee with her. Since both of us are alone and have no man to drive us, we thought we could share the driving. Before we head out, Elschen also has to have some tests. We'll have to see how things work out before we finalize our plans.

The drive to Tennessee didn't work out since Elschen had to have some minor surgery. Instead, we decided to fly to Florida and visit Friedchen and Helmut [her sister and brother-in-law]. Before heading out, I needed to get a few more tests and X-rays so that they would be available for an appointment with Dr. Koshy on December 6.

December 6, 1995—Dr. Koshy has been anxiously trying to reach me. When I saw her, I asked why she was so anxious to reach me? Did she have good news for me? She replied, good and not so good! The good news is that my bone density has increased; the bad news, that they have detected a spot on my liver, and I have to start chemo again!

1996—The first round of the new chemo was on December 28, 1995, for four and a half hours. This time it is different from before. At first, it wasn't too bad. Three days later, all my bones ached, followed a couple of days later with very severe back pain, which fortunately left after another three days. I felt quite good until I got a call that my white blood count was down again, and I had to take the Neupogen shots again. On January 29, I'm to have my second round of chemo.

My hair again began to slowly fall out. The comb and brush were already full of hair after the first chemo. On Friday, January 12, in the shower, I lost the rest! They just rinsed themselves off my head. As I came out of the shower and looked into the mirror, I was bald! So, my covering these days is again the turban and the wig. Be interesting to see how the hair will come back this time.

February 5, 1996—I hope tomorrow I'll have to have my last shot. With tomorrow's shot, I will have had eleven shots since the second round of chemo. I'm scheduled to have the next round of chemo on February 14. After that, Dr. Koshy will decide if I will need another round.

February 14, 1996—Unfortunately, I will need a fourth round of chemo starting March 6. For twelve days, I again receive the shots and feel good enough to drive myself to the hospital, but in two days, I'll have the chemo and will again not feel too good for the next two weeks. It will take some time after the next round to figure out if I need more chemo and how I'm doing.

May 5, 1996—In a couple of days, on May 8, I'll start my seventh round of chemo. After my last checkup, Dr. Koshy told me that the spot on the liver had shrunk. It seems the chemo did help! I asked her if that meant that we could now stop the chemo? She replied, "Not yet; we don't want it to come back!" I worked out in the yard a little bit each day. I have to take it easy because after a while, I can feel the pain in my back and have to rest. Nevertheless, it feels good to be able to do a little gardening.

June 19, 1996—I have my next appointment with Dr. Koshy and chemo. I'm hopeful that the news will be good and that I'll be able to stop with the chemo for a while.

June 23, 1996—It's been four days since the chemo and my shot. I don't feel very well. I hurt all over, my stomach is upset, and I just want to sleep. Tomorrow, the fifth day, things will begin to get better. By Thursday, the eight-day, I can stop with the shots. The exam on June 19 showed that the spot on the liver has shrunk again, but Dr. Koshy still believes it's too early to quit yet, so I had my ninth round of chemo that day.

September 11, 1996—Had my thirteenth chemo today! Dr. Koshy said I'm doing well. When I asked her if we could quit chemo, she said: "I can't force you; it's your life; but if we quit too soon, it could recur." She wants to give it another try in October or November. Starting with the fifth day, things are again beginning to look up again. I can quit after about nine shots, which is good because that will give me ten to twelve good days in between.

Since she said I was OK, Elschen and I decided to fly out and see Helga in New Jersey on October 12. We flew out of Benton Harbor, through Detroit, into New York, where Helga and Arnold picked us up. We had a beautiful and restful week out there. The weather was good enough that we could eat our lunches out on the patio. Friday the rain started, and it rained hard enough Saturday that even some of the streets flooded. On Sunday morning, the sky cleared, and we all went to church. Afterward, Arnold took us all out to lunch at a German restaurant. We loved the food and were full. By the time we got back, we were all ready for an afternoon nap. After that, we looked at some homemade videos and old albums, which brought back many childhood memories.

December 19, 1996—Had a checkup with Dr. Koshy today. She told me that she was afraid we'd have to start chemo again in February. I was shocked and upset! I asked her why, and she said my cancer count had not gone down, but we'll give it until the end of January to see what happens. She said not to be too upset since it has been only four weeks since I started the new medication, which for some people takes six to eight weeks to kick in. I hope and pray I won't have to go through chemo again! I feel momentarily much better and much stronger and try to take it easy as much as possible. My hair is starting to come back, and I hope that I'll be able to go out without a wig by spring. I've even gained some weight, and everything tasted really good to me.

February 1997—The exam showed I do not have to go back to chemo. X-ray of the liver and intestines did not show anything new, but Dr. Koshy was still concerned because the cancer count had not dropped but was "stabilized." Meaning, it hadn't gone up or down. She now wants me to wait until April and run further tests at that time.

Unfortunately, we couldn't wait until April, since mid-February I started having some very sharp pains on my right side. I tried to ignore it for a while, tried everything I could think of to make it go away, but nothing worked, so I ended up calling Dr. Koshy. She said she wanted to see me immediately. She checked me out and ran a series of tests—X-ray, etc. The next day I received word that everything was normal.

March 6, 1997—Saw her again yesterday, and she gave me the results of the bone scan and ultrasound. The bones have not improved. They found I had gallstones and kidney stones. She wanted me to have another MRI to examine it more carefully.

March 12, 1997—Saw Dr. Koshy again, and the news wasn't good! I still have the pain on the right side, and she said that could not be from the gallstones alone; it would not have lasted this long. The MRI showed that my bones are deteriorating, and she wants me to get another X-ray of my right side. She also ordered me to start chemo again on March 19, for three months.

I was so proud of all of my new hair, and now I'll lose it again! No matter, I won't give up and hope for the best.

Mutti took the pain and other side effects of cancer treatment bravely, rarely complaining. However, the loss of her hair bothered her greatly. We all thought she looked good. She had never been a vain person, but the loss of hair signified a loss of dignity to her.

March 19, 1997—On Wednesday, I started to new two-to-four-hour therapy for my bones, followed by chemo. I thought I had to have the bone therapy for thirteen weeks, but Dr. Koshy told me the bone treatment is only once a month, but the chemo is every week. The chemo will take only ninety minutes this time, instead of the three hours last year.

In 1994 I had seven chemo treatments. In 1996 I had fifteen. This time I'm supposed to have thirteen. After completing that series, Dr. Koshy wants me to have another bone scan to check for any change. Everyone wonders how my body can put up with all this! For some, it seems impossible. You just have to trust and have faith!

April 15, 1997—Today, it is two days after my 72nd birthday, and I had my fifth chemo. Don't feel too bad today, but it takes two to three days to hit me. Last weekend, for my birthday on Friday, I felt pretty good, so I made two cakes, some appetizers, herring salad, and some other treats. I took it easy. What usually took me two hours to make now took me six. It was a lot of fun! I took it easy, rested in between, and put my feet up. Just doing it gave me renewed energy.

"*Just doing it gave me renewed energy.*" It is important to consider this comment. This woman had been through hell for the last three years with chemo, radiation, and other medications. Her body was slowly but surely losing its capacity to recover. However, her comments are testament to the kind of person she was and how she lived her entire life. She wanted to bring joy to others!

When we came to visit, she made "two cakes, some appetizers, herring salad, and some other treats." She made the birthday treats she described in that entry when we came to visit. That was her idea of "taking it easy"—not sitting in a chair, watching TV, or even knitting, as she loved to do. This is who Mutti was—giving joy to others and cooking!

April 15, 1997, continued—On Friday, Manfred came down and took me to chemo and to get my shots. In the evening,

Tracy and Brian came down for a visit. I made dinner even though Manfred insisted on us going out. But I argued that if I cooked, it would distract me and give me something fun to do, so they gave in. It took some work, but I felt good. I made Rouladen, and for dessert, we had the cake I made. We really had a good time.

April 30, 1997—Today, I had my seventh chemo and surprisingly do not feel that bad. The last time I became very depressed and down. I asked myself how long can this go on??? I made myself a guinea pig. For two days, I've tried to go without Compazine medication. With the new chemo, I didn't feel good. I got sick at night and just felt bad.

So, we'll see how that turns out. Again here, God will be with me and protect me!

June 13, 1997—On the eleventh, I received my thirteenth and last chemo and today my last shot. I am glad to be done since Elschen and I have planned a vacation to Anderson, Indiana. Her church is having a big conference planned there. I've never been there before, so we decided to rent a trailer and attend. We had a really enjoyable time. Elschen took really good care of me and helped me a lot.

Using a wheelchair, she took me all over and to all the lectures and presentations. It was very interesting and informative to hear all of this. The candlelight service on Wednesday was very inspirational. Almost 7,500 people participated.

August 19, 1997—Received a call from the Clinic. Dr. Koshy wants to see me and talk to me about the lab results. I don't think it will be good news again! I will see her on the 24th, but in the meantime, I can't help but wonder what news she has for me now.

One can only hope for good news, but deep down, there are always worries!

That was the last entry in her diary. Her tests came back, showing cancer had invaded her entire liver and was affecting the spine. I received a call from Dr. Koshy one day in late August, telling me there was no good news. While it was possible that Mutti might live for another six months, it was more likely to be three to six weeks, and that I should prepare myself for it.

How does one prepare for the inevitable? You really can't! Even though I had known it would eventually come.

I decided to leave work and spend as much time with her as I could. She and I had some serious conversations about her wishes for once she was gone. She called her sisters to let them know the sad news. As the time got closer, her siblings arrived to help with her care.

Karen also came down from Marquette one weekend, bringing Anna and picking up Tracy, who was living in Kalamazoo. Knowing the state Mutti was in was hard on them, especially Anna, who is a very caring and sensitive person.

As the end came close, Helga and Elschen stayed with me at the house to take care of her, giving medication, bathing her, and changing clothes. Other close family members living in town came by during the last two weeks to say goodbye, bringing food and helping in whatever way they could. It was another sign of how much Mutti was loved.

Helga described Saturday, September 25, in the diary she kept and will use in her forthcoming book:

A little after 3 p.m., Elschen, Manfred, and I sat around Trautchen's bed. The hospice nurse had left us instructions on what to look for when someone is dying. At 3:15, we heard what has been described as a "death rattle." Elschen started saying the 23rd Psalm and a short prayer. But the

time the Psalm was done, no more breathing could be heard.
We closed her eyes and let her sleep.

She died in peace, knowing she was surrounded by the love of family and belief that she would see all of them again.

The vision in the cloud showed me that she was OK.

CHAPTER 14

REUNION

I rubbed my eyes and squinted as the sun streamed into the room through the half-open blinds. Maria's large bedroom window looked out over a small yard onto the garage and alley behind it. The window was high enough so that no one could see in, even standing in front of the garage. Maria and I liked to see the stars in the evening and the sun in the morning, so we rarely closed the blinds fully. I didn't know what time it was, but by the way the sun lit the room, I knew it was late in the morning, so we both slept in. I considered how the burnt-orange and yellow stripes alternated with dark shadows of the blind against the wall. *So, this is what a sunburned zebra looks like*, I thought, and laughed quietly at my own joke.

I gazed at the walls and recalled how one morning not too long ago, after some thoughtful examination, I had turned to Maria and offered to repaint the room. Sleepily but politely, Maria asked why I felt the room needed painting. I explained I had been looking at the walls while waiting for her to wake and noticed that their adobe-orange color had been unevenly applied. I assumed that she didn't know how to correctly paint a wall.

Gently, she asked, "Do you know anything about painting walls?"

"Of course," I answered proudly, and listed the virtues of all the painting I had done over years of homeownership and helping friends. "Have you ever heard of sponge painting?"

"What's that?" I asked, perplexed.

Looking me straight in the eyes, Maria raised herself unto her right elbow and explained that sponge painting was an easy faux finish that produces stunning pattern results. She was very proud of how the room looked.

"Oh, really," was all I could muster in response. I had just put my foot in my mouth by underestimating Maria, showing my ignorance and male arrogance. It would not be the last time.

Maria, I had learned in just a few short months, was a woman of great depth. On the surface she was a self-assured professional woman, not to be toyed with. But beneath that surface lay her great understanding of art and items of beauty and her magnificent intellect, which she hides behind her professional persona. Maria is most protective of her great sensitivity and shares this deepest layer of herself—the vulnerable little girl who wants to be hugged, held, and protected—with only a few people. This is no surprise, considering the trauma and emotional turmoil she experienced as a child, teenager, and adult. Totally opening herself up to others was not something that she did readily or naturally.

Turning away from the sunburned zebra walls and the thought of my old embarrassment, I smiled turned to look at Maria, still peacefully asleep. After the events of the previous night, when she experienced a bad nightmare, I was glad she was getting the rest. It was not the first time she had a nightmare that took her back to earlier days in Chile. I laid my head back on the pillow, listening to her calm breathing. Mere months ago, neither of us remembered the other's existence. Now it felt as if we had been together for years.

Eight months earlier, on March 13, 2005, I was shaking hands and accepting congratulatory remarks from audience members at a national conference of brain injury professionals in Baltimore, Maryland, having just finished my presentation. I had half an hour before the luncheon started, so I quickly went up to my hotel room to wash up and check my emails. I booted up my laptop and then stepped over to the sink. As I dried my hands, I heard the familiar Windows *dahding* and signed in to my email account. At that point, internet connections were made over landlines, so it took some time for my emails to load. I skimmed through the usual messages from coworkers and professional colleagues, and then one—subject line "One of those voices from the past"—caught my eye.

I had only about ten minutes before lunch started. Though I was anxious to get a good table, curiosity overcame my usual discipline and I clicked on the strange message. It opened, "Hi, I don't know if you remember me, my name is Maria, and we went to school together." *Maria who?* was my first thought. Then it struck me; could it really be *that* Maria?

My God, I thought, *it can't be her.*

A simple message, yet here was a person I had not seen or heard from in almost thirty-six years! A flood of memories raced through my brain. It was like one of those movie scenes where a person looks back on his or her life in a montage of images, people, and sounds rushing by in a swirl of my college days, friends, the time she and I had spent together studying or working. I also instantly flashed back to my two ex-wives, who had been housemates with Maria.

No, it really can't be her. It's been too long. Why would anyone look up somebody after all these years?

Maria had read in our university alumni magazine that I was speaking at the conference and spearheading Michigan's traumatic brain injury program. Even though she had not heard from me since our argument in mid-1970, she knew there was only one Manfred who went to that school at that time. She assumed that I would ignore her email, but she took a chance on renewing our acquaintance.

I knew I didn't have enough time to reply properly, and furthermore, I was skeptical about the authenticity of the message. I decided to type a quick response and see how the sender would react.

"No shit, it's really you?" I typed out. I hit send and left for the luncheon.

As I made my way through others already seated in the large ball-room, my mind was still speculating about the email. Dodging waiters carrying lunch on big, round aluminum trays, I finally found my assigned table, where colleagues and a couple of other presenters were seated.

"You won't believe what just happened to me," I said, sitting down at the last remaining chair. Skeptically, I described the email I had just received from a girl I had known thirty-six years ago in college.

"Are you the father?" one of my male companions sitting across from me asked with a chuckle.

"How did she find you?" asked one of the women.

"How well did you know her?" asked another woman, throwing out the same implication her male companion had.

Patiently, I explained that she had been a work-study student in the college language lab I supervised, also on work-study. I explained that she was from Chile, and I had taken her under my wing—that she was like a little sister to me, in protest of the implications thrown out earlier. Before I could explain further, a waiter delivered plates of chicken breast covered in a white gravy, five twigs each of asparagus, and delicious looking red potatoes in front of us. Looking at the gravy, I decided to double down on the breadbasket and make the potatoes my entrée. Besides, a mouth-watering slice of chocolate cake to my left was calling me to save it from abandonment.

Still, I could not let the implication go unanswered. "Seriously, after I left college, I never heard from her again," I mumbled as I stuffed a potato into my mouth.

"Well, obviously, you were memorable enough for her to look you up after all these years," said one of the women. She shared a sly smile and wink with the woman across the table, who agreed, "A woman would not go through all this effort, after all this time, unless there was something special there!"

"Really, you think?" I asked, mystified.

The two women gave each other a look that made it plain they thought I was clueless. Through the rest of the afternoon, I tried to figure out what to do next. Should I reply to Maria, or should I ignore her? I wanted to know more about her. Why had she contacted me?

By the time I got back to my room, it was after four thirty. I took off my suit and tie, washed up, opened a soft drink, and then heeded the siren song of the laptop. While it was booting up, my mind wandered back to the good times Maria and I had shared.

One email can't hurt. Be polite and respond!

I intended to approach her as objectively as possible. I had no clue about her current marital status. I did not want to get in trouble with a jealous husband or start something with a wife dissatisfied in her marriage. I wrote her a second brief note, thanking her politely for contacting me.

Seven days later, on Sunday, March 20, 2005, I received the following reply to my initial email:

> *This is interesting. For the last 30-some years, I wanted the chance to sit down and say to you that it was important for me that you understood this "kid" thought you walked on water. Now that the chance is here, I am not too sure how to start.*
>
> *My arrival at college and the years that followed were not only a middle-class family sending their daughter to study abroad, but there was also more to it. As I try to make the sentences, I realize that nothing makes sense if what I assume you thought at the time is not real. So, let me start there. For the two-plus years that we worked together and spent a considerable amount of time in each other's presence, you took on (or I placed you in) the role of a father/older brother. You were also the only man in my life. Often our conversations dealt with what relations were about,*

about men and women. You were my first boss. You taught me how to work, to be responsible, and to do the best job one could. To be responsible! You pretty much expected that, and I wanted to please you. I wanted you to like me, but under all this, there was another person. One that thought of herself absolutely unacceptable to a man like you. At the time, I could not have told you why, but I knew that I was "bad," and you did not know it; and that because of that, I could not let you (or anyone) get close. Therefore, periodically out of nowhere, I would do bad things, stupid things, which would leave evidence for others of how bad I really was, so that distance will be maintained. I know today that you must have cared for me. It never occurred to me then. I loved you with that pure sense of the unreachable. It was so easy to love you as long as I did not have to deal with myself.

When I got to know Judy and her roommate, I promptly stole from them, not because I needed it or anything else, but because you would know. Then you would not like me anymore, and I would not have to deal with how I felt about you. Complicated, I know! Strange, I feel like I am baring my soul here to a man I have not seen for 30-some years.

Life went on. I had a short, failed first marriage. Over time, I understood that I sabotaged relations on purpose. In 1978, I met a man I wanted to marry. Before I could blow the relation up, he was killed in a car accident, and I truly spiraled down into a bad depression. I went home. A year of painful therapy with a psychologist in Chile helped me put stuff in perspective and understand why I did what I did and how I did not need to keep doing it anymore. Dr. Kunifer (umlauts over the u) was Austrian; his parents had immigrated to Chile. There was a bearing about him that was so much like you. Over the course of therapy, your name and my relationship with you came up, and we talked about my wanting just to talk to you. To let you know how you had helped me survive at a time when it was so hard.

I was so lonely, so "on my own," and you were there. It was not until I was 30 that I asked myself for the first time, what was there for you? Why devote time and effort to this Chilean kid? You came and took me out for ice cream on weekends; talked me into studying in the library, and even once, when I was going to quit French, furious at the prof, you taught how the best revenge was to force him to give me an A. That has been a lesson I have used time and again.

I guess I want you to know that it did not go unnoticed, that the care and the time and patience fed my soul. There were times I got going in the morning because I had a lab to run, and you would be there. So sure of yourself, so willing to say, "Let me show you how." I always thought you were "older." How much older could you have been, a year or two at the most? I was 18, were you 20? Did this man really love me, and I was so screwed up that I missed it? Did I?

Did I really keep a warm spot in his heart for me, or did he just dismiss me as a "bad person," screwed up, and simply weird? I recall that once, over my dating someone or another, we had a heated discussion about sex. You were adamant in defense of virginity. You closed the door and practically yelled at me that I could not just throw myself away to any passing Joe. I had to "save" it for someone who really mattered. That love was what made it so special (another one of those forever lessons). I remember thinking, I wish that were true and that you really did not know about me because I could not afford for you to know me. I had not been a virgin since I was seven. Part of why I came to the US had to do with a broken engagement because I "confessed" I was not a virgin.

This message was the beginning of a flood of emails with each other.

"I had not been a virgin since I was seven." What did that mean? What was Maria trying to tell me? I read the message, and the shock of what I just read hit me full on. I had been so sure that I knew all about Maria, my little sister. Indeed, that's how I had always thought of her!

I pushed that comment aside. Her next email arrived:

> *Christ, this is longer than I expected it to be. Yes, I wondered over the years what happened to you. My being pissed at Judy, at the time, had to do with my knowing I loved you better, and there was no way to say that. I hope your marriage to her (did you did marry her?) went well, at least for a time. You deserved a good marriage. So here we are, so long past the time we saw each other every day for 3, 4, or 5 hours a day, in small little rooms. I wonder if we would even recognize each other. Could I pick you in a crowd? Would you know who I was?*
>
> *Take care, have a kiss 36 years or so late!*

I reached for the glass of white wine sitting to my left on the computer desk and absentmindedly took a large gulp. The taste of the Chardonnay going down created a comforting feeling as it hit the pit of my stomach. I was overwhelmed. I read the message over and over, each sentence taking me back to those times in college. My fingers scrolled the mouse up toward Maria's description of our days together. What were my feelings about her back then? Maria had never been more than someone who needed to be cared for, and taking care of people, whether they want it or not, is what I do. It's in my DNA!

I strongly believe I inherited this caring trait from my maternal grandfather. I hardly knew him because he lived in Germany, but in the few times we met, I learned that he was the kindest man on the face of the earth. He was a religious man who truly lived his faith. During World War II, even as his own family struggled for food and security, he took in a Jewish family until their escape from the Nazis could be arranged. He had to work hard all his life and had few comforts, yet he always had a positive and a spiritual outlook. Looking back, I believe I inherited some of his outlook on life. Therefore, it had been only natural that I would help my coworker Maria and anyone else who had a need or want.

Opa Ferdinand Lenk and aunt Helga.

Rereading Maria's note for the fourth time, something began to make sense. One time, at the end of my almost twenty-six-year marriage, my wife Karen accused me of carrying on an affair with Maria. Her assumption was based on a call she had received one evening from a Hispanic sound-ing woman who asked for me. When I came home late from work, she asked me if I knew where Maria was living.

"Who?" I asked, and then "Why?" I had not thought of Maria in years, yet here I was, standing in our family room, accused of being in contact with a woman I had not seen or heard from in decades. Now I won-dered, had Maria called that evening? Had she reached out to me before now? How did she know where to find me?

Occasionally, over the years, I had wondered what had happened to her after our argument. I envisioned her as a stay-at-home mom with a couple of children, married to a nice Catholic husband. Every few years, I would be reminded of Maria as I cleaned out my nightstand drawer and saw the small, decorated box of souvenirs Maria had brought me from Chile while we were still in college. It contained a set of silver spurs, casta-nets, and a bookmark. On the top shelf of the closet I kept the poncho she had given me; it still looked new more than thirty-six years later because I never wore it, preserving that keepsake from her.

I could not let Maria's message go unanswered. I replied to tell her about my intervening life. That small act started both of us on a new path that changed our lives.

March 30, 2005

Maria: *It is so weird to have you not be in my life for more than 35 years, and now we have almost daily contact. Food is a passion we share, though you must do something to counterbalance. In the picture, you looked as you did in school. My parents are doing great, still live in Chile. Up until the previous year and for the last 10 years, they came every year for 3 months and stayed with me. Last year, my mother was very ill, at death's door, really. She recovered, but for the foreseeable future, it's doubtful that they can make the trip back here. It is so far away, and such a long trip really is taxing on her system. Particularly, if you are 86 and 87 like they are. So instead, I just went to see them and will go back in December.*

April 8, 2005

Manfred: *Tell me more about yourself. Where do you live? In the city or suburb? Can you send me your address & phone number?*

Maria: *I live in a little house in N.E. Minneapolis. We have been here for about nine years since we moved from Michigan. It is a nice neighborhood, much quieter when we moved into this place, and even though there are some problems (minimal compared to other places), it is still a good place to live. We know our neighbors; the kids have "block friends," all of whom have grown up in my house. For their early teen years, my house was the gathering place, so lots* of them call me "Mom." Now that they are all moving out, working, etc., I don't see them as much, but they are still around.

April 12, 2005

Maria: *Now, I want you to think about this. For more than 36 years, you have had a special place in my heart. I am not sure why or what it is, and it does not need to be defined. It just is! However, I do not know you in the sense that an entire lifetime has gone by, and your thoughts and feelings have been shaped by your experiences. I am sure during all those years, there are things that you are not proud of, that you would want to have a do-over, or places and times where you did something that hurt someone, maybe even on purpose. So, have I. Welcome to life.*

I do know who you were at 20. Much has no doubt changed since then, but there was a core of decency, kindness, and love of whom you were that time, and experience does not change that. Nothing you say, do, think, or believe is going to change that. I might disagree with some ideas and will tell you so. Maybe even have a lively discussion about it, but it will not change the way I feel about you and would not turn me off so that I would stop being in touch. I want to make a deal with you. Nothing that you say or tell me will make me stop communicating. I want the same from you. We don't have to agree on everything, but I don't think there is any-thing that would justify stopping communicating either. If the time comes when either one of us wants to move on and stop communicating, let's talk about it and say goodbye like friends. It will not change the feelings that have been there for 30-some years. That will just go on. This became much longer than I thought. Sorry about that. Take care :-) Maria

As time moved on, each email became more serious, delving deeper into our lives. Finally, I suggested that we meet up in person to get to know each other again. I was, as usual, very formal about my approach, and she wasn't sure of my meaning.

April 18, 2005

Manfred: *Maria, I must eat some of my words! I have a BAD habit of not being able to spit out what I really want to say with some people. I need to explain my statement about "not feeling as comfortable talking on the phone and preferring the e-m." What I meant but didn't say was: I'm so happy and excited to see you that I don't want to take a second away from sharing everything that has happened to both of us since we last saw each other in person and do it by looking into your eyes and seeing that wonderful smile of yours again.*

April 19, 2005

Maria: *I was not going to have this conversation with you, mainly because I am enjoying this lot, and I do look forward to your emails on an almost daily basis. I do love the attention, but because I do like it perhaps a bit too much, I wonder if I am reading this right. It is considerably harder to read the intent of something said in an email than it is on a phone call. What I am trying to tell you is that your emails are not sounding like you are coming to visit an old army buddy, or a college buddy, or your little sister! You are tremendously complementary and somewhat seductive. Are you doing this on purpose? Is it just the way you talk to all the women in your life? This email stuff has many shortcomings. We can't laugh together. You can't hear if I am making a joke about anything or if I really mean it, and of course, you skip all the parts you want, and I can't hear your voice when you say the things you say in the email.*

April 20, 2005

Manfred: *Maria, I don't know! I have found our "synchronicity" fascinating. I, too, love to talk to you and check for emails. Quite honestly, in my mind's eye, you are still that girl in the AV room. I have refrained from again looking at your picture because there is a more mature and nicer looking woman than I remember. I'm just looking forward to spending time with you and catching up. I do recall your giggle and your smile and would love to see and hear it again . . . so yes, that is what I meant. However, I would be very dishonest if I did not share that somewhere deep inside of me, there is a wondering . . . has fate done this? Even so, that's playing with fire, so I try to stay away from that one. Lastly, maybe yes, I find the possibility of phone conversation threatening—you might lose faith in me, or it could go the other way—so, yes, opening deep inside of me . . . this form of communication does allow for a level of "protection" to avoid unintended intimacy.*

April 21, 2005

Maria: *I find it interesting that you think I could lose faith in you. What will I discover that you are human? That you, like most of us, are not all good, kind, well-intended, etc. That like most of us, you too have a dark side that you don't particularly like and try to hide from people. So, do I. Do most people that have the courage to look at themselves in the mirror and really see themselves?*

The truth of the matter is that you scare the bejesus out of me. Your term "cosmic Karma" has not escaped me. I, too, am taken from all the coincidences that our lives have had.

This might very well be a case of letting me scare you before you scare me more than I already am. Of what, I am not sure! I am a grown woman. I know myself, my needs, and wants, but you have such an advantage over me. I am trying hard to keep perspective on this. It occurred to me exactly as you said, knowingly or unknowingly, we were playing with fire, and I just wanted to put it out there. Are we setting ourselves up for a big letdown? No one is as wonderful as when looked at through the mind's eye. Are we memories of each other's past, when we were so much more innocent and have not gone through the hurt of failed marriages and separations? I loved you then, you know it. Now I could get hurt, and that scares me.

How Quickly Things Moved Along!

That first email was the plug in the dike of lost memories and feelings. As we connected via daily emails and then phone conversations, the three and a half decades between us were nothing but a lost day of conversation. I knew it was an argument that broke up our friendship years ago; yet try as I might, I could not remember what the fight had been about. I hoped Maria would not ask!

Late one the evening, near midnight, glass of wine in hand as I finished reading her most recent email, I found myself wondering, *Is this still a friendship, or is it becoming a relationship?* Both of us had gone through two marriages. If, by chance, this was going to turn into a relationship, the issue of trust and intimacy had to be addressed early on.

Maria, however, knew what she had to do if we met again. A bond existed, unmistakably, born thirty-six years earlier, and she needed closure.

During one of our daily conversations, she casually asked, "Would you like to go to a wedding with me?"

"Sure, when?" I replied without hesitation.

Her heart raced. *This is crazy!* she thought. She had not expected me to respond positively. For the first time in thirty-five years, she would be seeing me again.

May 11, 2005

Manfred: *I can just see both of us oldies but goodies on Friday night, a couple of glasses of wine, a dinner, and by 10:30 we'll be snoring in bed*

By the way in case I haven't already told you . . . THANK YOU for the invitation! I'm really glad you invited me to the wedding to meet your family and close friends. I'm truly looking forward to spending time with you at both.

Love, Manfred

I looked at the keyboard in front of me and realized I had just pushed the send button, telling a woman I had not seen in decades that I loved her! Not only that, but "We'll be snoring in bed" implied an assumption about our relationship and escalating it to a new level.

Now what? Well, it's out there now, and I can't take it back.

I absentmindedly stared at the screen, trying to grasp the implications of what I had just sent out. Distracted, I took another sip of wine and then tipped the glass onto a pile of papers as I set it down on the desk.

I scampered into the kitchen, desperately looking for some towels to clean up the spilled wine. Bringing papers into work smelling of wine would not be acceptable. After cleaning up the spill, I swiveled the chair away from the computer and glanced around the apartment and out the large patio door into the night sky. I wondered if I had done the right thing, signing off with "Love?"

Where did that come from? What was on my mind . . . in my heart? Did I really understand the step I had just taken? When, in this crazy interval of two months, had I fallen in love? Had it been there all along? Why, at this moment in time? If I really felt that way, should I have waited until we met face-to-face? Could I have told her the same words?

Ridiculous, I thought, realizing I had not consciously intended to close with that term. It came from my heart. Standing in front of the desk, I looked at the clock on the computer and I realized it was after midnight. I went to bed, wondering how Maria felt. What expectations had I created?

It had been only two years since I divorced Karen, the mother of my three grown children and former roommate of both Maria and my first wife, Judy. Since the divorce, I'd had an occasional date with dinner and a movie, but building a new relationship was not on my radar. Emotionally, I felt alone. I've never been a person who had a lot of buddies or hung out with other guys. Perhaps it was growing up as an only child. During last few years of my marriage to Karen I found a friend, Kathi. I got to know her through work—someone I could confide in and who provided me with emotional support. She was a school social worker and therapist at one of the mental health agencies with which I worked, and later at a school in the same community. She was my lifeline as I struggled with the loss of my parents and the stress my job imposed on our marriage. Kathi got to know Richard and was a member of the TBI group I chaired. With her in my corner, I felt comfortable being alone.

Suddenly, with one keystroke, I had potentially changed my life again.

Coordinating calls and even emails was tricky because we lived in different time zones. Although I was tired, try as I might, my thoughts would not let me sleep. I began to go back over the email and phone relationship we had developed. Slowly, I realized how every day I longed for a call or message from her. During the workday, I checked my email to see if she had sent a note or if she responded to the one I had sent the night before. Turning my head into the pillow, I drifted off to sleep from exhaustion, wondering, had I actually fallen in love with Maria years ago and never realized it?

On May 12, 2005, the next day, Maria's response was:

How can I miss you so much? I don't understand it!

About Friday, you know it is very possible that a couple of glasses of wine, good food, and I will fall asleep on you. That is why I thought we could change the order of the events, but you insisted on keeping it this way. By now, I think you are right, though I don't know how much I am going to be able to concentrate on the meal. Couldn't we have dessert first and then go out for dinner?

I also can't wait to see you. I want weird things. I want to smell you and touch your face. I want to see you laugh, look at your eyes, and feel your hands touching me. It is the strangest feeling to feel that I know you and not have seen you for so long. To feel so intimately connected, I really have a hard time getting past the first hour with you. I am aware that all this can blow up in smoke, but it is hard to conceive that it would. In the meantime, I am enjoying the attention, the feelings, and the care you send my way more than you can imagine. It is like not having realized how thirsty I was until there was water, and now I can't stop drinking it. Does that make sense?

No, thought I, *it does not make any sense!* We had not seen each other for over three decades, yet after only two months, it felt like we had been friends throughout all that time. This new level of intimacy made me anxious about meeting her. I wondered what she really looked like. We had exchanged pictures, but in person no one ever looks the same. We were going to meet and spend a weekend together—not only a weekend, but also her nephew's wedding. I would be meeting her entire family, including her two children, in one fell swoop.

Fate Finally Wins!

As the plane roared down the runway on its way to Minneapolis, I thought, *What was I thinking?* Agreeing to see a woman I had not seen for thirty-six years is one thing, but attending a family wedding on the first date is nuts! *What will it be like?* I wondered as I watched the spring earth pass below the wings of the plane.

I got into Minneapolis midafternoon. The front desk and lobby of the downtown Marriott Hotel in Minneapolis are on the second floor. An atrium area overlooked the front door and concierge station. I registered, went to my room, unpacked, and took a short nap in anticipation of being up late. Waking, I realized that I was still nervous, thinking again, *What did I get myself into?* Through the large window I could see the sun starting its dip into the western horizon. The bright ball was fading but still visible between the tall buildings of the cityscape. The sheer curtain allowed enough light into the room that I didn't have to turn on any lights. I showered to refresh myself and rinse away the grogginess of the nap. I laid out fresh clothes, unsure of what to wear to impress Maria; should I dress casually, or should I wear a tie? *No,* I thought. *She probably still thinks of me wearing a tie during our college days in the sixties.* I would meet her as the new me: tie-less, nice shirt, and casual slacks.

Cleaned up, I went down to the lobby to wait for Maria. We had exchanged pictures, but would I recognize her? Maria had probably dressed for dinner and made herself up, so she would look different from her picture. Would I make a fool out of myself, not recognize her, and then stammer something stupid? Did I look OK?

Why was I so nervous?

I peeked over the atrium railing to see if I could catch her walking in. I don't know what made me think that she might be walking in just at the moment I looked—anxiety, probably—but no one was there. I found a place to sit in the second-floor lobby where I could observe the elevators.

I kept watching the elevator doors open, but no Maria came out. *This is nuts! How long can I just sit here and stare at the elevator, hoping she would appear?* It had been Maria's idea to meet in the second-floor lobby, and from here we could find somewhere close by for dinner, since downtown Minneapolis has many wonderful restaurants. I hoped, though, that we could have a drink to settle our respective nerves before we went to dinner.

I started to pace the floor next to the lobby bar. Knowing I had to calm myself and kill some time, I ordered a glass of Sauvignon Blanc from a passing waiter. After he brought the wine, I realized I was still pacing, now with wine in hand! Comprehending the futility of my actions, I sat down on one of the leatherette couches. From there, I could turn to look at the elevators whenever I heard the chime announce an arrival. In due course, I decided to distract myself by watching the college basketball game on the bar's big-screen TV.

The young men running up and down the court reminded me of my days in college. Two of my roommates had been star basketball players, and I was the team statistician. It had been a long time since I had thought about them. Memories of those days started coming back. Why? Just seeing a game had never done that to me before; could it have anything to do with the eagerness to see Maria again?

What was there about Maria that made me interested in her? I took a long drink of wine. Why had I not just ignored her emails a couple of months ago? Maria had told me early on that she had fallen in love with me in college, but oddly, I had never really explored how I had felt about her. Of course, exploring my feelings was not one of my better traits. With the wine taking its effects on my empty stomach, I began to relax and let my mind retrace the day we first met in 1968.

Where had the time gone? It felt as if I was meeting Maria again after only a few weeks of absence! My anxiety generated crazy thoughts like hiding behind the large potted plants to check her out first, but then what? Leave? No, that was not an option. I had flown all the way here to meet a woman I believed I had fallen in love with over the last two months, so I had to go through with it.

The *ding* of the elevator door opening brought me back to reality. I looked at the crowd of people stepping out of the elevator.

Out stepped a crowd of people laughing and talking among themselves. I carefully scanned the group, but they were all younger couples in their mid-thirties. Then the crowd moved on, and I saw another person, a woman in a dark dress, with long dark hair, carrying a big purse, Staring around as if looking for someone. *This must be Maria*! I thought.

"Hi, there, at long last," I said, walking up to her. Maria turned, and we embraced.

"Oh, it is so good to see you!" she exclaimed. "I cannot believe you are really here! We're here. Oh, wow!"

Maria hugged me tight, and then we parted so we could admire each other. Nervously, we exchanged pleasantries. She asked about the flight, and I asked her about her day. Did she have any problem getting to the hotel?

"Well, I'm a little late because I had a hard time finding a place to park. Sorry!"

"I wasn't worried," I said, holding up my empty glass of wine.

"Oh, that looks good."

Taking her cue, I suggested that we go to the lobby bar and have a drink. As we walked toward the bar, however, it occurred to me that we could have some wine brought to my room. I asked Maria what she thought about that, never thinking about how forward it might have sounded. Without hesitation, she agreed. While she waited, I went to the bar and ordered two glasses of wine to be brought up.

Once we reached the room, she put her purse on the bed and we moved to a small table by the window overlooking downtown. The sheer curtain made the city lights sparkle and shine—a Christmas like glow in May that had engulfed the city just for us.

We started out with giddy small talk about how we each looked and how well we had aged. I talked about my flight and Maria about how busy she had been with several clients that day. Soon, we heard a knock on the door, and room service delivered two large glasses of white wine.

"I should warn you," Maria said as we sat back down, glasses of wine sparkling in front of us, "I haven't eaten yet and am a bit tired, so this may knock me right out. I might fall asleep on you."

"If that is the case, maybe we should just order room service and eat here," I suggested.

We did, and we didn't leave the room again that night!

Four Hundred and Six Days Later. . .

On April 22, 2006, a gorgeous, warm and sunny Saturday afternoon, Maria and I stood in the front room of the Minneapolis home of two of Maria's friends. The ornate three-story home was old and lovely, situated on a hill that overlooked downtown Minneapolis. The sun streamed in through the large windows facing the west.

Maria wore a beautiful burnt-orange dress, her hair tied in a bun, and curls hanging down each side of her head. I wore my black suit and a burnt-orange-and-brown tie Maria had given me for the occasion. We stood in front of the officiant, ready to say our vows, surrounded by a small group of friends; my daughters Tracy, Anna, and Marie; and Maria's children Amanda and Bob. Maria was nervous, and I was confident. I knew this was the right thing to do.

The officiant looked at both of us, and my confidence immediately melted. She started with "Maria and Manfred, you have written your own vows, which I will now read to each of you. I will then ask each of you whether you will take each other into this marriage."

She continued:

We bless this marriage with the virtues of communication between your hearts, minds and bodies, fresh beginnings with the rising of every day's sun, and the value of the wisdom of sharing silences.

We bless this marriage with the virtues of a warm and welcoming home, the delight of your heart's passion, and the ability of both to lighten the darkest of times.

We bless this marriage with the virtues of the deepness of the lake, the swift flow

You each possess the parts of life that the other needs in order to experience the fullness of life, and you share in common your love and appreciation of each other's special qualities and your goal of sharing your family and your future together.

An unknown future stretches out before you. That future, with its hopes and disappointments, its joys, and its sorrows, is hidden from your eyes. But it is a great tribute to your belief in each other that you are willing to face those uncertainties together.

Please face each other and hold hands and each repeat your vows after me:

We promise each other that:

-We want to define our relationship from this day forward as the most important learning opportunity in life.

-We want to be close to each other and are willing to do whatever it takes to do so.

-We want to put the relationship above our respective quirks, hereby choosing our relationship above any resistance to it.

-We promise to tell the truth to each other—no matter what—to overcome what we have become skillful at—hiding our feelings.

-We are committed to our own separate development as individuals, wanting our relationship to be a facilitator of our growth.

-We promise that whenever we find ourselves complaining about something, we look into ourselves for the source, rather than looking for the source of the problem outside ourselves.

-Finally, we promise to each other that we will have fun! No one precisely knows the meaning of life, but surely it's not to have a bad time.

This we PROMISE each other today before, family, friends, and God.

With cracking voices, we each said, "I do!"

The officiant then made the pronouncement: "We know that it is by the power vested in you, by your heart and soul joining love that, I now pronounce you husband and wife. You may seal your promise with a kiss."

We did so, and then we accepted congratulations from everyone there.

The rest, as they say, is history.

ACKNOWLEDGMENTS

I tried to find the voice for this book for several years, never fully satisfied with what I had put on paper. Three years ago I took a class at the Loft Literary Center given by Laurie Hertzel, senior editor for books at the Minneapolis *Star Tribune*. Although I had taken other classes, it was Laurie's Socratic method of teaching that opened the door to completion of this project. She provided me the courage and freedom to express myself and tell the story that had been hiding in my head and heart. Laurie gave me the courage to write the story from my heart.

While I assisted my friend Laura Moyer in teaching a class of adult English learners, she surreptitiously teaches me. Every day, I listened and learned from her, skills I had long forgotten since those early English classes in high school. She didn't know it, but I have been her student as much as those that sat before us.

Thank you to Ernie, Michael, Ken, Kathi, Roger, and Hugh, for reading the first draft and giving me feedback. Even more so, thanks for the encouragement to go public with this story.

This book would not be possible without the support of my aunt Helga Arndt—"Helga." She read and reviewed rough drafts for over ten years, encouraging me to complete this project along the way.

Most important is Maria, my wife and life partner, who, encouraged me despite great skepticism. In the end, she helped me to write a better story, correcting errors in my description of her life. Although the book is about both of us, she reminded me that I could only write the story I actually knew.

Until I finished this manuscript, I never knew why authors lauded their editors so much. After all, it's the authors who are responsible for the words on the page; right? No, having had the pleasure of working with Kellie Hultgren, the editor on this book, I now know how invaluable a good editor is. She cleaned up the grammar, understood what I wanted to say, and made suggestions that made this a much better document both in content and readability. Thank you Kellie! Angie Drennen, thank you for putting the final finishing touches on the manuscript.

In the end, the book would not be without my children and grandchildren. They are the reason I have worked so long to complete this journey.

I love them so very much.